River Voices

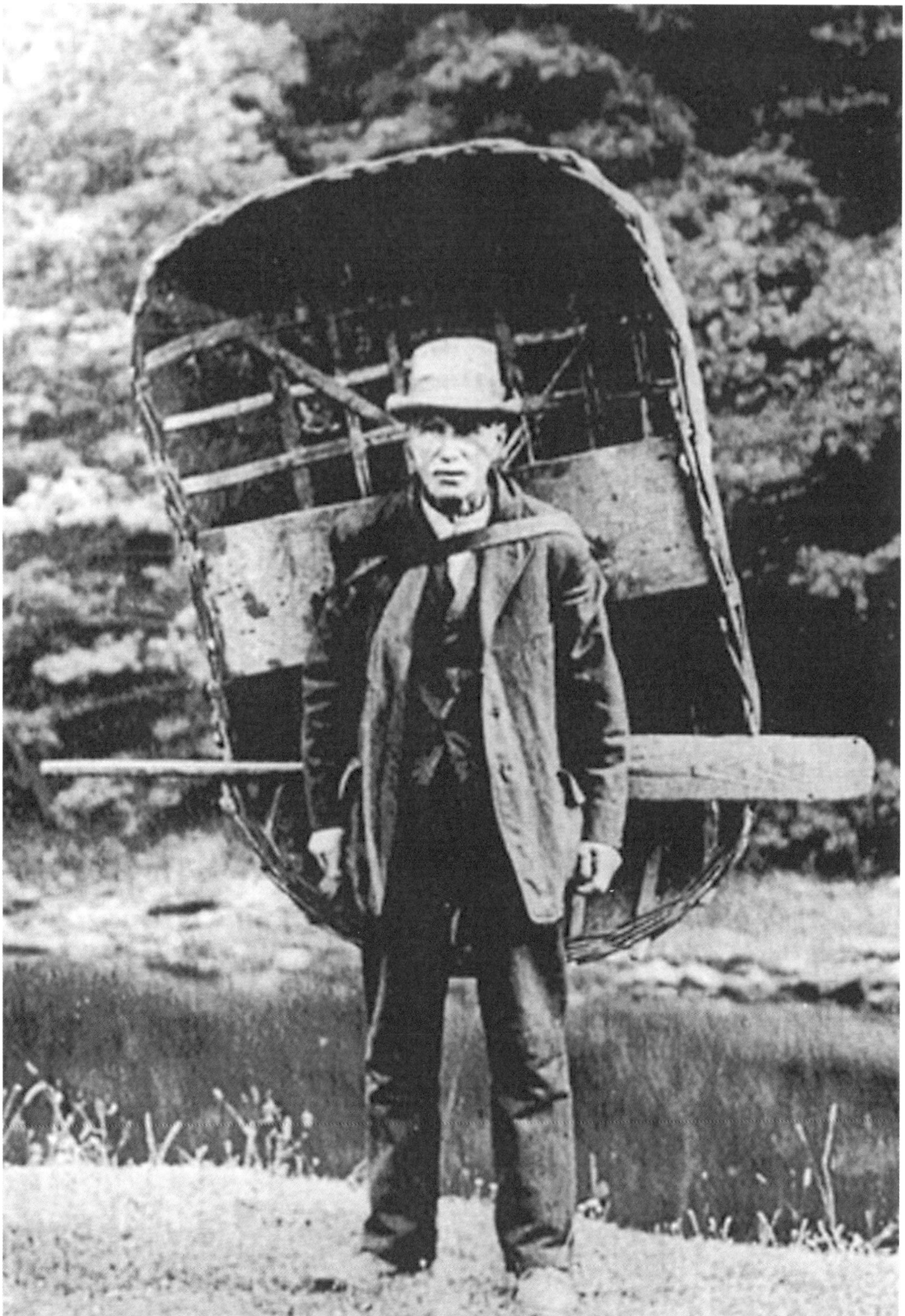

River Voices

Extraordinary Stories from the Wye

Marsha O'Mahony

LOGASTON PRESS

FRONT COVER (clockwise from top left): Fishing at Brockweir (*Chepstow Museum*); Wye Bridge (*Derek Foxton*); Fisherman with salmon (*Ross Gazette*); Janet Preedy and sisters (*Janet Preedy*); Hunderton Bridge (*Derek Foxton*); Hereford Rowing Club 'Eight' (*Frank Ford*); 'Hereford Beach' (*Derek Evans Studio Archive/ HLTAL/ HARC/ Hereford Libraries*); The Vaga rowing team (*Janet Preedy*)
BACK COVER: Tom Preedy (*Janet Preedy*)
FRONTISPIECE: William Dew and coracle (*Herefordshire Libraries*)

First published in 2018 by Logaston Press
The Holme, Church Road, Eardisley HR3 6NJ
www.logastonpress.co.uk
An imprint of Fircone Books Ltd.

ISBN 978-1-910839-31-7

Text copyright © Marsha O'Mahony, 2018

All rights reserved.
The moral right of the author has been asserted.

Without limiting the rights under copyright reserved above, no part of this publication may be reproduced, stored in or introduced into a retrieval system, or transmitted, in any form or by any means (electronic, mechanical, photocopying, recording or otherwise), without prior written permission of the copyright owner and the above publisher of this book.

Designed and typeset by Richard Wheeler.
Cover design by Richard Wheeler.

Printed and bound in the UK by Bell & Bain Ltd., Glasgow.

Logaston Press is committed to a sustainable future for our business, our readers and our planet. The book in your hands is made from paper certified by the Forest Stewardship Council.

British Library Catalogue in Publishing Data.
A CIP catalogue record for this book is available from the British Library.

CONTENTS

ACKNOWLEDGEMENTS	vi
FOREWORD	viii
INTRODUCTION	ix

1	*Swimming*	1
2	*Fishing*	21
3	*Ghillies, Bailiffs & Poachers*	73
4	*Wye Valley Otter Hounds*	95
5	*Boat-Building & other Crafts*	103
6	*Navigating the Wye*	123
7	*Ferries across the Wye*	159
8	*Bridges & Trains*	183
9	*Ice Age & Biblical Floods*	203
10	*Pubs, Clubs & Missionaries*	215

VOICES OF THE RIVER	230
REFERENCES	234
INDEX	237

ACKNOWLEDGEMENTS

With grateful thanks to National Lottery Players and the Heritage Lottery Fund for helping make this project possible, and to our match funders, Terry, Carol and Wesley Mason, Hereford City Council, Monmouthshire Building Society Community Fund, New Grove Trust, William A. Cadbury Charitable Trust, and the Wye Valley Area of Outstanding Natural Beauty (AONB). Herefordshire Lore Committee, the Project Steering group: Bill Laws, Heather Allan, Kate Bower, Eileen Klotz, Julie Orton-Davies, Lynda Ward and Harvey Payne. Interviewers: Beverly Clark, Vicky Connaughton, Jo Henshaw, Jeanette McCulloch, and John Rose. Project photographer Emma Drabble. Website designer Voodoo Chilli. Special mention to Hugo Mason, Terry Mason, and George Woodward. Photographs and images from the: Derek Foxton Collection, Keith James, Herefordshire Archive and Records Centre (HARC), Herefordshire Histories, Herefordshire Libraries, Landscape Origins of the Wye Valley, Herefordshire Life Through a Lens, Derek Evans' Collection, Hereford Museum Resource Centre, the *Ross Gazette*. And for their stories and support: Gordon Amand, Andrew Blake (AONB), Rosemary Brown, Brian Butcher, Lynne Butler, Fred Carpenter, Jack Catchpole, Tim Chance, Karl Chattington, Lyn Cobley, Howard Copping, Terry Croaker, Peter Daines, Major Patrick Darling, Donald Davies, Peter Davies, Robert Davies, Brian Dean, Simon Dereham, Bob Duberley, Liz Everall, John and Chris Fishpool, Frank Ford, Father Christopher Fox, Geoff Franks, Nick Frost, Vic Gammage, Nicola Goodwin, Dave Green, Tricia Hales, the Hammonds family, David Harper, Julie Hardman, Tom Henderson, Hereford Rowing Club, Deborah Hill, Marie Hills, Ron and Kit Hodges, Caroline Hodgeson, Adrian, Janet and Mark Howard, Maurice Hudson, Rebecca Huggett, Trevor Hulme, Robin and Caroline Hulse, Ray Hunter, Heather Hurley, Deborah Jarman, Derrick Jones, Dylan Jones, Philip and Patricia Jones, Phil Jordan, David Joyce,

Ed Kelly, Doris Kershaw, Lizzie Knock, Sarah Laws, Fiona Lloyd, Joan Lloyd, Gary McLeod, Hannah McSherry, Mandi Matthes, Mill Hill Missionary Society Archive, Nina O'Mahony, Margaret Morgans, Les Moses, Tony Norman, Lindsey and Ray Norton, Simon Owen, Cara and Shona Palmer, Gerald Parker, Richard Pennington, Hannah and John Pickford, Mary Powell, Janet Preedy, John Pullen, Peter Redding, Charlotte Reynolds, Ian Rivers, Ross Rowing Club, Jo Scrivin, Ron Shoesmith, George Smith, Joan Snell, John Symonds Fly fishing, Maggie and Graham Taylor, June Thimblethorpe, Tom Vaughan, Hannah Vernon, Bruce Wallace, Ruth Waycott (AONB), Dave and Shona Warnes, Margaret Wilce, Philip Wilcocks, Jean Williams, Lynn Woodward, Andrew Wynne, the *Hereford Times*, Felsted School, Nichola Geeson, Bill Jackson, Lynn Jones, Keith James, Dorothy Joyner, Terry Preedy, Ben Ray, Bob Tabor, Rodney Walker, Meldon Kysow, Dave Avery, Diane Bone, Julian Owens, Innes Jones, Maurice and Julia Hudson, Gordon Diffey, Richard Shaw, Graham Andrews, Terry Halford, Matt Woodman, Terry, Carol and Wesley Mason.

FOREWORD

Forty-two years ago, I settled in the Wye Valley to find that very soon the beauty of the river and its wildlife began to creep into my whole being. Not only did the river become a place to work but a place to be admired and respected. My early working days as a ghillie on the Wye gave me an opportunity, not given to many, to enjoy the river in its many varied moods; days spent in the company of fishermen and others from all walks of life who shared with me a profound feeling for the environment of the river valley, some of whom became life-long friends. It is a sad fact that the great Wye salmon and the river characters have declined during my years spent on the river. As the reflections in these pages will show, we lived through the best of times. I for one, given the chance, would willingly do it all again.

George Woodward

INTRODUCTION

In 2010, working as a reporter on a weekly paper, I was sent to interview a retired River Wye water bailiff. He was George Woodward. We met in a coffee shop and started chatting about his work and experiences on the river. A couple of hours later, and with an anxious editor eager to get me back at my desk, I tore myself away, promising I would return. I wrote my two hundred words for the article, but I knew then there was a much bigger story waiting to be told. He was just one character with an extraordinary story. How many others are out there? I have discovered that there are many, and they just keep on coming. We have just touched the surface but, my goodness, what a group of people they are. I feel touched, privileged and fortunate that they have entrusted their stories to me. I hope you enjoy them too.

Marsha O'Mahony, 2018

x   RIVER VOICES

1 Swimming

It is a long-held superstition in Herefordshire that the river 'will take, then leave alone for another year'. This was brought home with a vengeance in news reported in the *Hereford Times* of January 1940. While the country was preoccupied with the onset of the Second World War, a tragedy of epic proportions occurred much closer to home, with the deaths of four children in the river from drowning. They had been playing on ice opposite the Bishop's Palace. The sequence of events played out in newspapers is almost too much to bear. Two years later, in the summer of 1942, pupils of Felsted School, who had been evacuated to the safe havens of Goodrich from Essex, were enjoying 'bathing' practice in the Wye, when a 15-year-old member of their party drowned. Much later, in the summer of 1974 at Symonds Yat, another two drownings prompted calls for an outright 'swimming ban'. The appeal came to nothing.

Yet the lure of the river holds strong. Despite the obvious dangers, generations have discovered, and continue to enjoy, the delights of swimming in the Wye in its most breathtaking scenery. On a summer's day, soft grass underfoot, the lapping sounds of water, birdsong overhead, the Wye is at its most tempting and seductive, as many have found.

Janet Preedy, 79
I must have been taken on the river from the day I was born.

Three generations of the Preedy family ran the Hunderton Ferry, Hereford's last river crossing service, rented from Hereford Council. Janet, who can still read the weather from the river's appearance, recalls forgotten swimming place names, busy summer Sundays, her father pulling a drowned child from the river and almost drowning herself.

Janet still lives within minutes of the former Hunderton Ferry launch. Access to it is now overgrown and little that surrounds this once bustling river crossing gives any indication of its past life. When she was a girl, she had an early and frightening lesson:

> I must have been about ten and I put a ring around my waist and I dived off this landing stage on the opposite side of the river and of course it slipped and went around my feet and I couldn't get my feet out and I was being held upside down. I was nearly drowned. It was my fault. If it hadn't been for my sister's fiancée jumping in I think I would have drowned. But it's a funny thing, when I first went under I panicked a bit and then I got calm and I thought, "Oh somebody drowns every year under the water," and I stopped panicking. And the next thing I knew I was breathing in fresh air!
>
> All the years we were children, the river was our playing ground. But we were always taught where to go, where not to go, and always stopped in groups of three, 'cause in groups of more than three one isn't missed. So never mind how many children were in the river you always stopped in groups of three. And all the years I've been growing up on the river I can only remember two children being drowned and they didn't do as they were told and that's how they come to be drowned. That was by what we called the 'Big Boys'. They had to be strong swimmers to swim there, right opposite the Water Works.

There are hundreds of salmon pools up and down the Wye, each with a name telling a story all of its own: Pope's Rock, Coldwell Rocks, Island Pool, Martin's Pool, Priors Pool, Oak Run, Bridge Run to name just a few. How or why they are named so is unknown, but the clue is in the name, mostly. But swimmers haven't missed out in creating names for favoured swimming 'pools' either.

Janet again:

> There was the 'Big Boys', where the stronger swimmers went. Next door to that was what we used to call the 'Bab's Pool'. You weren't allowed to go there because it was sandy, but all of a sudden there was a shelf and the current used to suck you under. Then we used to go on up, on the bend, and that was what we used to call 'Sandy Bay', where it drops off from one

side to the other and that's where most of us children went to play. It's like the Victoria Bridge. There was one at Breinton Springs, because that was pretty shallow, but you had to be careful there because all of a sudden there was a drop.

Top: children playing in the river at Breinton. Bottom: family group at Breinton
(photos: Doris Kershaw)

The Second World War saw hundreds of gum-chewing American GIs coming to camps across the county. They really did 'smell nice', had lots of chocolate, liked to jitterbug, and brought a few local girls back home to the States with them. While here, they also had time to play, and the river drew them in too.

Janet Preedy:

American GI in a boat at Symonds Yat
(photo: Terry Halford)

> We used to sit on the wall and ask them: "Got any gum, chum?" And they used to give us some. It was like sweets to us with the War on. I can remember my dad; I was in the boat with him and there was an American and he was diving off the tree by the 'Big Boys', so my Dad goes up there, and I was in the boat with him, and he says, "If I were you mate, it's all right to swim, but don't dive because there's rocks on the river bed." I can hear the American saying, "Oh go on old man, I've jumped off here half a dozen times and I'm perfectly all right." He was impressing a girl that he had sitting on the bank. Dad said, "Well I'm only warning you." The American broke his neck, didn't he? He was all right after, but it stopped him.

Drownings across the decades have featured in contemporary newspaper reports. The shock never seems to fade, an innocent day ending in tragedy. For a few, there are memorials to those lost to the river. Moss grows on some and weather has worn away the lettering on others. They remain a painful reminder of lives cut short.

JOHN FISHPOOL, 72

John was born and brought up in the riverside village of Brampton Abbotts. His late father, George, was the village wheelwright, undertaker, coffin maker and, as if that wasn't enough, Chief Inspector of the Special Police Constables. In the summer, bedecked in his smart uniform, he directed the endless traffic going up to and down from Symonds Yat Rock, a busy tourist destination. Of his two sisters, one worked in the ticket office of Ross Railway Station and the other was Ross's first ever policewoman (it made the national news at the time). Today, he lives high above the Wye, with wife Chris. The view from their home is spectacular.

'I used to go swimming at the island below Foy suspension bridge, a short distance from Brampton. Our parents didn't warn us away. It was part of life then.' Just upriver from John's riverside playground is Backney. When the Great Western Railway company still ran this line, Backney Halt was an industrious place. Today, it's quiet, an idyllic spot. Only the red brick supports remain of the old railway bridge. On the side of the river is a plaque: it's worth taking a moment to stop by and contemplate. It is dedicated to the former Rector of Brampton Abbotts, Revd H. St Helier Evans. On 4 August 1904, he set out with four children to go bathing in the river for respite from the summer heat. When his son and a young girl got into difficulty, St Helier Evans rushed to save them, bringing them safely to the bank. Sadly, he was to die shortly after from heart failure.

As a teenager, John and his father remembered the man and his brave act, by repainting the plaque annually. It is still there, but faded now, still reminding.

Bob Duberley, 86
I had a couple of uncles and the one, he was nobody's fool.

Bob Duberley was brought up in Bishopswood, a short distance from the busy Kerne Bridge Railway Station. The River Wye ran past the bottom of the garden of his family home. The Duberleys were well known for their chain of butcher shops in the Forest of Dean. Bob's father was a former coal miner there, and a cider maker of some repute. Evacuees to Bishopswood during the last war insisted on trying some freshly pressed cider, despite warnings from Duberley senior that their 'bodies wouldn't cope'. There were many urgent visits to outdoor loos in Bishopswood that evening. 'They really should have listened,' said Bob.

> I remember, when I was a boy, my mother was never keen for us to go in the river. Every year someone was drowned. But I remember my elder brother and my two older sisters, they used to swim in the river. Old Storey, from Bishopswood Estate, went down with a police inspector once to tell them he didn't want them to swim there and my uncle said: "Well, I've swum down there for a number of years and I know a man who is 80 years of age and he swam in the river when he was a boy". And old Storey said, "May he drop dead!" They carried on swimming regardless. Storey put up notices saying, "no swimming", but eventually my father pulled them up and used them for firewood!

Boys playing in the river at Hereford (photo: Derek Evans Studio Archive/ Herefordshire Life through a Lens Project, courtesy of HARC and Hereford Libraries)

MARGARET MORGANS, 74

Margaret was the daughter of Kerne Bridge licensees, James and Winifred Horsley. The pub, now a private residence, was the centre of village life in Bishopswood. A well that provided fresh drinking water for several cottages, was in their kitchen. Margaret remembers the frequent visits from neighbours: 'They had to come through the back door to get to the well, carrying their pails.' A perfectly normal arrangement for a young Margaret.

Living very close to the river, she was forbidden to go near it unaccompanied:

> I used to paddle and sometimes bathe, but not swim in the river. The river could be dangerous. My parents used to swim in it when they were younger; but not me. During summer, we often took picnics to the banks of the river. The Wye meadows in front of the house were also fertile breeding grounds for mushrooms and I used to pick loads when they were in season. There was hay-making on the banks of the river too. When I was very young the river meadow was stacked in hay ricks. Somehow it made me think of Thomas Hardy. But one of my greatest delights was to catch minnows with a jam jar tied with string. I loved it.

Hereford's Hunderton Farm was known locally as Walls Farm after the farmer, Mr Sid Walls. He allowed generations of children to play in the woods on his land and fish in Newton Brook with jam jars on string or small fishing nets on bamboo canes. At the point where Newton Brook entered the river from the south, almost opposite the Broomy Hill water intake, there was often a rope hanging from a tree on the river bank, which had been rigged up by much older children to form a swing. The outcomes were either a perfect return to safety on the river bank, a not so good landing in the brook itself with shoes full of water, or a very wet walk home after landing in the river, which was seriously addressed by parents regardless of the age of the child.

Children playing in the river in the 1940s (photo: Doris Kershaw)

HEREFORD BEACH

No need to head for Weston-super-Mare or Barry Island when Hereford had its own beach. There isn't much of it left now, but it was there, a sweeping stretch of shingly beach opposite the old General Hospital. On a summer's day, this was the place to be. Families, harassed mums in cotton frocks; dads, braces pulled down, open-neck shirts, ciggie in mouth; excitable children – they would all flock to the 'beach', claiming their spots for the afternoon. Laid out on plaid rugs were baskets of greaseproof-wrapped sandwiches of egg, ham or cucumber, pork pies, squash and flasked tea stewed to within an inch of its life. Stretchy, neoprene swimsuits were still in the future. Back in the day, bathing costumes, often knitted by Granny, caused acute embarrassment and lasting psychological harm! Della, 93, recalled her woollen onesie 'stretched beyond belief after one dipping and I never wore it again'; while Tom Henderson, 80, improvised: 'I got an old pullover, tied it up with a piece of string, and sewed up the middle!' It did the job.

The peril of the hand-knitted swimming costume: cue maximum embarrassment!
(photos: Doris Kershaw)

Joan Lloyd, 95
Oh, I loved the water. I was always swimming in the river. I've been swimming even when it's in flood.

For some people, old habits are hard to shake off. When is it time to finally hang up your swimming cap and goggles? The answer is never! In her youth, Joan Lloyd's favoured swimming place was the river. This astonishing 95-year-old still swims daily, though in the warmer municipal swimming pool. Brought up close to the Wye, she is one of the last surviving members of the extended Jordan family, builders and hirers of pleasure boats on the Wye. Joan used to be a regular at Hereford Beach:

I love the river. I think it's because I was brought up on the river, practically. Even when my daughter was old enough, I used to take her down to the Victoria Bridge paddling. My grandmother, who was over at Wyebridge House, used to sound a gong to say it was lunch-time. We used to pack up then and go over for lunch. We did all sorts there, like diving off the end of the canoe. I knew where all the holes were up the river. Up past the Wheatfield stream there's like a pool and we used to swim in there. And before you get to Belmont there was a farm, Walls Farm, and I used to take our Alsatian up there and swim across the river with him and back.

– Such free and easy times, where the days were long and the sun shone all day.

Families flocked to 'Hereford Beach' in the late 1950s
(photo: Derek Evans Studio Archive/ HLTAL/ HARC/ Hereford Libraries)

BRUCE WALLACE, 76
We used to climb over a stile and walk down to the beach opposite the old General Hospital. We went there and we caught minnows and got wet and had a really good time.

In 1948, schoolboy Bruce Wallace left war-damaged Coventry with his family and moved to Hereford. His garden backed onto Bradbury Lines, later to become the Special Air Services (SAS) camp:

As boys, we used to roam everywhere, even at a very early age. Today you wouldn't be safe to do it.

There were about six or seven of us lived in the road and we were friends and a lot of these friendships went on for decades. We used to walk down to the river through the Hinton estate. At that time, where the King George's playing fields used to be, there was a farm and there were cows in the field, we used to climb over a stile and walk down to the beach opposite the old General Hospital. We went there and caught minnows and got wet and had a really good time.

Children jumping off Victoria Bridge in Hereford
(photo: Derek Evans Studio Archive/ HLTAL/ HARC/ Hereford Libraries)

Bruce again:

> The one thing we wouldn't do was jump off the Victoria Bridge, but a lot did. There wasn't much in the way of casual clothing about then and we would get our shoes wet and get into trouble when we got home. We had jam jars of minnows, with a piece of string round as handles, which we took hours trying to get the knots right before we headed off. My father used to help. He was a fireman and he was very good with knots so he used to help us. And off we'd go, with a net. Our parents didn't worry, nobody worried, and, going away from the river, we used to cycle to the top of Dinedor Hill on three-wheel bikes and we'd take cold tea in a bottle and off we'd go and we'd have a drink and came back down eventually. We would take toast down to the river as well. I couldn't swim initially when I first went down there. We were all about the same age, the boys, and there was one older boy who could swim and I suppose he was nominally in charge. We all survived.

While Bruce didn't jump off the Victoria Bridge, there were many who did, risking life and limb. Among them Diana Bone, 'but only from the Mill Street side, where the water was deepest'. Dave Avery was 15 years old when he jumped off, 'with a packet of cigarettes in my pocket which four friends had chipped in to get and then going up to Castle Green toilets to dry them out!' But for some, the Victoria Bridge just did not cut it; they were looking for bigger and even more dangerous jumps. Meldon Kysow: 'Victoria bridge was nothing; it's where kids jumped off to build their confidence up before walking to the new bridge or Eign Bridge. I even witnessed a friend climb a lamppost on Greyfriars bridge and then dive off it! Crazy kids!' Matt Woodman was one of those: 'I remember standing on a mate's shoulders and jumping off the Eign railway bridge. A copper caught us the one day so we legged it across Goodwins field!'

GARY MCLEOD, 75
There was always something going on in the river.

Gary McLeod is a proud Hundertonian, living just a few short strides from The Vaga, where his father Gordon was landlord in the 1960s. The pub is an honest-to-goodness, backstreet inn, part of a dying breed, site of bare-knuckle fighting in its day, allegedly, and it remains at the centre of the community in its riverside location.

Gary McLeod:

I learnt to swim in the Lugg. But there was Hereford Beach down opposite the General Hospital. Families would go down there, sandwiches, thermos flasks, fishing nets. Didn't matter if you lived south or north of the river, you would go home with jam jars of minnows, put a string round the top, carry them home.

Minnow hunting, enjoyed by little boys and girls everywhere
(photo: Derek Evans Studio Archive/ HLTAL/ HARC/ Hereford Libraries)

ROSS BEACH

Hereford wasn't the only place with a beach; Ross-on-Wye had its own too. Who needs a swimming pool, when you could learn to swim in the Wye? Ross Rowing Club life member Brian Dean was one youngster who took his first strokes in the river:

> When I was a child we always had the pebbly beach, just above the Rowing Club. In the summer, all the kids would be swimming and the more adventurous would build a mud slide into the river. I mean the river in those days was a joy. I was taught to swim in it by a Land Army girl. Where the motorway bridge is now, that was known as the Lions; that was deep there. About there, where the stream comes out from Scudamore's opposite Benhalls Farm, that was known as the 'Diving Board' because there was a tree there and a rope and they had a plank going out from the tree and it was used as a diving board.

Ross Beach (photo: *Ross Gazette*)

THE BASSOM

Municipal swimming baths equals swimming in the river, a match made in heaven? Oh, how times have changed.

In the early part of the twentieth century, the Bassom, on Bartonsham Meadows, was the municipal bathing station and the place where many dipped their toes before taking their first tentative strokes in the Wye. Schools held their swimming galas there and individuals, like Margo Edwards, swam there

Bathers and changing tents, Bartonsham Meadows (photo: Derek Foxton Collection)

every morning at 7 a.m., with her aunt, before they started work at the laundry in Rockfield Road. Early pictures show sagging canvas structures that represented the changing quarters on top of the bank.

Yet the Wye, as we have seen, isn't always the swimmer's friend. Even a place like the Bassom couldn't escape the river's might. Gordon Lamputt, who died in 2017, was swimming at the Bassom at the start of the Second World War and witnessed a distressing scene:

> We were swimming at the Bassom in 1939 or 1940, by the bathing hut. These army chaps from Bradbury Lines were being rowed across in a boat when the damned thing overturned. Their heavy uniforms dragged them down and we were diving to try and get them up but we couldn't. I always wondered how many survived.

Schools today make swimming and water safety a compulsory part of the National Curriculum with the dictum that pupils should be taught to swim 'competently, confidently and proficiently'. I wonder if the Bassom's chief attendant would have got past the interview stage in twenty-first-century recruitment?

Spectators gather to watch swimmers at Bartonsham (photo: Derek Foxton Collection)

His 'just get in and get on with it' teaching style wouldn't really cut it with current school practice, would it?

In a previously recorded interview, Alf Evans recalled the chief attendant at the Bassom during the First World War years, a man not given to pleasantries or any notion of safety. Alf, however, took it all in his stride:

> An old man was the chief attendant of Bassom bathing station. He taught me to swim with a rope. The diving plank was a long wooden strip going out almost into the middle of the stream where it was deeper and then he had a flexible plank at the end and that's where he used to walk along there. He'd put a rope round your shoulders and push you in; that's how you learnt to swim.

It's unthinkable today that children would learn to swim in the river but it's where Marie Hills was taught. She lived at Hunderton and the river was 'just across the road'. Swimming a mile up-stream to Breinton with a neighbour was considered good practice then. 'We swam back down the river 'til it was too cold, then I would have to get out! I'd rather swim in the river. I mean you know where the bottom is.'

Adrian Howard, 74
It's the best place to learn. Plenty of water!

Adrian Howard worked for the Woodland Trust as a maintenance and woodland manager for 27 years. Most of his work was on Little Doward. Now semi-retired, he continues to look after the Woodland Trust's cattle there. He was born in the lower lodge of the Wyastone Leys in 1944. His grandparents lived in the riverside cottage below the grand house selling drinks to passing tourists as they walked to and from Monmouth to Symonds Yat. When it came to swimming lessons, sometimes the 'chuck them in and see if they float' method worked – for some anyway (not a practice we would advocate, by the way).

Adrian:

> I learnt to swim in the river as a child. Down by Huntsham Bridge there was a pebble beach, but it's gone now. The bigger boys always chucked you in. I should think most of the local kids swam in the river in those days. It's the best way to learn, to find the dangers, climbing trees and all that. Going back some time, the old headmaster at Whitchurch School actually went down to the river once to try and find somewhere that would be safe for kids to teach them to swim. But he couldn't find anywhere safe so they ended up going to the swimming pool anyway.

It wasn't all just messing about in the river. The Wye has also hosted competitive swimming races too. In the 1960s in Ross-on-Wye, the Brewster Cup Wye Swimming Race was a big sporting event, demanding attention from spectators on the river banks and reports in the local paper. One family, the Scotts of Hereford, claimed the title five years running. The Race, over a course of 300 yards, had its own dramas: in the 1968 final, a Mr A. Green was disqualified when 'his poor steering caused Arrowsmith to collide with him'. Tea provided by the ladies' committee afterwards hopefully provided some commiseration to the exhausted swimmers and overwrought parents.

There was another race of sorts in the summer of 2016 when a trio of plucky swimmers decided to strike out for their own title. Nicola Goodwin, Ian Rivers and Julie Hardman claimed to be the first swimmers to take on the length of the Wye, from source to sea. They started on the peak of Plynlimon, the highest point of the Cambrian Mountains in Wales, a massif that dominates the countryside of northern Ceredigion – it is also the source of the River Wye. Two weeks later, the trio emerged from the tidal water at Brockweir, walking the last stretch into the frontier town of Chepstow. In the process, the swimmers raised around £3,000 for St Michael's Hospice – no mean feat.

Julie Hardman, Nicola Goodwin and Ian Rivers (photo: N. Goodwin)

Nicola is a swimmer and triathlete and a former European age-group champion at middle distance Triathlon. She is coach and club secretary at Hereford Triathlon Club and represents the GB age-group squad across the world. After university, Nicola was a rugby player and journalist and part of the England Women's Squad. After retiring from rugby, she joined BBC Hereford & Worcester. She was born in Herefordshire and lives next to the River Wye.

When Ian was seven years old, he nearly drowned in a swimming pool on a caravan site in Tenby, whilst on holiday with his family from London. His uncle pulled him out of the pool and thought it was time Ian learned to swim properly. Fast forward to the age of 19, and he did the commando swim test as part of the 'All Arms Commando Course' – a stiff test and challenge, but one he passed and enjoyed immensely. Ian is also a coach at Hereford Triathlon Club.

Julie Hardman's love of swimming began early as a member of Hereford Swimming Club. She later became a swimming coach. In the Army, she was a physical training instructor and swam for the Army and Combined Services. Like Nicola and Ian, she is a coach at the Hereford Triathlon Club. For all three the Wye swim was a chance to explore the adventurous side of swimming. 'A truly wonderful adventure,' said Julie. 'Mole, Rat and Badger exploring the Wye.'

Nicola:

> It was a crazy idea hatched over a few years and then suddenly it became serious. I thought it would be something cool to do and the other two felt the same. I found out that nobody had done it, which seemed really weird. A gentleman back in the nineteenth century wrote some diary entries year on year, but he did different sections each year, so he did the whole distance, but over a period of 15 years.

Anyone paddling the Wye will have noticed the need for some portage along sections of the river, and inevitably this adventure involved some walking too, but the trio were never far from the water.

Ian:

> We did it in two weeks, but we did three days walking at the start. The source is literally a hill with a stream. The only amphibian we saw for the whole two weeks was a frog at the very beginning! The first day was the longest, I think about 25 miles, walking around eight hours. And then on average six or seven hours walking a day. Then probably about eight hours a day in the water. I think from beginning to end it was about 158 miles.

Don't get the idea that this trio are novices when it comes to open water swimming. They are regular river swimmers, and very fit too. However, when their epic swim passed close to Nicola's home at Rotherwas, it was particularly testing:

> For me, swimming that stretch was the hardest day because we got out at my house and we were due to get in and swim to a friend's house, which is at Lucksall near Fownhope, and we were just cold and wet and tired, and that's really hard when we were swimming past my house.

Julie:

> We had to practise low water swimming, which is a very different action, a sideways action, and then to practise what you do over the fast rapids, which is like torpedo style. So, you put your feet first and then you lie and go like Superman! Ian used the Global Positioning System (GPS) so we knew exactly where we were at any given time. But I think my favourite place was going from Nicola's down to Hoarwithy. Pretty much all the

times we've been down there you can guarantee you will see a kingfisher. Ballingham is just so beautiful. We were training there in the summer and it's just so shallow there. It was more walking and scrabbling rather than actual swimming. But it really did feel like we were in a *Wind in the Willows* adventure and an adventure on our doorstep.

All three were sad when their challenge came to an end after two weeks. Battered, bruised, cold and sustained by cheese and marmite sandwiches, and friends offering hot tea and blankets on the bank-side, they arrived in Chepstow with a new-found respect and love for the Wye. Nicola: 'The one thing I knew all the way through was that I would never forget what we had done. And being able to share it with really close friends was very special.'

SNORKELLING

Snorkelling isn't just about coral reefs, crystal blue waters and exotic fish. There are some who have donned a mask and breathing tube to venture under the waters of the Wye and found some interesting relics. Some 30 years ago, Tim Chance of Newent was delighted to uncover arrow heads and musket balls in the river below Wilton Castle in Ross, and the remains of a trow at Symonds Yat. Up river in Hereford, the Rotherwas munitions factory also left traces of its production in the Wye.

Up to 6,000 women worked at Rotherwas munitions factory through two world wars, making bombs, shells, land-mines, torpedoes and weapons of modest, if not mass, destruction. During the Second World War, the importance of the factory increased as did the demand for labour. Workers arrived in their thousands, attracted to the decent wage. But it could be dangerous work, with some workers being christened 'Canary Girls' because their skin turned yellow from the noxious chemical they were working with, picric acid. Alternating shift patterns kept the production line going 24 hours a day, to keep up with the war effort. Workers descended on the factory from all directions, with various modes of transport: bus, on foot, bike and sometimes by boat. Alfred Evans lived at the Wye Hotel in 1912 and remembered a bridge across the river for 'bicycles and people to walk from the town to the river, at the bottom of Hampton Park hill, attached to the railway bridge. They put a path all the way along the river and fenced it in so that nobody could fall in.' No bodies in the water, but what about items?

Peter Redding is a familiar face in the St James area of Hereford; he is the man carrying a coracle to the river. He loves being in the water, and *under* water too, and loves finding things. And he's found an item or two. This isn't South Sea island conditions. It can be cold, the water silty, and the appearance of a snorkeller might draw the odd comment or two. But can you imagine the countless items dropped or washed away in the water? Pete has had a few finds too:

> Quite a few years ago, I used to spend a lot of time snorkelling in the Wye and the Lugg and I found a First World War shell case from Rotherwas. My great aunt was actually one of the Canary Girls so it was a good find. And in Glasbury I found a gold engagement ring under the river bridge but never found the owner.

Other snorkellers, according to Gary McLeod, included the 'men from the Regiment' (the SAS):

> On Hunderton railway bridge, the SAS used to put a rope across and the lads would get all their frogman gear on and they used to handline themselves under the bridge and the water right to the other end. Well, a couple of young boys were up on the railway bridge, where they shouldn't have been, and they'd seen these frogmen get in, and you could see bubbles coming up from their oxygen tanks. Well, somebody must have told one of the kids that if they see bubbles it's a fish. So they started chucking these boulders in on top of them. Well, there was hell to pay. By the time the frogmen had got out and onto the bank, the kids had already scarpered!

Hunderton railway bridge (photo: Janet Preedy)

2 *Fishing*

> Followers of the "gentle craft" still find ample occupation in the salmon fishery of the Wye, though the prince of fishes is no longer plentiful as formerly, when it was considered necessary to insert the indentures of a Hereford apprentice, a clause providing that he should not be compelled to live on a salmon more than two days in the week!
>
> (*Nooks and Corners of Herefordshire*, H. Thornhill Timmins, 1892)

It stretches the realms of belief now, but there really was a time within recent memory when an afternoon's fishing on the Wye could easily land an angler a draught of decent salmon. It was that simple; they were that plentiful. But not any more. Apocryphal tales of the Wye 'churning with salmon' abound. Maurice Hudson, 85, could safely be described as an 'old man of the river', and he's unlikely to disagree. Reminiscing about his 75 years of fishing on the Wye, many of those spent on his own river beat, he does remember the river 'rippling with salmon'. It's a very different picture today. Numbers have reduced dramatically. As a salmon river, the Wye is a pale imitation of its former self. Once upon a time anglers would talk about how much their last salmon weighed; today it's more likely to be how many months since they last took a bite. If you are lucky enough to land a 'pink un' these days, it has to be released.

Gentle craft, noble sport, this beautiful river of ours has tempted and teased huge numbers of a very particular audience to our river banks. When commentators said we were a 'classless' society, it is evidently not true when it came to the glory days of fishing for salmon, the 'gentry' fish. Anglers paid big money for a 'rod'. A fitting equivalent could possibly be polo today and its select audience and players.

The Wye has entertained royalty (Emperor Hirohito's visit is anecdotal; we're still looking for evidence!), World leaders, captains of industry, senior military personnel, politicians, and, at the other end of the spectrum, poachers. It is a different scene for salmon fishing today, as it slips down the angling hierarchy. It is coarse fishing that has taken the lead and is proving to be of greater importance to the local economy today. But many still fantasise about landing the 'big one'.

Maurice Hudson and father (photo: Maurice Hudson)

From Hay-on-Wye to Symonds Yat, a distance of 60 miles, the River Wye meanders and only drops 160 feet. In bygone times salmon were plentiful on this middle section, but nowadays the numbers of running salmon are low and so they are spread out thinly along the Wye.

George Woodward, 74

Our Atlantic salmon are going thousands of miles. It's the equivalent of taking a small child when he was three, putting him in the Amazonian rain forest 'til he was about ten, then saying, "Make your own way from here lad". It's just beyond comprehension really.

Retired river bailiff and ghillie, George Woodward, is a Lancaster lad who was tempted down to the Wye with the promise of wildlife riches in 1976, the great drought year. He's still here and it's unlikely he'll ever leave now, for he has already made his own funeral arrangements. He wants to be buried sitting up, looking over the valley to the river below, with a glass of whisky balanced in his hand. It's all arranged and his

George Woodward
(photo: David T. Grewcock)

George Woodward in his living room (photo: Emma Drabble)

wishes will be followed. He's made sure of that. Today he lives on the Courtfield Estate, Goodrich, a short distance from the river. His home is a testament to his love and knowledge of the countryside, although not necessarily a politically correct one! Jostling for space in his living room with his many successful attempts at taxidermy, are several (hundred) bottles of whisky, gifts from grateful guests. He has lost count of the number of people he has taught to fish over the years. The original country man, he is also a talented writer and artist, though he is too modest to admit it.

George:

> Before arriving in Herefordshire, I had read a bit about the Wye and I knew it was one of the most well-known salmon rivers in England. I had heard it referred to as the beautiful Wye. After I first arrived here on a Saturday, I got up on the Sunday morning and walked down through the wood at the back of the house, straight down to the banks of the River Wye and was confronted by torrents of sludgy brown water, and I thought, "Well this

can't be the bloody Wye, it's just a muddy, dirty ditch." But of course, I had not realised at the time that there was quite a major flood on and it wasn't at its best! To this day, I still think down Coldwell, below Yat rock, is where the river is one of the nicest places in the whole Wye valley.

There's something about the salmon – its mystery, its elusiveness – that fascinates. George has hauled in his fair share over the years, but they continue to intrigue even him:

> It's very likely people know more about the dark side of the moon than they actually know what happens two feet under the water of the Wye, because you don't see salmon and fish on a regular basis. Lots of people think it's just a river, it's got fish in, but they don't know or understand the life-cycle of those fish. David Attenborough makes marvellous films about the migration of the wildebeest on the Serengeti plains of Africa, and people sit there and think, "oh, isn't that marvellous?" Those wildebeest are only going a few hundred miles at most. Our Atlantic salmon are going thousands of miles.

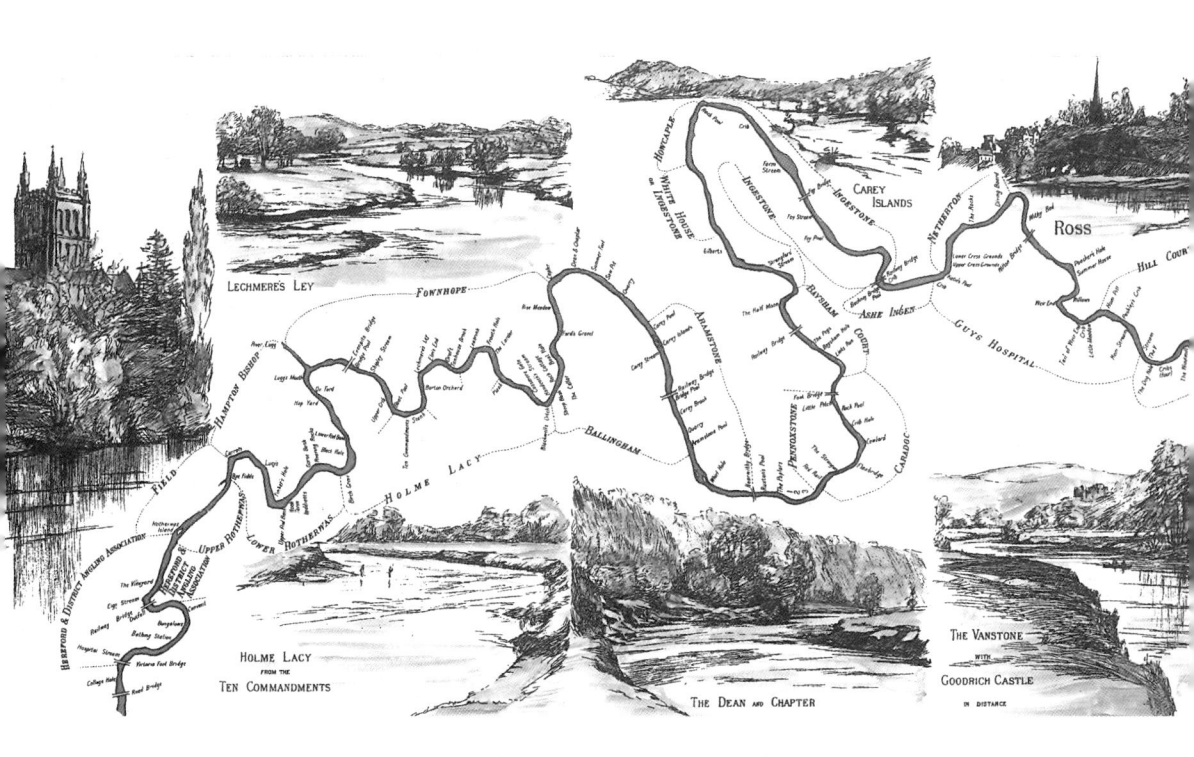

Beat map of the River Wye (photo: The River Wye Preservation Trust)

Maps draw you in, don't they? Geographical features, monuments, place names, they all tell a story. Fishing beat maps of the Wye do the same, but with an added allure, telling tales about the hundreds of salmon pools along the length of the river. Some have acquired legendary status (Cowpool in Winforton is one, the place where the largest ever salmon was caught) and others read like places out of a folk tale: Oak Tree, Pope's Rock, Bert's Hole, Pashley Crib, Dipples Pool, Dog Hole, Bridge Run, Coldwell Rocks ... They have their own characters and qualities, favoured by some, and avoided by others. George Woodward again:

> Salmon could be lying in the same pool in 1989 as they did in 1889. The pools, particularly on the lower Wye, have not altered an awful lot in thousands and thousands of years. Some are a lot more prolific than others. There's some that produce more fish than others; and in some, you stand a better chance if you're standing in her; some are good fly fishing waters; and then you might get another pool that, at certain times, is a good spinning pool or a good fly fishing pool. And then there's the ones where you struggle to catch any fish out of the river, or there's others where you struggle for a period of time, thinking, *I hate this bloody place, it's useless*, then all of a sudden you start catching fish out of it and then change your opinion again. But I think everybody who fishes will have their favourite bit.

George Woodward with daughter Lynn and Jack Charlton (photo: George Woodward)

Reports of impressive catches often featured in the news section of papers and were never demoted to a corner of the sport pages. The season salmon rod catch was one of those frequent items. In 1967 the *Ross Gazette* reported:

> The 1967 salmon season on the River Wye produced the highest rod catch ever recorded and the best net catch since 1962. Sales income from salmon easily passed the estimated figure of £3,000.

A year later in 1968, and again in the *Ross Gazette*, news of the sale of a Wye Fishery was reported with the headline: 'Sells for £38,000. Part of the draw for the Strangford End Fishery, sold at public auction, was the salmon catch for the previous four years which totalled 302.' Norman Owen, who took over the running of Hatton's, Hereford's pre-eminent sport fishing shop, was a respected fisherman, whose prowess was used to good effect when a stretch of water came up for sale. He would often be invited in by owners to fish. His inevitable successful haul would help bring up the 'beat' catch, thereby bringing the sale price up too. This was common practice.

MAURICE HUDSON, 85
I've been fishing since I was a youngster. I had no choice but to take up fishing.

Maurice has caught more Wye salmon than anyone alive: 2,400 salmon at the last count. An ex-pupil of Monmouth School for Boys, he went on to a career as a physics master at Seaford College in Sussex for 35 years until his retirement. But he still made time to return regularly to his home patch for a spot of fishing. He has owned the same stretch of river bank for over 50 years and can be seen there most days during the season, with his wife, Judy, and their faithful pooch.

Maurice Hudson and his father
(photo: Maurice Hudson)

Maurice:

> My father was a fisherman and his father was a fisherman. Where we fished, the Duke of Beaufort owned the fishing rights. It was my grandfather who leased the fishing rights off the Duke of Beaufort. In those days, it was a source of food for us. You caught your food in the river, grew it in your garden, and you shot it in the woods. The river provided an awful lot of food in those days. We always had more salmon than we knew what to do with.
>
> Methods were very cruel in those days. There wasn't all the tackle. Rods were very rudimentary and you had to be skilful to catch any fish. I used old greenheart rods and wooden sea reels. Flax line used to stick on the rod, but if you had a lot of money you bought a silk line. But there were plenty of salmon back then. My grandfather netted the river and going back for generations the Wye was netted. The nets then were made of hemp, natural fibre. Because hemp rotted and it wasn't as strong, the nets couldn't gill the salmon, unlike those modern nylon ones. They were about a hundredweight when dry and 500 hundredweight when wet and you had to have a truck or wheelbarrow to bring them back. Grandfather used to throw the salmon net over the chicken pit at night to keep the hens safe from foxes. During the 1960s and 1970s we were catching 6,000 salmon a year. There were so many. I used to come home for summer holidays and catch 60 or 70 with no problem.

It's no stretch to say that salmon fishing attracted a variety of characters and eccentrics. Where to start? How about Peter Clay Snr of Fawley Court, a salmon fisherman of note on the Wye. His stretch of river has to be one of the prettiest along the whole route, but it's up against some stiff competition. Hugo Mason of Brockhampton has enjoyed fishing on the late Clay Snr's beat since he was a boy growing up in Brockhampton, and remembers quite a character:

Hugo Mason, 1979 (photo: Hugo Mason)

Mr Clay cannot pass by without mention: an exceptional angler by any standards, especially with the Devon Minnow, a salmon lure, in the spring and the fly in the summer. As youngsters, we always had to get permission from him to fish for coarse fish and if any of us misbehaved, then we risked having the permits withdrawn. He was an avid salmon fisherman and a keen shooter. He nearly always wore a leather waistcoat and drove an open Willys jeep. Once a trailer slipped into the river by Lilley's Lane and, without hesitation, he stripped to his underpants and dragged a chain in so that the trailer could be rescued. A tough character, that's for sure. In 1998, when he was 84, he caught a lot of summer salmon. Both he and his sister, Bridget, who was 87 at the time, fly fished from a boat on their Dean and Chapter beat under Capler. They were both taking considerable risks, but I am sure that was entirely second nature.

FIRST SALMON

Your first kiss, passing your driving test, getting married, they are all rites of passage. Much like new mothers will always remember their baby's weight and

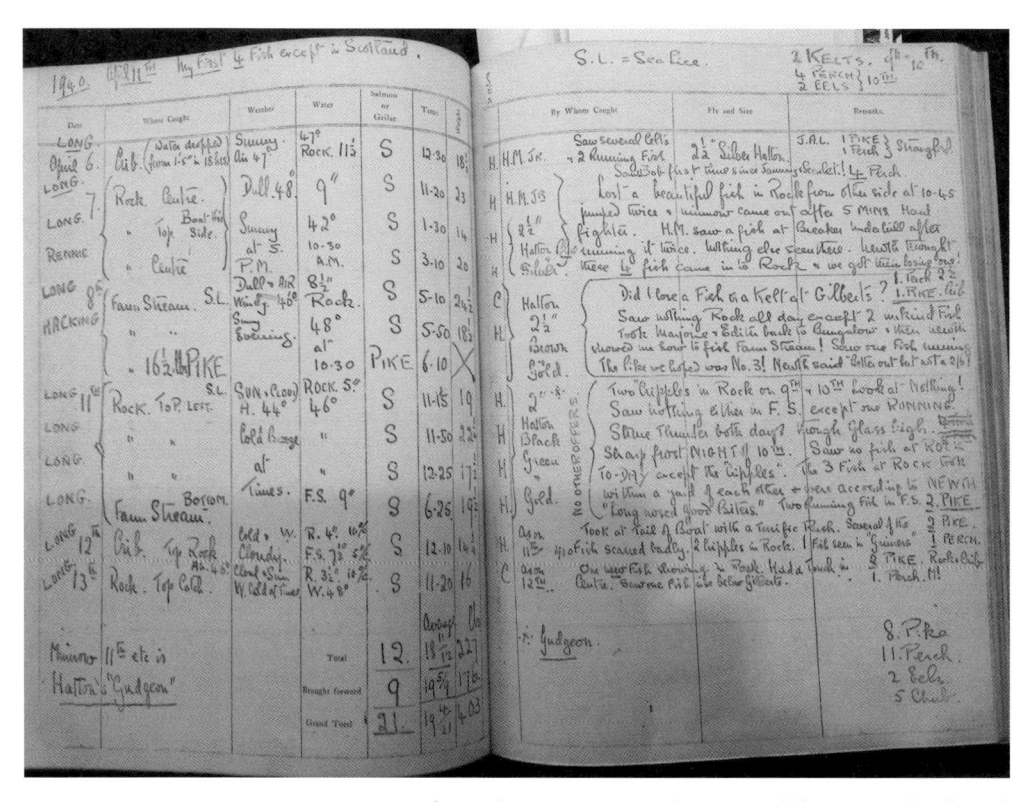

Extract from the Ingestone Fishing Log (photo: M O'Mahony)

time of birth, anglers will never forget the moment they land their first salmon – and its weight too. They are also likely to take a photo! The moment becomes seared on their memory, like the first child: where, what weight, what pool and which fly. And it's got to be recorded. Some records, like Ingestone Fishery's at Foy, are beautifully leather-bound, a three-inch-thick fishery record. Owners come and go from Ingestone, but this document remains with the fishery. The copperplate handwriting can be hard to decipher, but the lines and loops hold secrets. Careful detection reveals that in 1924, a gold-painted Hatton Minnow was used by Philip Moreland, of England's Glory matchbox fame, in the Rock Pool. He owned Ingestone at that time and on his death in January 1940, the fishing record included his obituary: 'Phil caught 2,212 fish on the Ingestone Fishery between 1899 and 1939, his biggest 45lbs from the Fawley Stream in 1928.' It's business as usual on 11 April 1940 when the writer records: 'Saw nothing all day except two unkind fish. Took Marjorie and Edith back to the bungalow.' It's a charming account. Also in April,

Fisherman with salmon and gaff, 1930s
(photo: *Ross Gazette*)

> Molly, Sam and Bob to lunch. Newth's duck eggs are excellent. Lost a pike of 9–10lbs in the Farm Stream. SJM on leave. Molly drove him out with Bob. Bob walked and talked!

A year later and in 1941 the record logs an arrival: 'Bill arrives from Sandhurst with his first PIP!' It's not just fish the writer also pays attention to, but the glorious nature around the fishery when he observes in the spring of 1941, 'Saw first swallow at Farm Stream on April 20th and heard first cuckoo at How Caple, Perrystone, April 22nd.'

The river telegraph was alive and well when the Wizard of the Wye, Robert Pashley, is reported to have 'had 1 on Tuesday up river'. The wider world comes home with a thump when the deaths of two friends are recorded in the summer of 1944: 'Two very good friends whom we hold in affectionate memory. Charles Ogilvie Rennie and F.W. Duart Smith. Bill is mentioned in dispatches, and another, Sam, wins the Military Cross.'

Tony Norman, 71

Tony Norman is a country farmer and wildlife lover. In 2015, an 11-year-long project, in which more than a 1,000 volunteers removed 111 tonnes of rubbish from over a 1,000 miles of river bank, came to an end. It was initiated by Tony in his role as a Wye and Usk Foundation trustee. He feels a huge responsibility to the environment and wildlife. He is also a member of the Golden Valley Fishery, an initiative designed to introduce the endangered eel back into the Wye.

Tony:

> My dad farmed beside the Berkeley Canal and the family fished on various places on the Wye. In the 1960s we fished almost exclusively at Whitney-on-Wye, Captain Hope's estate. So, we fished there with the family, all the brothers and friends, and between us all we covered most days of the week. It was quite a drive from Gloucester to go there, but we did it because we caught a lot of salmon. I was five or six when I first started going. Sixty-five years ago – Christ! I do remember the first salmon I caught was at Whitney. The older generation probably celebrated in a liquid fashion. I don't remember anything else, but they were catching fish all the time. They never used worms, they just used spinners or fly on bait (prawns).

Major Patrick Darling, 59

A stretch of river frontage at his farm in Sellack was a 'tremendous bonus' for Patrick Darling when he moved to the area: 'It's a delight to have a river, particularly such a pretty part of it.' He always fished while growing up in Northern Ireland. When he was in the army he fished wherever he could if there was some going. He is Chair of The River Wye Preservation Trust, an organisation that ensures that the river continues to be an unspoilt part of our natural heritage in Herefordshire, Monmouthshire, and Powys.

The Wye salmon has special appeal. Patrick Darling again:

It's just the magic of the salmon. It's a wild fish and its ecology is so amazing; how it spawns in the river, the way it is nurtured in the river, its fry, then its 'parr' [young salmon], then its 'smolts' [salmon aged between two and five years], then it goes out to sea. The Wye is a big river and probably should be England's premier salmon river. I think at the moment the Tyne is, but potentially the Wye, if we get it fully restored, should be the best. It's quite a slow river. Up in Wales there's some lovely fly water. Once it flows into England, the Welsh, rather contemptuously, refer to it as the "English ditch". That really is referring to the fact that it gets quite slow flowing, meandery, not particularly good for fishing for salmon with flies. So the salmon fishing, traditionally, has been done with minnows and spinners, and in previous days, banned shrimps and worms. And very effectively – people would catch a lot.

I caught my last salmon on the Wye about five years ago now. The reason for that is I really haven't had time to go fishing, and this year I haven't fished on the Wye at all. I think the Wye salmon spend quite a lot of time at sea and come back very big because of their migration route. So there is a tradition in the Wye for some very big fish. Certainly, if you go to Aramstone you will see the British record for the two biggest fish caught in a day. They are both enormous, in plaster casts up there. Fishing as a sport is a lovely way to clear the mind. It is a wonderful, relaxing sport.

In his book, *The Tale of a Wye Fisherman*, H.A. Gilbert discusses the salmon fisherman's ultimate ambition: the 'portmanteau', the 40lb salmon. In the past, anglers often referred to big fish over 40lb as the 'portmanteau' because of the slow movements of a very large fish when hooked was supposed to feel as though a heavy suitcase had taken the bait. Fish weighing between 30lb and 35lb, however, are called 'ladies handbags', because they can be dealt with much more easily. But there is another holdall-like category if you are lucky enough to land a 50-pounder (rare even when salmon were plentiful), and this is the 'American Travelling Trunk!' We can only wonder if this is what Miss Doreen Davey felt she was bringing in on 13 March 1923 at the Cowpond, Winforton, when she landed the river's record-breaking (still to be beaten) salmon, coming in at a hefty 59.5lbs.

A portmanteau was certainly the dream of Richard Pennington's father:

> We lived in Winforton and fished near there. My dad must have caught hundreds of fish and I think his best was a 36-pounder, but he would have

Left: Mr Pennington of Winforton (photo: Richard Pennington)
Right: Ivor Williams holding a 44lb salmon (photo: Robin Hulse)

loved to have caught a portmanteau. I don't know why, I suppose because they were heavy. To catch a portmanteau was the ultimate ambition for salmon fishermen.

Some tried for many years with little success, while others, like the Wye's most famous fisherman, Robert Pashley, caught 14. It was his first portmanteau that he recorded thus: 'My first 40-pounder was killed on Guy's Hospital water with a £2 season ticket!' He had hired a small pleasure boat from a gentleman known only as Davies, at Ross Dock, who was later to meet an ignominious end a few years later, when he drowned while clotting eels at night!

How do you memorialise your greatest salmon catch? You could go the way of hundreds of fishermen and women and have it cased, (as we heard from Aramstone earlier) mounted and stuffed, in a naturalistic setting of course – de rigueur in castles, grand houses, pubs – and the odd terraced house in Monmouth? The latter is the unlikeliest of places to see a mega salmon cast.

John Francis Thompson posing with his 44.5lb salmon (photo: Nicholas Frost)

Off the street, in through the front door, up some rickety, quite ancient stairs, and into the first-floor living room, and here a sturdy coffee table dominates. On it, rather incongruously, is a preternaturally enormous salmon, mouth agape (*Jaws* comes to mind). Glass-cased, this 1907 Symonds Yat catch is immortalised forever. So large was this salmon that it had to be carried from the river to the house on a stretcher fetched hastily from the nearby Symonds Yat station. John Francis Thompson was the gentleman credited with landing the 44.5-pounder. The photograph immortalising the catch was taken at Thompson's seasonally-rented property (specifically for the salmon fishing season), which later became the Wye Rapids Hotel, Symonds Yat. He was assisted by his groom, Edgel. This somewhat disgruntled the local ghillies, who would have gained great kudos had they been involved in landing such a fine specimen. Thompson's salmon landed live in a net and, having been despatched, was got ashore with some difficulty up to the station for prompt weighing. As the parcel's scale was calibrated only to the nearest half pound, and the tail tended to touch the ground on one side of the scale, the exact weight will never be known, but a contemporary edition of *The Angling Times* accepted the figure.

Thompson's wife, Emily, hearing a commotion from the river bank below the house, called her daughter, and they saw a solemn procession returning home with what appeared to be a body on a ladder, carried by two men. Fearing a drowning, Emily wanted to pack her young daughter off indoors, but joyful shouts soon changed their mood, and the party was excitedly welcomed back to the house. There was no time to be lost – the photographer, Dickie Davies, was summoned from Ross (presumably by Railway telegraph and the next train), Thompson was suitably spruced up, the supporting pole was fashioned and the catch was recorded with a plate camera for posterity (albeit with the supporting pole subsequently airbrushed out). With commendable speed, the fish was cut up and the bulk of it despatched by a returning train to Burton-on-Trent cold stores, arriving there perfectly fresh the next morning. The Thompson family based in Burton were then able to draw down salmon whenever the occasion justified, in the comfort of their family homes. The legend of this Edwardian-era catch survives today in Monmouth with Thompson's grandson, antique dealer Nicholas Frost.

Geoff Franks, 76

Geoff Franks is a ghillie on the upper Wye and one of the founding members of the Wye Ghillies Association. He started making fish casts in 1992 after landing a respectable 32-pounder, but first he had to ask permission.

Geoff:

> I rang up my boss and told him I had just caught a 32-pound fish that morning, and he said, "well done; can you take it into Hereford and get it smoked for me?" And I thought, "I'll never see it again" So I got a bag of plaster and made a cast of it and that really was my first attempt. Once I had done that fish I started doing casts for other fishing people as well and it's just gone on from there.

SALMON AS FOOD

There is only so much salmon any self-respecting fisherman can eat. So there comes a time when finding a buyer is the best option. At one time in Hereford there was Mac Fisheries and Sid Wrights selling fish. But the man of choice was 'Fishy' Gardiner. His shop, on the corner of King Street and Bridge Street, made a striking impression in its day, becoming a Hereford institution. Across the shop front a shoal of fish hung from above. More were laid out on tables in front, or resting on marble slabs inside, all jostling for space. If you couldn't get to the shop then Fishy could come to you. For several years he delivered fresh fish from his van all across the city. His method for keeping fish fresh was

Fishy Gardiner outside his shop in King Street (photo: Derek Evans Studio Archive/ HLTAL/ HARC/ Hereford Libraries)

a reliable if now outdated method. Julian Owens of Arkwright Owens Estate Agents remembers, 'Messrs Gardiner renting a garage and underground brick vault as a cold store', which still exists and is still called 'Gardiner's Store' to this day. Fishy's King Street shop closed its doors for the final time on Christmas Eve 1989, the business moving across to the Butter Market.

Speaking some years ago, Fishy Gardiner, also long-time member of the Hereford Rowing Club, remembers the heyday of the salmon market:

> We used to get wonderful salmon from the Wye, wild salmon. Twenty or thirty years ago, during the salmon season, we'd have lots and lots from the river. Local anglers would bring them in each morning. Every Good Friday everyone wanted salmon, so that would be a busy time for us. And I would also smoke salmon too, round the back of the shop.

Tony Norman was one of those who took his freshly-caught salmon to Gardiners:

> We took quite a lot of freshly caught fish to Fishy Gardiner. All these fish were laid out on slabs, and he had dozens and dozens of Wye salmon there. He supplied all the restaurants and hotels and anybody who wanted a fish went to Fishy Gardiner. And he was also an expert at smoking them. You could take a salmon there and two weeks or a month later, you would pick up two sides of salmon, smoked. I'm not sure where he smoked them, but I think it might have been round the back. It was an amazing shop.

When Gordon Diffey was a teenager he would sell fresh catches to Fishy for a few extra 'bob', 'as long as you could show him a valid fishing licence'. The promise of a few extra pennies led to inspired 'enterprising' activities from some youngsters. Innes Jones' shenanigans have all the trademarks of the Artful Dodger:

> I sold Fishy Gardener a large pike once. I had found it dead on the river bank and splashed some water on it from the Castle Green toilets to make it look fresher, and brought it into the shop. I think I got about £3 for it. I was around 13 at the time and with two friends, Tony and Merrick, we found the fish on the beach by Bartonsham Farm. It may have been caught the day before or early that day; it was very dried out and it was so big and heavy we could barely carry it, so I draped it across my cow horn bike handlebars. We found a cup from somewhere, probably a bin, and filled it with water from the toilets. Just before arriving at the shop we poured the

The Mac Fisheries shop opposite All Saints Church at the end of Eign Gate
(photo: Derek Evans Studio Archive/ HLTAL/ HARC/ Hereford Libraries)

water over it which made it look fresh from the river, they weighed it then gave us the cash which we split and spent on cans of shandy.

Besides Gardiners, Hereford also had a 'Mac Fisheries' shop – one of a national chain of fishmongers' shops founded in 1918.

Ross-on-Wye, too, had its fishmongers, with Metcalfes vying for business with Gwynnes. Mr Metcalfe's shop was in Gloucester Road and he is remembered as a proper old-fashioned gentleman, always wearing a trilby hat and he would habitually raise it whenever a customer walked into his shop, and even when speaking to women customers on the telephone. Fishmonger David Gwynne's shop was around the corner in Broad Street, a colourful shop front, with rabbits and birds hanging outside.

Fishy Gardiner may have cornered the Hereford market when it came to fishmongery, but he wasn't the only one smoking salmon by a long stretch. Huts and sheds in woods along the length of the Wye were all engaged in the craft. The smoky tang, wafting through the trees, must have been a familiar smell once upon a time. Norman Owen, former rod maker at Hatton's of Hereford, was also a well-known and much sought-after salmon smoker, and 'Wizard of the Wye' Robert Pashley also got in on the act. He didn't get his hands dirty though. That was the job of his ghillie, Jack Whittingham, as Jack's son Mike recalls:

> There was a little old cottage where Mr Pashley lived at Kerne Lodge, opposite Goodrich Castle, up the back, but it was derelict. There was a tin shed near it and I seem to remember dad smoking salmon in there. He used to gut the salmon and open them up like a kipper and he'd hang them up in there. He'd get all these wet leaves so they created this tremendous smoke. And I think one year the leaves must have dried out quick because it went up in flames and the salmon, they were hung up by rope, and it just went. Of course, being wet, the leaves used to smoulder, but these dried out and burnt the salmon.

RON HODGES, 91
There was a limit: if the salmon was not a certain size, you had to put it back. But old Cal, he had this overcoat with huge pockets and most days he'd come to Mrs Curtin, who I was living with, and say, "Annie, would you like a small salmon?"

River users have netted some unusual and not so unusual finds: cameras, canoes, safes, rings. Ron Hodges probably beats all when it comes to least likely catch: a sting ray in the Severn estuary. Gulf stream, continental drift, or just plain lucky. Poor little sting ray, but a great story for Ron to dine out on. Yes, not strictly in the Wye, but worth a mention nonetheless. During the war, Ron used a fish cellar as an air raid shelter in Chepstow and worked with a fisherman straight out of the pages of *Moby Dick*.

'Stop net' fishing at Brockweir, 1950s (photo: Chepstow Museum)

FISHING 39

Ron:

> Mr Childs was in charge of the fishing in Chepstow. I think they were called Wye Fisheries, or something like that. But they had rights over the river, commercially, for catching salmon. There was an old boy who I was billeted with. His name was Caleb Cumper. In those days, the fishermen didn't dress up. He used to have his overcoat on and a scarf around his neck and used to get in these boats, rather large rowing boats, and they'd anchor them sideways on, facing the incoming tide. Then they'd have two poles, like that, crossing over, and a net over the bottom half. And so, they'd anchor fore and aft, sideways on and then tilt the poles up and wait for the salmon to run into them. There was a limit if the salmon was not a certain size and you had to put it back. But old Cal, he had this overcoat with huge pockets and most days he'd come to Mrs Curtin and say, "Annie, would you like a small salmon?" So, she'd give him a sixpence, or if it was a bigger one, a shilling, then take it out of his pocket, and so we used to dine well on fresh salmon.

Mrs Curtin wasn't the only one to enjoy some salmon perks, as former bailiff for the Wye River Authority, George Smith discovered:

> We had our own netting station at Chepstow then, which belonged to the authority. We used to have stock boats, big wooden boats covered in tar about the length of an average sitting room, weighing about a ton. They'd row them out into the middle of the river and they'd put these big poles down into the middle of the river in the mud to hold them there, and then they'd have these big nets that they'd drop into the river to catch fish. The authority did it up to the mid-80s I suppose. Then they'd go off to Billingsgate or somewhere like that and sell the salmon and that would help pay for the fisheries enforcement on the river. And part of our salary when I first started was all the bailiffs had a salmon every year. I would go up there and choose one myself.

FISHING HUTS

A refuge from the sun, rain, snow, or even prying eyes, fishing huts of every description and persuasion hug the banks of the Wye. Some are grand affairs; others more modest, like the frequent shepherd huts that appear, and a few leaking, creaking remains of a caravan. One shepherd hut relic on the Middle

Left: fishing hut (photo: M. O'Mahony). **Right: Mr Clay's Fishing Hut** (photo: Hugo Mason)

Wye was once a navvies' shelter for Irish labourers working their way up the newly built canals. These mobile huts were once horse-drawn, with their original swivel mechanism for steering the front pair of wheels. The walls of these fishing huts are invariably hung with rods, nets, line, flies, waders, spinners, and plastered with photos of previous catches. Many an angler must have stood in the doorways of these huts, waiting for the kettle to boil, looking to the river wondering what it held in store for them today.

Around 100 years ago, near the village of Aberedw, one well-known fisherman never ate his sandwiches unless accompanied by a glass or two of port. It was reported he overindulged one day and when he started fishing after his midday break, he fell into the river, turned turtle-like, and floated off downstream, but buoyed up by the air in his waders. Thankfully, his ghillie saw what happened and ran downstream, gaffed him by the seat of his waders and hauled him out like a large salmon. The fisherman was quite unaffected by the experience, heartily sustained by liberal quantities of port, and had little recollection of the trauma.

Hugo Mason of Brockhampton remembers Peter Clay Snr's fishing hut next to the Wye under Capler:

> It was something of an icon. He even built an extension on it to save him dismantling his long salmon fly rods! On many occasions, there would be a couple or more salmon on a white marble slab by the door. It was full of fantastic tackle. Unfortunately, it was a target for thieves and finally it

FISHING   41

Herbert Charles Hatton (photo: Hatton Family/ John Symonds)

Left: Hatton's Shop Front in St Owen Street. Right: Mr and Mrs Hatton behind the counter
(photos: Hatton Family/ John Symonds)

was abandoned altogether. Sadly, it was burnt down by vandals on a summer's day after Mr Clay's death in 1993. All that now remains is the floor slab and chimney stack. It had a fireplace to make it more comfortable to fish for salmon in the bitterly cold months at the beginning of the season. Another bit of history lost.

HATTON'S OF HEREFORD

Hatton's of Hereford cannot pass by without mention in any book on the River Wye. A legendary destination for sporting fisherman, the doors to the St Owen Street shop are long closed, but the impression left behind continues to linger.

Writing in 1955, C.V. Hancock (*Rod and River*) insisted, 'the name of Hatton must recur in any history of the Wye salmon fishing'. And he is right. In its time, Hatton's reputation, like the salmon fishermen it served, was world-wide. When the shop closed its doors for the last time in 2001, it was described as the 'end of an era'. Certainly, anglers old enough to remember this 'Aladdin's Cave', describe the shop and the Hatton family – Herbert, Margaret, their son John, and later much-valued assistant (and later owner) Norman Owen – with great affection. Among the many illustrious customers to step over its threshold were some royal guests, including Edward VIII, when he was Prince of Wales, and George VI when he was Duke of York.

The patriarch of the business, Herbert Hatton, who died in 1955, founded the shop at the turn of the nineteenth century and steadily built it up into one of

Left: Mrs Hatton painting Devon Minnow lures. Right: Split cane rods being worked on
(photo: Hatton Family/ John Symonds)

the best-known of its kind in the world. In his obituary in the *Hereford Times*, he was described as 'arguably the king of salmon fishing on the Wye and his customers and many correspondents from all over the world dredged him for knowledge until his deathbed in 1955.'

Hatton's had customers in the Americas, China, Europe and the Middle East, and Herbert was a fishing consultant to some of the largest households in Britain. The high number of salmon in the Wye sustained the business and, with so many anglers beating a path to the river, the business attracted a stream of often monied customers. Game fishing wasn't a cheap sport and the salmon was therefore known in some quarters as the 'gentry fish'. Entering the shop, customers found an interior that resembled a fishing hut in many respects, with stuffed salmon immortalised forever in cases on walls, gaffs and nets propped up in corners, lures and spinners of many descriptions, including the famous Wye Devon Minnow, laid out under glass counters, rods on display, and an array of reels and lines – and of course maggots could be bought by the pint. The upstairs of Hatton's was lined with oak panelling and glass cabinets hugged the walls.

The Hatton handmade split cane rod and hand-tied flies were made in the back rooms. All were designed for use on the Wye.

Herbert and Margaret Hatton at Capler (photo: Hatton Family/ John Symonds)

Herbert honed his craft from his own experience as a fisherman, landing no fewer than 14 salmon over 40-pounds in the Wye with the Wye Minnow, a lure he designed and patented in 1907. It was painted by his wife, Margaret, who worked from a back room. She was a respected fisherwoman in her own right, described in contemporary reports as the 'Grand old lady of Hereford angling'. Her father-in-law had rented five miles of river bank at Fownhope and here she learned almost all there was to know about catching salmon. Her greatest catch was in the 1930s, a 38lb salmon at Fownhope, and she tore the seat of her trousers on a barbed wire fence doing so. Herbert founded the Hereford & District Angling Association in 1921, and he and Margaret were made life members in 1937.

Their son John took over the running of the shop on the death of his father in 1955 and followed in the family tradition, garnering great respect in the angling community as an authority on fishing. He appeared in several TV angling shows in the 1960s. During his tenure, the shop remained unchanged, with hundreds of fishing floats, fly trays, rods, reels and spinners on every shelf, and the obligatory stuffed fish in frames. Together with his business partner, Norman Owen, they showed great skill in rod making and they became the only representatives of the fishing tackle trade in the Guild of Master Craftsmen. In the 1960s alone, the shop repaired more than 3,000 rods every year, with orders coming from all over the world. And there were many more, handcrafted, made-to-measure models. Hatton's is some act to follow.

Hugo Mason is a retired director of Hook Mason architects. The conservation of churches and historic buildings was at the forefront of his work and included a major refurbishment of All Saints' Brockhampton in 1999. He is a lifelong angler, gardener, and wildlife, countryside and dog lover. Thoroughly practical and supportive of good art, colour, creativity and exceptional craftsmanship, he was a customer of Hatton's:

> Nothing about the Wye would be complete without mention of Hatton's. From my very first day's fishing, Hatton's was the place where most people, especially salmon fishermen, used to buy their fishing tackle. It was in St Owen's Street, approximately opposite the Town Hall. Very soon after I started to go there, they were joined by a competent local angler and rod builder, Norman Owen. This was good news as the Hattons were getting older. I had a 'Hatton's Hereford' built cane fly rod at the time, but didn't know how to use it. Norman offered to give me two lessons at Hoarwithy, where he lived, for free, and so this is how my life's fly fishing really began. I remain extremely grateful to Norman for his help in those early days. When he took over the running of Hatton's I helped him design and seek planning permission for his Walenty Pytel shop sign.

The Hatton shop sign, rediscovered during research for this book
(photo: M O'Mahony)

It is believed that Norman was the last person to study for a City & Guild qualification in rod building. He joined Hatton's straight from school at 14, but had been fishing for salmon years before that from his family home, Quarry Cottage,

From left to right: **Norman Owen with a salmon; Norman with his sons, Paul and Simon** (photos: Paul and Simon Owen); **Norman in Hatton's** (photo: Hatton Family/ John Symonds)

in Hoarwithy, almost within casting distance of the river. His son Simon won't eat salmon today; he had too much of it when he was growing up, 'nearly every single day,' said Simon:

> Dad was born in Hoarwithy and he was always fishing from a young age. When he was a kid, there was a surgeon who used to come down to go fishing, but would actually spend all his time in the pub. Before he went back home he would ask dad and dad's friends to bag a few salmon for him so he could bring them home and show his wife that he had been fishing!

Simon is no great fan of fishing, but does remember his dad's skills:

> He used greenheart wood for the rods, and sometimes used old lock gates, because they were made of greenheart too. He did everything by eye and didn't use measuring tools and always, always got it right. He would mend rods too, and he made the famous Wye Minnow. They were complicated to make; each one was composed of at least 20 elements and was the equivalent to a couple of week's wages, so beyond most people's pockets. One of his customers was the chap who owned Booths Gin. As he left he would always say to dad, "drink Booths Gin and live forever!"

Norman finally moved the shop to smaller premises further along St Owen Street where it was eventually acquired by two brothers, who ceased trading after a few years. Norman continued fishing of course, working up to his retirement as a well-loved ghillie at the Cardora beat, downstream near Whitebrook.

A fisherman for over 60 years, Tony Norman is another angler who remembers Hatton's with some fondness:

> Old Mrs Hatton taught me how to make mounts. When you have a spinner, you have a hook with a long piece of cat's gut and then a swivel on the end and that's what you tie onto your line. And she had a special way of making these mounts all out of cat's gut. When I was a boy, she used to take me round the back into her workshop and show me how to tie flies, while my father and uncles were chattering. There was also a bench for making mounts and painting spinners. In the end, she gave me a whole lot of cat gut to make my own, even though she was doing it herself.
>
> Mr Hatton, he was like a sponge. He knew all the bits of information coming up and down the river. There were no computers in those days. So, you called into Hatton's and found out what was going on on the river. Oh, he would know all the information because the ghillies would go in there and at that time there were a lot of water bailiffs as well, and so there was plenty of information travelling around. You didn't need the internet in those days. All we had to do was go into Hatton's for a catch up – any excuse to buy a few little bits.
>
> I've got several Hatton rods. One or two I used to use then and I've still got my Hatton gaff and I've got a really old Hatton rod, which is called a splice rod, which is a fly rod. It doesn't sort of fit into a socket, the two ends; the two pieces overlap and they're bound up. A very old-fashioned way of doing it. They were good rods; they knew what they were doing and Norman Owen was absolutely excellent at repairing rods. They had all sorts of their type of minnow. Every fishing man had their favourites, sort of blue and silver or a yellow belly, black and gold or whatever. And they had their own special ways of painting them up. A lot of them were wooden. A bit technical this, but you've got a fishing line and it goes to a lead to make their minnow go down. It's called a Wye lead. So, there'd be diffrent weights of Wye lead that would pull it down.
>
> This lead was shaped in such a way that it would bump over the stones on the river bottom. Well, from the lead there is about a yard of line to the minnow and a lot of the Hatton minnows were wooden so they'd float off the bottom. What you were trying to do is just swing it round in front of where the fish is lying. That was the theory of it anyway.

'Putcher' basket used to catch salmon (photo: Black rock lave net heritage fishery)

The Wye was such a famous river. It was not only Pashley catching thousands; there was a chap called Hutton, who fished down near the Bunch of Carrots in Hampton Bishop, who was writing books extolling the virtues of the Wye as well. And the Wye was running thousands of fish every year. That wasn't just the ones caught on rod – there were further thousands caught by nets or 'putchers', which are baskets used to catch salmon. It was an exceptional river.

Yorkshire man and ex-miner Phil Jordan, 66, has been river keeper at Garnons for the last 40 years, and knew all about Hatton's:

> We used to share information at Hatton's. I loved to hear that Hereford Anglers, for example, had caught 15 fish on one day because it meant that the following day the run of fish would reach me up-river and we would have a good day. The hazel wood used on the Hatton Devon Minnow came from trees here at Garnons. The minnows were all hand-made. They were sent worldwide for a long time. And then of course the sport stopped spinning and that was one of their livelihoods gone, just like that.

Jack Catchpole is an irascible 85-year-old and a seasoned fisherman. He wasn't Hattons's greatest fan, but he has reserved some good words for the other angling shop in Hereford, Perkins:

> Old Fred Perkins' son got drowned at Eign. He was in a punt with his dad fishing and he fell over in the water. He was only 14. Very sad. Fred Perkins was a smashing old boy; he was a compatriot of my dad. I preferred Perkins. It was only a little shop, but Hatton's were a bit up-market for me.

Jack did his dad proud when he was a boy, when his dad sent him down to the river to catch the family's supper one evening. It was a special moment to be entrusted with his dad's rods:

> The Hospital stretch was a good one for salmon. Jack Daffern, a retired copper, was the bailiff there. I was very proud because I had dad's rods and managed to catch four little trout and Jack Daffern appeared and said, "hello young Catchpole", because he lived opposite us, and I said, "I've got four little trout!" "You haven't," he said, "you've got four little salmon. Now, don't you do it again." So, I went home and we ate them anyway.

COARSE FISHING
An eel skin garter worn below the knee will prevent cramp.
The Folk-lore of Herefordshire, Ella Mary Leather, 1912.

'What is more beautiful to behold, more agreeable to smell, or more pleasant to taste than the grayling,' wrote Giraldus in 1188. His enthusiasm for the umber, or the grayling, is a reminder that the Wye produces fish other than just salmon, which has often proved too expensive for many anglers, put off by the cost of a 'rod'. It was a 'gentry' fish after all. The decline in salmon numbers in recent years has seen a rise in coarse fishing, which has brought in precious revenue to the local economy – a complete turnaround from the buoyant days of salmon fishing on the Wye. In 1954, the Woolhope Naturalists' Field Club reported that,

> The salmon of the Wye provides a by no means unimportant addition to our national food supply. Nor should it be forgotten that a considerable amount of money spent by anglers for house rent, food, servants, ghillies, car and horse hire. The fisheries of the Wye are really of great economic importance to the whole of the district.

Eign railway bridge (photo: Derek Foxton Collection)

On a sunny and bitter February morning in 2018 up to 40 coarse anglers took up their places for a competition on the Hereford Anglers beat. One Welshman has been coming to the same stretch of river for over 45 years. He wouldn't give his name: 'I don't want the wife to stop me coming!' The new footbridge is a godsend, he said. No more dodging trains. That's how keen these anglers are to get to their fishing grounds: up and over the railway bridge. Jack Catchpole remembers well:

> Earlier on you could go over that railway bridge with permission from the railway people as long as you recognised the time of the train. Down at Eign was where all the people who were on the dole and things used to go and earn beer money. Then you used to have your fish weighed in at the Brewer's Arms and you sold them. It was the official weigh-in place for Hereford Anglers. It was cheap to be a member. I used to go to Eign occasionally and when the sun came up you could see all these little red dots where all the men were smoking. And there were postman coming off night shift, railway people, all those sorts of people. It was an easy way to earn money. Before the Brewer's Arms, the Hereford Anglers had their AGMs and meetings upstairs at the Whalebone Inn. Then they went to the steak place on King Street and then for years and years they were at the Rowing Club. I became a member in the fifties, when my father was a member.

Lyn Cobley, 75
Fishing was a bug. I was working in Hereford and I took a job nights so I could fish throughout the salmon season.

Lyn Cobley, a former South Wales' coal miner, is a ghillie at Ingestone, Foy. Can there be a greater contrast in his choice of workplaces, from dark coal caverns to this sublime stretch of river? He must pinch himself every morning. He has been on the river at Foy for 39 years and shows no inclination to retire:

> I've fished all my life and my dad introduced me to the Wye when I was five years old. There wasn't much fishing at home in South Wales as the rivers were black with coal dust. My dad used to bring me up to the Wye and we'd get a bus and fish there and all we used to catch were trout and sand dabs, but up on the Wye we used to go all over with the Angling Club, and we used to catch the chubb and dace and God knows what. Fishing was a bug. I was working in Hereford and working nights. How the hell I used to get through the season I don't know!
>
> Coarse fishing – you go in and you catch fish in freshwater and then put them back, and when we used to come to the upper reaches of the Wye at Builth, Glasbury, and Newbridge-on-Wye, the condition of fishing them was you had to take the fish from there, so you caught the fish and took them home. They were buried in the garden but thank God none of that goes on now.
>
> The Wye was about the best river in the country for coarse fishing. You could come in and catch about 30, 40 pound bags a day of roach. You're talking about 50, 70, 80 pound bags of chubbs, and when the barbel come in, it altered it. There's no doubt the barbel made big inroads into the Wye. It was introduced into the Severn, but it's a fish that comes from abroad originally. It was put in the Wye illegally and now we get people from all over the country to fish for barbel. They'll catch the other fish but the majority is barbel.
>
> It brings in a lot of revenue. I would say for the Wye as a whole now, coarse fishing brings in an equal amount, if not more, than the salmon fishing. The salmon angler, he comes one day a week, drives up here from the Cotswolds or whatever and drives home at the end of the day; but our coarse fishermen come and they'll stop a week, so they'll get all their groceries in Ross-on-Wye and their bait and they'll buy a lot and it's a fishing week. People come from all over the country. Coarse fishing is worth a fortune and unfortunately we anglers don't make enough noise about the income it brings into the Wye Valley.

THE EEL

The eel: snake-like, slippery, slimy, what's to like? Well, at one time quite a lot actually. They were easy to catch, there were lots of them, they provided a cheap food source and, we are reliably informed, tasted pretty good. But there is a problem with our eel population. Their dramatic decline makes for shocking reading. The shrinking salmon population pales into comparison when it comes to the eel. Words like *devastating*, *catastrophic* and *irreversible* are bandied around when talking about the 'slippery one'. The statistics really do speak for themselves. One group is trying to do something about it.

Guenter's sister with an eel catch at Wilton
(photo: Mandi Matthes)

TONY NORMAN

Tony Norman is part of The Herefordshire Eel Project, a collaborative effort between the Golden Valley Fish and Wildlife Association, the Lugg and Arrow Fisheries Association, the Wye and Usk Foundation, the Environment Agency and supporting groups and sponsors. It is trying to increase the numbers of eels in the Wye:

> The eel's population has dropped by 95% in 30 years in the Wye. I can't remember the exact figures, but I think in the 1970s it was something like 50 tonnes of elvers (baby eels) caught on the Wye. Last year there was just one kilo. A dramatic difference.

The Project has restocked county rivers with elvers and is campaigning to stop the fish being exported. It remains to be seen whether this effort can replenish the Wye of the elver that has been fished, almost to extinction, over several generations. There is scepticism from some about their attempts. What is undisputed is that they have quite a job on their hands. It's a sad and poignant story. As one old-timer put it: 'There's none left and that means little boys can't bring an eel back home and show mum anymore. We all used to do that.'

Bruce Wallace, 76

Bruce loves the River Wye. A keen sportsman, he has rowed, played squash and rugby, and swam too. During his working life, he was Production Engineering Manager at Rank Xerox in Mitcheldean, spending some of his time at the company HQ in Webster, New York. Now retired, he lives in his riverside home with wife, Jane, at Breinton Common.

As a boy he was taught a rather unusual but effective tactic to catch eels:

> What we did was get a sheep's head and we put it into a sheaf of corn, at the narrow end, where the grain is, and tie it to keep it in there. And then we would put it in the brook or the stream with the head of the stook facing downstream. You'd have to string round both ends, coming across to the bank. You'd then leave it there overnight, and in the morning you'd come back and you would have eels in there.

Easy then? In preparing a plate of grilled eel, recipes call for the creature to be salted then skinned. No doubt Fishy Gardiner would have done this in a blink of an eye. There were many methods. One particularly brutal way was to nail it to the door and then set to work and pull the skin off. Many more children brought them home to mum, putting the writhing mass into the sink in the scullery. When ready, the eel was grabbed, head chopped off ('put your foot on its head and then chop it off'), salt it to give some purchase, and then start to roll the skin down a little way. After this slightly tricky start, the skin can be pulled down fairly easily and came off in one piece. Simple once you know how, we suppose. As recently as the early 1990s, Meldon Kysow was night-fishing for eels:

> I lived on Hinton Road, a stone's throw from the River Wye, so I fished all along the Bishops Meadows/ Bartonsham Farm stretch and Rotherwas from a young age from the mid-eighties. Back then when fishing for eels, I'd stay out the whole six weeks of school holidays, night and day, fishing with friends. We used to take our catch to Fishy Gardiner's in the Butter Market early the next morning and we would stuff some of the eels with

pebbles to boost the weight! All money raised would be spent on more fishing tackle from Hatton's/ Perkin's, mainly hooks as eels swallow them, and cigarettes ready for the next night to do the same again.

The fruits of Gary McLeod's eel fishing exploits in Hunderton were enjoyed steaming hot and served up on a platter to an eager audience in The Vaga Tavern:

> We used to go eeling down on the ferry steps, at the end of Villa Street, Preedy's ferry. We used to come out of the pub at night, get two flagons of GL cider or something, and we'd be there all night eeling, and you'd come back in the morning and you'd have a whole bag of eels. You'd bring them home and mum would do them: skin them, cut them up, put them in the oven. You'd sort of fry them off, but you wouldn't put any fat with them because there was fat in the eel. Then pull them out, damp them off in a tray, put them back in for a minute until they are dried off. When an eel is done it's as white as cod, white as snow and it's beautiful. When it was ready I used to take them across the road to The Vaga on a Sunday, where dad was the landlord. All the lads in there said they didn't like the eels, but I'll tell you what, there wasn't much left when they started on them. All you had left was the bone and they'd suck that, the meat off the bone. I'd bring a big bloody tray over to the pub and they'd get stuck in and then they'd buy me a pint!
>
> Eel was a popular thing mind. We just used a rod and line and anything rotten. Someone came up with an eel trap and we would go and get something dead, some old guts, and chuck it in. The trap went down to a narrow point and they couldn't get out. You would probably leave it in there for 24 hours and there were loads and loads of eels in there when we came back.

There were certainly plenty of eels to go around. Down-river in Bishopswood, Bob Duberley would set night lines. But watch out – the eels had a bite.

> We used to fish for eels quite a lot from the bank in Bishopswood. The other thing we used to do was set night lines. Well, you put a line with a hook on and you put a good big worm and then you put a peg in the side of the bank and you put the line in the river. And on night lines you always seem to catch bigger eels. The next morning you would check and you'd often catch something worth having. You got the big ones and you had to chop their heads off pretty quick because they were on the nasty side. You'd get

a big piece of newspaper on the table then you'd chop their heads off, and get some salt just behind the fins and then you pull the skin right off them. Then we fried the eel. It's quite nice, like a white meat. But the best time to catch eels was when it was thundering and they'd be a bit like mad.

Eels though, as many have already remarked, are as 'slippery as hell!' And they didn't go without a fight.

Adrian Howard, Crokers Ash:

> You'd have a job holding onto them; they've got a slime on them. It's horrible if you get an eel. They wrap around your arm and sometimes around the line. Bit like you get a trail with a snail – it's a bit like that. The Garron used to be full of eels and they used to be a damn nuisance. We went down there once after a thunder storm and we caught 18 in three quarters of an hour. We ran out of worms then and we broke the last worm in half and we had an eel each on that.

The Garron (photo: *Ross Gazette*)

A young Hugo Mason of Brockhampton was another night-time eel fishing fan:

By the time I was 12, I was well into fishing and this increased as I reached my teens. Being good with my hands, I soon learned to make my own fishing rods out of old tank aerials, which were totally unbalanced, but all that we could afford.

The main season was early May to the end of June. Ledgering was the favoured method, using worms for bait. Rising water was always good. I used to fish under Capler, below the Iron Gate, down to The Boards or The Stones and it was nothing for me to catch a bucketful of eels in a four-hour session. These eels would wriggle all over the place and took some handling. I fished for eels until 1965 and caught many over 3lbs in weight. The big draw of eel fishing was going at night. This I used to do very often.

Hugo Mason with two eels
(photo: Hugo Mason)

The night I remember best was the day I left Ross Grammar School at age 15, without any idea of what I was going to do with the rest of my life. On this occasion, I fished at Seabournes, Much Fawley, and having got permission from Tom Gaskell, the owner, I cycled from home to the river a couple of hours before it got dark. I left my bike at Brace's farm before walking down to the river. I always took a little split cane fly rod with me in order to catch a few dace and bleak [a small, slender fish, found in most streams, lakes and the slower moving rivers, but prefers open waters] for bait. Then I would settle down with two rods, each illuminated with torches, so that I could see when I had a bite. In the daylight, eels will usually only take worms, but when it gets dark, chopped up bleak and dace suit them so much better. The big bonus is that larger eels come on the feed after nightfall and it was nothing for me to take a bucketful home before it got light the next morning. Big eels are very powerful fish and develop an extra strength when they have the tip of their tail under a rock or in a weed bed. And what did I do with all these eels? Occasionally my mother could be tempted to skin some, and we would eat them. Better than that though, the farmer at Ladyridge, Harry Phillips, simply loved them and would give me as much as ten shillings (50p) for a bucketful.

Tony Norman enjoyed smoked eel:

> As a boy we would set the net in a small stream and catch the silver eels heading off to the sea, and my friends, other farmers, would have eel traps on their weirs and things which had been set for the same thing. Then we would hang them up and skin then, and we had a smoker at the time, smoke them and eat them. Eel is delicious, soft succulent, a quite oily meat.

TWICE IRON CROSS DECORATED GERMAN POW

The Second Battle of El Alamein (23 October–11 November 1942) was a battle of the Second World War that took place near the Egyptian railway halt of the same name. With the Allies victorious, it was the watershed of the Western Desert Campaign. Living in peaceful retirement outside Ross-on-Wye is one of the commanders who took part. General Sir Thomas Pearson KCB, CBE, DSO & Bar (born 1914) is currently the oldest living British full General and was awarded a Bar to his DSO on 19 August 1943.

On his opposite side at the Battle of El Alamein was a handsome young German, Luftwaffe paratrooper, Guenter Matthes. Born in Berlin, he trained as a baker after leaving school, but his youth and career was interrupted by the war and he was soon fighting for the Führer. During his army career, he was awarded the Iron Cross First Class twice and was captured twice by the Allies: the first time in Europe (although he managed to escape), and the second time in North Africa, when he was fighting under Rommel and opposite Sir Thomas. After he was captured in North Africa, he was shipped to a POW camp in North America. From New York he was taken across the US with other POWs to a camp in Sacramento, California. After escaping a second time, he was brought to a POW camp in Ross-on-Wye.

Guenter Matthes in his uniform
(photo: Mandi Matthes)

At the war's end he stayed on in Ross, never returning to his German roots. His family, meanwhile, had been separated by the Berlin Wall. One of his brothers-in-law, Herman, worked for the Stasi in East Berlin, the official state security service and one of the most feared and repressive intelligence and secret police agencies during the Cold War.

In later years, his parents and sister did come to visit Ross-on-Wye, where he introduced them to the delights of eel fishing on the Wye, often on the river bank at the White Lion in Ross. He is still remembered by many as one of life's characters. In his photographs, at the helm of a boat, or holding up his latest eel or salmon, swashbuckling in appearance in his waders, he took English country life to his heart, dashing around to the envy of some on his Norton Dominator motorbike. It is extraordinary that he went on to work for a short period as ghillie for Sir Thomas, his opposite number on the field of war. Guenter's daughter, Mandi, remembers a man who rarely talked about his wartime experiences:

> He did tell me he was let out of the camp to work with fellow prisoners on local farms. He worked as a barber in Ross for a while, but he felt the war had robbed him of his youth and he didn't want to go back. He worked for Rank Xerox until he retired, but was a ghillie on the Wye and that's what he loved, shooting and fishing. I have fond memories of him bringing fresh eels for breakfast. Delicious.

From top: Guenter's parents;
Guenter working as a ghillie at Kerne Lodge in the 1960s;
Guenter on the river later in life
(photos: Mandi Matthes)

Les Moses, 58

Les Moses is a former salmon poacher. When the salmon population began to decline, he turned to eel fishing and made a good, and legitimate, living from it for eight years. He only stopped when he realised the consequences of what he was doing, and there were no eels in the river anymore.

> It all started when I was listening to an old chap, the one that made nets for us in Bridport when I was salmon poaching. He kept saying to me all the time, "Forget the salmon nets, buy these eel fyke nets". Eventually, I bought some – they were all legal. And so he put me onto the eel side of it, and me and the wife did that for eight years. She actually rowed the boat. This is how ironic it is. I started asking the landowners if I could net the river system for eels and promise not to touch the salmon. And one or two let me have a go. And of course, once I got on well with some of them, the others could see it was better for them to let me work with them than against them. But it was big money with eels again. The first owner who let me on – I won't name him, he's dead now, but his son hated me – I said, "Whatever I earn I'll give you half." And he said, "I don't really need it. Just leave the salmon alone, that's all I ask, and I'll give you a chance to turn a new leaf sort of thing." I admire the man for what he done for me. In the end, I had 56 miles of the Wye, legally, to net eels.
>
> I started having all that permission and started earning a lot of money. I had some big landowners, Hoarwithy way, all the way through. They kept going up, because once you empty a place of eels, they take four years or more to fill back up. I had an agreement with all of them: me and the wife would turn up in the evening after the salmon fishermen had gone and we'd put the nets in for the eels, sit on them all night; we'd pull them out, and I was talking 40 to 50 fyke nets then. It would take you hours to put in, in a rubber dinghy, a good one. We would go out every night then, and we started making our way up the river. We had trailers, into tanks, waiting for the lorry, all the pumps going, load them up. But when I tried to go back over ground I had done, there was no eels there.
>
> I was earning big money on the eels, £5 a kilo. I used to meet the lorry from Holland down at Chepstow once a fortnight. In the end, he was coming once a week to my house, taking 300 to 600 kilo a week. I had tanks up here holding the eels – nobody knew I was doing it. When I do something, I look into the finest detail to get it right. If you're going to do something, do it proper. But then what happened was the eels weren't there no more.

Les had his own unusual and highly effective method for catching these slippery fish, using a combination of umbrella and dental floss. It worked very well:

> This was an old way from years back. I used to thread worms onto cotton wool and make a mop and tie it like a fishing rod, and then bob it into the river and the eel would take a bite and I would lift it into an upside-down umbrella. But I changed from wool to dental floss, because it caught in the eel's teeth better, and floss was easier to sew worms onto. You would drop this floss mop in the river and pull it out and it was amazing. Most times I would get five or six eels each time and the most I've ever had on one mop was 11. There were plenty of nights when I would make two or three hundred quid.

But these are still desperate times for the eel in the River Wye. Could there be reasons to be optimistic? The Herefordshire Eel Project presented a petition of nearly 2,000 signatures in 2016 to 10 Downing Street calling for an end to the commercial exploitation of endangered baby eels, so there is some hope for our silvery friend. But still a long way to go.

ELVERS

Elvers are amazing creatures. Small, transparent, worm-like fish, they arrive in the Wye and the Severn from the Sargasso Sea in their millions. They are a highly sought-after delicacy with the appearance of glass noodles. In Gloucestershire, they are commonly served with scrambled eggs on toast.

In Robert Gibbings' meander down the Wye in 1942 he enquired about elvers. In response, he was told: 'If you wants to see elvers, cut three inches off the ends of a hayfork, then you can get them proper.' (*Coming down the Wye*). You can see an implement of a similar description at Hereford Museum.

The promise of gold enticed thousands of prospectors to the Californian goldfields. It was a rough, tough, uncertain, and often violent existence. But there could be the occasional riches that kept the carrot dangling for far longer than it should sensibly have done so. Could we make similar comparisons to the Wye 'elver rush'?

Make no mistake, there was big money to be made and some rough and tumble on the riverside to secure it, with bullying, intimidation and even death threats. At one time, a kilo of elvers in China (where it is considered a delicacy and consumed in vast quantities) cost £6,000. That's more than Beluga caviar. But today the elver population is decimated. It's a salutary tale: if you want to fish the young in those quantities, there's going to be an impact at some point down the line. And it's being felt now.

The eyes of one Monmouth hairdresser still glaze over when he remembers striking 'elver' gold on the banks of the River Wye, leaving his competitors empty-handed:

> I stepped in to help a friend one evening. He and his usual elvering partner hadn't had much luck the previous few nights, so I helped when the other dropped out. At Brockweir we picked our spot, got the nets out and waited. There were other groups waiting like us, with their nets and that, upstream, downstream, on the opposite bank, all around us. It was quiet and we put our nets in the water. We had only been there ten minutes, when the elvers came, and they kept coming, net after net, bucket after bucket, tray after tray. We hadn't even been there an hour, but had to stop because we didn't have enough space for any more. The guys opposite and downstream hit nothing. In little under an hour we earned £10,000 each. Best night's work ever.

The stakes were high and it could get rough during the season as competition for prime spots reached fever pitch. Unconventional, and often flirting with the law, Les Moses took his elvering operation very seriously, employing some 'hard nuts' with the intention of putting 'the fear of God' into fellow elver fishermen:

> I done the elvering all my life from the age of 16. I used to go and just dabble, have a bit of fun. There was 300 to 600 people fishing there at one time. But the big money crept in on it. I shouldn't have done it at the time, but I banned all the locals from going on some land by the river that one of my relatives owned. They said, "You can't do that," and I said, "Watch me." So, I got three of the hardest nutters from down the Valleys and one of them was one of the hardest men rugby league players ever. They were fishing with me to look after it. I've had up to £480 a kilo at one time. The best they had down there was probably £380 a kilo. One time, the crew fishing for me, we had £52,000 in less than an hour one night. All tax-free.
>
> If someone was on the bank when you got there, it was their spot, or you'd fight them off it. On the other rivers, we've had drive-by shotguns, cars slowing down, window wound down and someone pointing a gun at

you. That was just how it was. There was a lot of money at stake.

Everyone had wooden trays. You'd fill your trays and you had to go to the lorry that pulled up at Bigsweir Bridge and sell them, and you'd stand in a queue. It was all cash. I'm telling you now, God's honest truth, I've seen over a million-quid's worth of elvers die, while people waited in a queue to sell them at Bigsweir. I estimated over a million-quid's worth, at the price I could have got, £480 a kilo. I had crews fishing other rivers for elvers that nobody else did. The only other crew fishing on the river was the Gloucester 'mafia'; they was old men and we never got into fighting with them because they was old and, fair play, they been doing it years before us. They'd all bought their houses before we'd even started it. They knew what they was doing on one little river. You could earn enough to buy a house. But it's ruined now, all the elvers are gone.

Major Patrick Darling farms above the Wye at Caradoc. It's also where a 15-year-old Les Moses was an apprentice national hunt jockey in the late 1970s, a long time before Patrick's arrival. Patrick agrees the eel is much reduced in number:

> They are a species that are struggling to survive. In the old days if you dredged out a pond, you would find eels in the mud. Much less so now. And by the old days, I'm only talking 15 years ago. And of course, it's sad to kill an old eel because it's probably taken ten years to get to that size and you want it to get back to the Saragossa Sea and have more elvers.

PIKE

And then there was the pike, the underdog in many respects in the river. They don't get the best of press. One observer was most unflattering in its description: 'It has the smallest of brains. It lacks anything of the innocence of salmon, trout or perch, which renders the creature so repellent!' (Gibbings, 1942). Its predatory nature is well known. Last century, a fisheries inspector, H. Cholmondeley-Pennell, recalls this example of the greedy fish:

> A night line had been set, and when taken up the next morning was found to have a large pike on the hook. In order to extract the hook this fish had to be opened, and it was then found that the hook was really inside a smaller fish, which had been swallowed by the bigger one. This smaller one was then opened, and it was found that yet another pike was inside its belly.

So, not very attractive, and a voracious bully boy in the river. Nonetheless, it certainly has fans, and Hugo Mason is one waving the flag for them:

Pike are amazing fish. I got to know the beat under Capler very well and I became very good at locating pike when they were feeding. In the Wye they can go up to about 30lbs in weight and are truly fantastic as they can move like lightning. I never got anywhere near 30lbs, but I did catch a lot in the twenty-pound bracket. One late autumn day in 1988, I took my nine-year-old daughter, Lucy, down to the Wye, where we fished for over an hour with a 'Colorado Spoon', a type of bait-fish lure. I really wanted her to catch a pike and just when I thought we were going to have a 'blank' a really fine pike took the spoon. Lucy played the fish with no help from me and it weighted 12.5 pounds. I thought that experience was a once and only, but was proved totally wrong when I took eight-year-old Damian on his very first fishing lesson in exactly the same spot some 27 years later. We hadn't been fishing long and were using a heavy rubber sprat as bait using the sink and draw method. Just as Damian was about to pull his bait off the water in order to re-cast, it was taken by the largest pike I have ever seen.

Lucy Mason, daughter of Hugo, with a 12.5lb pike (photo: Hugo Mason)

Pike are mainly caught on spinning baits, such as 'Mepps' and 'Colorado Spoons' and very often they will take your bait from right under your feet. I picked up most of my pike fishing skills from Eric Powell. Eric lived in West Cottage, only a stone's throw from my house. A local farm worker and keen angler, I now find his methods rather unacceptable. As well as the usual spinning baits, 'live baiting' was practised by nearly all anglers. You would either go out the day before or early in the morning to catch a few small dace or roach for 'live bait'. These would then be transported live in a milk churn or similar from spot to spot where you thought there might be feeding pike. The poor little 'live bait' would be mounted onto a wire trace with at least two treble hooks and then allowed to swim freely around, lie until found by a hungry pike. How disrespectful. West Cottage had a bathroom of sorts, but the bath was not plumbed into hot or cold water. During the winter Eric would keep his live bait in the bath. Quite how he and Mrs Powell washed I am not too sure! The more familiar pattern of pike fishing

Hugo Mason with Reg Cotterell and a 16lb pike outside the Yew Tree Inn (**Wood Pub**) **in Fawley, 1960s** (photo: Hugo Mason)

was going to the river on a Sunday morning with my next-door neighbour, Reg Cotterell. We would go about 9 a.m., walk down Lilley's Lane and after fishing would find our way up to the Yew Tree Inn (the Wood Pub) for a few pints.

Hugo Mason with a 19lb pike, under Capler (photo: Hugo Mason)

Richard Pennington from Winforton is a salmon fisherman who has some sympathy for the poor old pike, especially in his days as ghillie at Letton:

> When I was there the salmon fishermen, if they caught a pike, would just throw it on the bank. I chastised them in a polite sort of way. I said, "if you catch a pike give it to me". I knew somebody in the village who liked it, and we had one once or twice from Letton Court. It would be my job to get rid of all the bones. They are quite boney but the flesh is nice. I think it's as nice as cod. I used to make it into Dutch fishcakes, which was about 80% fish. Everybody would eat them. Salmon fisherman didn't like them because they ate the salmon. When I was a boy, my father and I used to do pike fishing. We used to apply for a licence from Whitney Court, a permit, and on it it said: 'All coarse fish caught must be killed!' When we applied for the next one we would tell them how many pike we had caught, and that stood us in good stead for getting another one. One of the fishermen who used to come down to Letton would very often catch a pike and he would take it back to London and they would have a dinner party with it.

Les Moses has felt the breath of many a bailiff down his neck over the years, but comes clean when it comes to the pike. It's not the thrill of the chase for him, but seeing the float go under:

> That's what does it for me. I started when I was 16. It was a winter thing. I would do it in the day and go lamping in the evening. I didn't have to hide anything. I had a boat on the Wye for doing it and I chased big pike for ten years. Loads of 25 pounders and 28 pounders. At one time, I was the only pike guide on the Wye. When I was doing the eel fishing the owners let me do the pike fishing as well and kids and their dads came along. I took a 12-year-old once with three months to live whose dream it was to catch a pike and he did. I'll always remember that. I used to photograph every pike I caught, had boxes in the attic. But the fish just aren't there any more.

FLYING PIKE

Hereford's very own coracler, Pete Redding has the distinction of seeing a 'flying' pike. On a hundred-mile canoeing adventure from Bodenham to the Severn Bridge, he arrived where the Lugg and the Wye meet at Mordiford:

> There was a standing wave, where the two rivers were actually different heights and we got out to check our route into the river and we stood on this corner near a small hawthorn tree. While we were trying to pick out the safe area to break into, as we came into the Wye, a pike hit the wave, flew out of the water and landed in the hawthorn tree. It paused for a second or two, wriggled, then jumped out of the tree and landed in the Lugg!

IRANIAN SIEGE HERO

Fishing the Wye, salmon or coarse, has attracted a great number of characters in its time. None more so than Tommy Palmer.

Long after the Tommy Palmer competition stopped, the Memorial Cup still exists. Highly polished, and with the names of past winners etched onto its side, it sits on a sideboard at the home of Caroline Hodgeson in her Wyeside village. Caroline, since remarried, is the widow of Tommy, one of the SAS Iranian Embassy siege heroes. He and his comrades featured in several iconic photographs of the Embassy balcony as the drama unfolded, holding a nation spellbound in May 1980, when a group of six armed men stormed the Embassy,

Left: Tommy Palmer. Right: Tommy and Caroline at Buckingham Palace to receive Tommy's medal (photos: Cara and Shona Palmer)

campaigning for Arab national sovereignty in the southern Iranian region of Khuzestan. They took 26 people hostage, mostly Embassy staff but also several visitors, as well as a police officer who had been guarding the Embassy. By the sixth day, frustrated that their demands were not being met, they killed one of the hostages. In response, the Government ordered in the SAS to rescue the remaining hostages. A nation watched entranced, as the 'boys from the Regiment' abseiled from the roof of the building and forced entry through the windows, rescuing all but one of the remaining hostages, and killing five of the six hostage-takers.

In one of the famous newspaper images, Tommy's balaclava had been pushed back, revealing his face. It was a shock for his wife back home in Hereford, who had no idea where he was. Home life in Hereford was a relatively simple one for Tommy. He loved to fish, even if his methods were unorthodox, so an angling competition in his memory, organised by his 'adoptive' dad, the late George Butler, seemed the most appropriate way of remembering Tommy after his untimely death in a car accident several years after the siege. The competition continued to run for several years, with large turn-outs, including appearances from his regimental mates, before it came to a natural end.

When he first arrived in Hereford as a young man from his home town of Edinburgh, Tommy didn't know anyone. But it didn't stay that way for long.

> TOMMY PALMER MEMORIAL CUP
> FISHING COMPETITION
> RIVER WYE
> FORCE & FERRY INN FOWNHOPE
> 10 A.M. TILL 4 PM. 19TH OCT 1986
> ENTRY FEE. £4.00
> PRIZES. CUP. TANKARDS. MONEY. 1st 2nd 3rd.
> PAY & PEG Nos. 9 A.M. AT INN. RING HFD 267743 OR FOWNHOPE 391

Tommy Palmer Memorial Cup poster (photo: Cara and Shona Palmer)

Caroline:

> He was only little, shorter than me! A little toughie. Determined. Oh, he was a character. A chap called Rhett Butler (named after the *Gone with the Wind* character), who was also in the Regiment, took him under his wing and Rhett's parents, George (born on the road to Mandalay – seriously) and Doreen, used to feed him. Tommy thought the world of them.
>
> Tommy was a keen fisherman when he was here, especially where you weren't supposed to fish! He was called the poacher in the regiment. I don't know if he was ever caught! It has been said he went fishing with hand grenades as well. I'm not sure about the Wye but he did in other places while serving abroad.

George Butler's daughter, Lynne, recalls a one-off:

> Oh my god, what a character he was! But Tommy wasn't a fisherman, he was a poacher! His friends told me, wherever they went in the world he would go and get a treat of some sorts, food or whatever. That was Tommy all over, a survivor. In Hereford folklore, he was the hero of the siege. When

the men went away, in those days it was for six months at a time, so we were a close-knit family. My brother Rhett was in the SAS as well, and him and Tommy were best friends. My family became Tommy's family. Then he met Caroline and they got married, and Cara and Shona were born, and we've always remained close.

Tommy was into everything; he could live off the land. I came home once and thought, what's that in my back garden? It was him with a rotavator. I went out and said, "What are you doing?" He said, "Lynne, I thought we could grow some potatoes". I said no, that's my blooming garden! But he said, "We could make a killing". And we always knew when Tommy had been around because he would post a flower through the letter box. He really was extra something else.

I remember another time when my dad and Tommy fell out because Tommy was home and he kept trying to get dad to go out, but George would say, "no, you're married now, you've got to behave; you don't go out drinking, it's not fair". Well, he phoned dad up on one occasion and said, "Will you come and baby-sit because me and Caroline are going to a squadron do." So, dad said yes and when he arrived Caroline wasn't ready. Fatal mistake. Tommy took dad across to the clubhouse while Caroline got ready and they returned hours later absolutely paralytic. Poor Caroline was sat there all dressed up and nowhere to go! She wasn't very happy.

Cara and her sister, Shona, were toddlers when their father died but they want him to be remembered as a hero and to keep his memory alive.

Cara:

I was too young to remember, but I've heard so many stories about him. He used to run (fitness was a big thing with him). He had to be fit. He'd go running a lot and cover 20 miles a time. It was hard on a lot of marriages. He was fearless really. When the Wye was in full flood, for example, he would jump in and swim in it. He would jump off a bank near Holme Lacy bridge. He made his neighbour go in once, who said afterwards, "Never again".

The fishing competitions were good days. There used to be a lot of people who came and it was a family day, with all the kids running around, up and down the banks much to the annoyance of the fishermen.

On the night of the siege, Caroline was at home, eyes glued to the TV screen with the rest of the nation as the drama unfolded.

Caroline:

> When it started coming on the telly I knew that's where he was. He was on stand-by and he was called and then it started coming on the news and I knew that's where he had gone. I think it was the first time, and probably for a lot of people, I realised what the regiment did because he used to go away and come home and what happened in between I never knew and I never asked. He never talked about it.

He got home around three in the morning, hours after the siege ended and Margaret Thatcher took the men a crate of beer in person.
Caroline again:

> All I remember is him being violently sick, like a delayed reaction to it all I suppose. I knew a lot more about the siege after he died. He just didn't talk about things. He received the Queen's Gallantry Medal. And I was told by the lads that if it hadn't been for him things may not have gone as well as they did. He'd come down the rope and the terrorists saw him, so he just had to think quick. They'd piled up carpets near the windows and set fire to it all. He went in and his gun jammed, and he caught fire, his shoulder. He came back out, ripped off his hood, went back in for the second time, and that was at a time when it was kicking off and they realised they had to do something about it. And one of the other lads above him on the rope, the rope caught fire and burnt his legs quite badly.

Lynne:

> Tommy was a survivor; he could survive anywhere, and then he was killed in a car crash. I remember it clearly. It was 1983, and he'd been in Northern Ireland. We were devastated. But dad, George, wanted to do something that would remember Tommy, so he decided that an annual fishing match in his name was the perfect memorial.

Caroline Hodgeson presenting the Tommy Palmer Memorial Cup
(photo: Cara and Shona Palmer)

Caroline:

We held it at the Forge & Ferry in Fownhope for several years, when a couple, Ben and Cherry, were running it. Then it went to the Moon at Mordiford. And then George moved it to Belmont Golf Club, where it was held for about two or three years. But then George started to get too old to arrange it and it just fizzled out.

Tommy's eldest daughter, Cara, has three sons of her own now and has a dream that they may start up the competition again one day. Let's hope so.

If a one-off like Tommy Palmer had to choose one of these for company, who do you think he would choose: bailiff or poacher? He would probably give the bailiffs a run for their money and then buy them drinks at the pub after!

SIEGE HERO DIES ON A SECRET MISSION

PAGE 10 — DAILY MIRROR, Friday, February 11, 1983

AN SAS hero of the Iranian Embassy siege has been killed on a secret mission on Northern Ireland.

Corporal Tommy Palmer received the Queen's Gallantry Medal after the siege in London. He was one of the first SAS men to storm the embassy.

He also worked behind enemy lines in the Falklands conflict after parachuting into freezing South Atlantic waters.

Corporal Palmer, 31, who is married with two young daughters, was watched by millions on television as the SAS ended the embassy siege in 1980.

Hurling stun and teargas grenades and with his machine gun blazing, Corporal Palmer, a former Royal Engineer, stormed his way into the room where the hostages were being held.

Five out of six terrorists were killed.

DRAMA: SAS men storm embassy.

Corporal Palmer's name was never revealed when he was awarded his medal.

By ALASTAIR McQUEEN

Few people knew he was part of an elite SAS team in the Falklands.

After parachuting into the South Atlantic, the team was picked up by submarine and landed on the islands before British troops closed in on the capital, Port Stanley.

In ten years with the SAS, Corporal Palmer was able to spend only about four months of each year with his wife and family.

He had served in Ulster several times and returned there on active service recently.

Tragic

He was killed when his unmarked car left the road during a secret mission.

Another soldier in the car was slightly injured in the crash.

Yesterday a former SAS colleague of Corporal Palmer said: "This really is tragic. He was a superb soldier with a great future."

The newspaper report of Tommy's death (photo: Cara and Shona Palmer)

3 Ghillies, River Bailiffs & Poachers

Ghillie: he who attends someone on a hunting or fishing expedition

Over the years, this lovely river of ours has enjoyed entertaining and taunting an illustrious roll-call of British royals (HRH The Prince of Wales, Edward VIII), Japanese royals (Emperor Hirohito, allegedly), Prime Minister Neville Chamberlain, captains of industry, military commanders (Colonel Sir Thomas Pearson, El Alamein), artists, writers, and he of Starship Enterprise fame, Captain Kirk! (William Shatner). Like the salmon they are hunting, they slip into the county unseen, and slip away again, leaving barely a trace.

Standing beside their guests is the ghillie, guiding, advising, nudging. His knowledge of the fly, the worm, which pool and where, is rarely noted. Respectful, sometimes silent, other times garrulous, he is one of country sport's greatest figures, alongside the gamekeeper. His knowledge is honed from years on his beat, paying close attention to the river and the landscape, noticing changes in his environment before anyone else. Many people will have been instructed in the art of salmon fishing by a ghillie, dressed in his regulation green, and would have taken their first salmon under his critical gaze.

For Lyn Cobley,

> A ghillie is there to look after the rods of his guests, his ladies and gentlemen, and to assist them. A true ghillie will never fish if he's got 'rods' (guests) there. If he wants to fish, he'll do it when he gets home, if at all.

Sadly, the decline of salmon, and changes in river management, have seen a related decline in ghillie numbers, but there's no protection order on them. Today there are just a handful of full-time ghillies on the Wye, as George Smith points out:

> If you can think, from Bigsweir, the lower end of the river, to just above Ross, which would be approximately 40 miles of river, there was 15 ghillies years back. It's doubtful now if there are even three or four full-time ghillies on the Wye.

Ghillies take their guardianship seriously. They know their river intimately and care deeply. And, it has to be said, there have been some pretty memorable characters among them. We have already met Guenter Matthes, the German POW who ghillied the Ross water. But there are others. Someone said this book is 20 years too late, for many have already passed and hung up their rods, but others are still with us. A roll-call of these river men includes: Sid and Anthony Robins at Wyesham, Ron Burford and Ted Gwillam at Lower Symonds Yat, Frank Rees at the Tunnel beat, Jack Hillman and Cecil Teague at Lydbrook, George Crouch part-time at Courtfield Water, Ivor Williams at the Priory, Trevor Watts at Goodrich, and Ron Moody at Weir End. That's just a few to be getting on with. Here are a few others.

GEORGE WOODWARD, 72
Basically, you're a school teacher looking after a small child.

In 1976, George Woodward arrived to take up the position of gamekeeper at the Courtfield Estate, before later graduating to a ghillying role. He has fished with thousands of fishermen and -women, and taught his daughter, Lynn, the tools of the trade. She was the first ever female ghillie on the River Wye, working under the expert eye of her dad. He arrived in Herefordshire in January 1976 to live on the Courtfield Estate at Goodrich (the home of Henry V between 1387 and 1394). George claims that he once had, 'the terrible misfortune to go to London, which made him physically sick. Even Goodrich School rush hour is enough and to be avoided!'

George:

> I think one of the attractions of Courtfield was that the River Wye borders the estate on three sides. We're nearly an island. If it wasn't for Coppett

George Woodward with Sir Bruce-Gardiner, Chairman of Guest, Keen & Nettlefolds
(photo: George Woodward)

Hill, we would be! I had read a bit about the Wye before I came down and knew it was one of the most well-known salmon rivers in England, and I had heard it referred to as the "beautiful Wye".

There were two local ghillies who fished what we loosely called the Estate water. Having an interest in fishing, it wasn't long before I got quite friendly with them, and after a short while they realised I liked my fishing and they would say, "Come on George". I had never been a ghillie before; I just had this big interest in fishing and I was really, really lucky with Jack Hillman and Cecil Teague because they were two really knowledgeable people and they were quite happy to pass that knowledge on. After I'd been going with them for a bit, and they got somebody new or a guest, I'd get asked to go and help out. So I got to know the river quite well. And then dear old Jack died and I got offered his job and it worked quite well at that time because Mr Compton, who had owned the shooting, had packed it up by then, so I then went doing a bit of part-time keepering and part-time ghillying, and that went on for a good couple of years.

He was there when he began to witness 'the beginning of the decline'.

George again:

> In those early days, the water belonged to GKN, and one of the interesting things was there would be five people a day that used to fish. And at the weekend they used to send company guests – the chairman of this or the managing director of that. The river could cope; there was that many salmon. I think we had a waiting list of 19 people who wanted to come and fish. Basically, you had to wait for somebody to die before you got the chance. Nobody hanged their rod up. I had a few good years when I was catching close on 200 fish a year, but you did see it go gradually less and less, 'til some years we struggled to catch 50 or 60 fish.

While George's guests had accolades, awards, titles as long as their arms, that didn't necessarily mean they made an equal impression on the river bank. On the river, the man or woman with the knowledge is the ghillie and he must be listened to – if you want to land a decent fish that is.

George:

> I always found it amazing how you could have a man who ran a multinational company, where he could sign a piece of paper which could earn or lose millions; where he could hire and fire hundreds of people; where he'd gone up the chain of command; where he had a huge, great house and a chauffeur, and one day a week he'd get a fishing rod in his hands and his bloody brains would go through his backside! Unbelievable. Sometimes you would think, How on earth did that man get into the position he got into? It's a great leveller.

These River Wye ghillies could tell a tale or two. They have been privy to some fascinating conversations, with some fascinating people – and, as in the confessional, they keep most of them to themselves. But not all of them!

George:

> Out of all the people I have fished with, and I have fished with thousands, I can only think of two I didn't really want to be with. But I've also fished with an awful lot of people who had done something with their lives. Not just achieved greatness in the business they were in, but, for example, fighter pilots from the last war, people who fought at Arnhem, or landed in Normandy. It's hard not to be impressed by their experiences.

Fishing waders on, fishing tackle present and correct, hat at suitably jaunty angle, anglers could surprise their ghillies however.

George:

> I once fished with a gentleman: I can see him now, his pipe in his mouth, a well-spoken chappie. After a while he told me he was captain of one of the convoys to Russia during the war. He described some of the convoys he had been on. It was months later and I was fishing with another gentleman and he said, "Oh, you've been fishing with Mr so-and-so, haven't you? Did he tell you about his naval experiences?" Yes, I said. "Hmmm, have you seen the film, *The Cruel Sea*? Nicholas Montserrat, who wrote it, was a midshipman on this gentleman's corvette, and after the war he wrote *The Cruel Sea* and based it on the gentleman you were fishing with." I remember getting the book out again and reading it with a different view of this old gentleman, who had mentioned not a word about it.
>
> And then there was Mr Smith, who had been in the Navy for donkey's years and he finished the war in the Pacific. He ended up going to Japan with the American 7th Fleet into Nagasaki. I remember him describing getting off that ship and wandering around Nagasaki and kicking the ground and clouds of dust coming up. He said they went back to the ship that night and showered. It was a wonder he didn't glow in the dark!

Lynn Woodward, 50, is George Woodward's daughter. She caught her first fish when she was five, and by the time she was 20 she was an expert angler, oarswoman and shot. In the early '80s, when Lynn applied for the role of assistant ghillie on her dad's stretch of the Wye, he told her 'not to be so bloody daft!' Undeterred, she was appointed as the first woman bailiff on the River Wye, working under the tutelage of her father. Today Lynn is married and lives on a sheep farm near Builth Wells.

Lynn:

> When I was 20 I had been working in a factory for three months and got fed up with it and wanted a change, so ditched it when I heard that there was a vacancy where dad worked as a ghillie. But dad working there didn't help me get the job at all. I'm an outdoor person, so I applied. People talk about sexual discrimination today; imagine what it was like then! At the interview, I was asked what I would do if I was in a boat and needed to pee, or did I like worms! Couldn't believe it. I was very apprehensive about getting

the job though and working with dad, but we got on fine and he taught me a lot. I had a good idea what I was doing. Some people come along and have all the gear and no idea, not a clue.

I started in the January, and was sat in a boat in freezing conditions, ice on the rod rings and all that. It wasn't pleasant at times. My first guests were a couple of experienced locals, and they knew dad and knew the fishery well. Those that were new to the fishery were a bit horrified when they saw me. I don't think they had a lot of faith in me to be honest, but they were very polite. I had to prove to them I knew what I was doing. In the end, we became good friends and had a laugh. They respected me. Some of them called me 'ghillette' because it's not often you hear of a woman ghillie!

Lynn Woodward and client
(photo: George Woodward)

It may have helped Lynn that her boss's wife was keener on fishing than him. 'She was a big supporter of mine. My first Wye salmon was when I was ghillying for her. She was delighted to have caught it.'

WYE GHILLIES' ASSOCIATION

It was the appearance of the Wye Invader on the river in 1985 that propelled Lyn Cobley and George Woodward to take action, cajoling their fellow ghillies along the Wye to help do something about the incursion of this beast of a boat. There was worry that the barge's successful navigation up the Wye could prejudice the livelihood of the ghillies, with the added fear that more like it could follow. They wanted to protect the river environment. The Wye Ghillies' Association's first meeting was at the now-closed Antelope pub in Hereford.

George Woodward:

> I remember me and Lyn Cobley had a little chat one evening and we decided we would get as many of us together as we could and form a Wye Ghillies' Association. And so that's what happened. We all met at the Antelope one night, had a few pints, Lyn became the chairman and Lynn my daughter

The Wye Ghillies before one of their dinner parties (photo: George Woodward)

(she was working on the river with us then), she was secretary. Pete Smurthwaite was treasurer and I sort of ran the anti-poaching bit, and that went on for a good number of years. Geoff Franks ended up as the Chairman of it, and now it's amalgamated into the Wye Fisheries owners.

Lynn Woodward wasn't too thrilled about being appointed to the 'women's role' of secretary: 'They had me writing letters and I got fed up with it'. However, she was soon where the action was and joined her dad on the Association's newly formed anti-poaching team. Poaching was getting out of control on the Wye in the 1980s and 1990s, and the tried and tested methods were not working. The expertise of the ghillie was needed and the Association set up their own poaching patrol to protect the waters. Lynn was one of them. However, while out on poaching patrol, some stereotypes did persist.

Menu card from the 'First Gillies Dinner Party', in 1978
(photo: George Woodward)

Lynn again:

> Ghillies started catching poachers because we were using skills that country people knew. We knew how to hide, how to camouflage and we wanted to catch poachers. First of all the other bailiffs said, "we better put Lynn in the support vehicle". I got fed up with that. I wanted to get down and dirty, hands-on stuff. And that's what I did in the end. I didn't think I had to prove myself. They accepted me as part of the team in the end. That I was a woman never came into it. I just mucked in and got on with things.

Of course, poaching has been going on since time immemorial. Ghillie Ivor Williams of Coppett Hill (he is reputed to have caught more fish than his near-neighbour, Robert Pashley), was often called upon during his early working years, from the 1940s through to the early 1980s, to catch poachers up-stream in the Rhayader area, taking the train from the Kerne Bridge Station near his Coppett Hill home.

In 1923, at the Cowpond pool at Winforton, Miss Doreen Davy caught a salmon weighing in at 59.5 pounds. It was unprecedented and she holds the record to this day. And that would be that, if it wasn't for a conversation with an 85-year-old fisherman in Hereford, a chat that has muddied the Wye waters somewhat with his claim: 'When I was a young man, I knew the ghillie that helped Miss Davy. And do you know what he said to me? He said it wasn't her who brought that fish in, it was him!' A sentence that could cause a revolution in fishing circles. There's no evidence of course, but it does go some way to highlight the 'invisible' ghillie.

Ivor Williams, a ghillie on Bishopswood Waters, said to have caught more fish than the legendary Robert Pashley (photo: Robin Hulse)

In May of 1939, fresh from the much-derided Munich Agreement, a rather beleaguered Prime Minister Neville Chamberlain was guest of Viscount Bledisloe at his Lydney Park estate. A local newspaper reporter described Chamberlain looking 'bronzed and fit and was obviously enjoying a weekend break away from the strain of international politics'. The report went on to quote Chamberlain: 'I am well acquainted with these parts, and frequently stay in the Forest of Dean and fish in the River Wye'. There was no mention of his fishing host on the Goodrich waters, Robert Pashley.

GHILLIE TO ROBERT PASHLEY, WIZARD OF THE WYE

Whether he was known as 'Wizard of the Wye', or 'Napoleon of Salmon Fishers', Pashley's prowess as a salmon fisherman has been amply recorded. He even made it into that River Wye classic, *The Tale of a Wye Fisherman*, by H.A. Gilbert, a staple on any self-respecting fisherman's bookshelf. His name lives on in the village close to his former home at Bishopswood Lodge. The village of Walford has the Robert Pashley Memorial Hall, and for many years at Walford School he provided the means to hold a Christmas party, where each child was presented with an orange! For school outings, he always provided a fresh salmon, caught by himself. When he died, in July 1956, Mr Pashley left his considerable wealth in a Trust for Walford School pupils.

Jack Whittingham, ghillie to Robert Pashley (photo: Dorothy Joyner and Mike Whittingham)

Neville Chamberlain with five salmon in May 1939 (photo: Dorothy Joyner and Mike Whittingham)

But what of the man also in the photographs with Pashley, the chap with the cap standing beside him, always present; the one controlling the punt, hauling the salmon out of the boat, gaffing the fish? Time and again he appears in the images, but, as Pashley's ghillie, he has, up to now, been relatively nameless. Shameful really, when it was he who helped wartime PM Neville Chamberlain land five salmon that May morning in 1939.

Jack Whittingham's name should take its rightful place in history. In his obituary of September 1970, Jack is remembered in glowing terms:

> A man who earned his place in the affections of some of the Wye's most famous anglers, was Mr Jack Whittingham, of Goodrich. For 47 years he was a ghillie on the Goodrich and Hill Court water and during his time there fished with former Prime Ministers, authors, leaders of industry. He was with Neville Chamberlain in the late 1930s when the one-time Prime Minister achieved his personal best, catching five fish off one fly. Jack worked for Robert Pashley, who claimed 12,000 fish from the Wye, right up to Pashley's death in 1956.

– Quite some accolade.

Jack's children, Mike Whittingham, 85, and his sister, Dorothy Joyner, 81 (another sister, Margaret Fleetwood, died in 2017 aged 87) live in Ross-on-Wye today; but as children, Goodrich was their home, near to Pashley's residence at Kerne Lodge, and close to the river. They are pleased that their beloved father is getting recognition at last. Dorothy remembers the secrecy surrounding Chamberlain's visit: 'Mother had to keep quiet about it. She wasn't to tell anyone.'

Jack was born in 1907 in Walford, a village neighbouring Goodrich, and was christened Frederick Vercall Whittingham, but was always known as Jack. A kind man, he had an uncanny knowledge of fish and wildlife.

Mike:

> They say that during summer nights, Mr Pashley would lie in bed with his windows open and could hear the salmon jumping so he knew they were on the move. Dad worked for him from when he left school and was with him most of the time, except for the war years when dad served with the RAF. After the war he returned to the river and continued to work for Mr Pashley until Mr Pashley's death in 1956.

Top and above left: Jack Whittingham and legendary salmon fisherman, Robert Pashley.
Above right: Jack Whittingham (photos: Dorothy Joyner and Mike Whittingham)

GHILLIES, RIVER BAILIFFS & POACHERS 83

> Pashley was like the Lord of the Manor really, because we lived in a tied cottage, so we had to almost treat him like royalty. He used to hire Mr Webb's taxi to take him and Jack to Glewstone Boat, where he fished twice a week. We were always told that if he went by in the car, because he would be chauffeur-driven, me and my sisters would have to salute. As children, me and my sisters, Margaret and Dorothy, would occasionally go up to Kerne Lodge when the river wasn't being fished and when dad did odd jobs, such as keeping the house fires burning. He also had to pump the water from a well to keep the tank full for the house use.

Jack's day started at 8 a.m. when he hopped on his bike and rode from his Goodrich cottage, crossing the river and on to Pashley's Lodge a mile away. On the days they were fishing that water, below Kerne Lodge, Jack and Mr Pashley would cross the road and the railway line. Pashley had special permission to cross the line in order to get to the river and his punt. Jack worked wonders manoeuvring the punt into the exact position Pashley wanted.

Mike:

> He used to get paid one shilling (5p) a fish. In one season, he had 400 odd salmon, so that year he had 400 shillings odd bonus. But he only earned £4–£10 a week. If he had worked on a farm he would have been paid overtime. I mean, he would often be on that river until dark. If the river was fishable, when it was in season, dad was working. It was a bonus when the river was dirty or flooded because he didn't go to work. I think in the winter time Pashley would go duck shooting and pike fishing. I remember coming home once and mother said, "Mr Pashley's in the wood shooting – why don't you go across there to pick up any he's shot." I went blundering along, stepping on all the sticks looking for him and I can see him telling me to be quiet! I was frightening the pigeons.

Dorothy, the youngest of Jack's three children, remembers their salmon suppers:

> We used to have to wait till the end of the season before we got any, and then we only had the head! Mother used to cook it and there were bits there. We never had no best. What we had was pink though. Lucky if we had a bit of tail. I do remember dad used to wear long stockings up to his knees over his britches and mother used to knit them. We used to hang them up for Father Christmas.

Jack in the Austin Countryman advert (photo: Dorothy Joyner and Mike Whittingham)

A diehard fisherman, Jack tied his own flies. Mike remembers:

> In our kitchen was a big old-fashioned dresser. It was a writing desk really, and you could pull the drawer out and it was full of old fishing stuff, reels and lines and flies. He made his own gaffs too. The local blacksmith made the hook and Jack fastened it on to a nutstick.
>
> When Pashley died, dad continued to work as a ghillie for Pinchin and Johnson, the paint firm later known as Courthaulds, at Glewstone Boat. They had the fishing rights to that part of the river, managed by Harold Collins. It was while working for them that he appeared in a national advertising campaign for the Austin Countryman.
>
> Dad died in 1970 at the age of 63. He was a wonderful sportsman who will long be remembered by all who were privileged to know him and will remember with pride that they all once fished with the greatest of the Wye ghillies.

RIVER BAILIFFS & POACHERS

'Poaching's not thieving; rustling sheep is thieving', announced a poacher to a journalist in *The Independent* of September 1995. Even more brazenly, H.L.V. Fletcher (*Portrait of the Wye Valley*, 1968) described people who lived by the river as 'poachers by nature'. He went on to say:

I am not defending them, and I am not saying the custom is a good one. But for thousands of years their ancestors have taken fish out of the river for food and the salmon population has not apparently been affected.

He might have been referring to Charlie Catchpole, a marvellous character and, according to his 85-year-old son, Jack, an equally excellent fisherman. He was also something of a maverick:

He used to poach a lot. I can remember Bullock Mill on the Arrow. Mr Passey, an agriculture merchant, owned all that area. We went there one day to do a bit of poaching and, without warning, dad suddenly threw the rod into the stinging nettles and put his binoculars round his neck. And I was stood next to him with a net and he snapped, "throw the net away!" and along came Mr Passey with his farm manager. He was dressed up with his spats on and all the crap. And he said, "Who are you?" "I'm Charlie Catchpole", said dad. "Well, what are you doing on my land?" And dad said, "We're birdwatchers". And I thought, this will never work. Then Passey looked dad up and down and said, "You can come on my land any time you like!"

Charlie Catchpole
(photo: Jack Catchpole)

That the salmon population has fallen dramatically is a given. Whether the prolific poaching along the Wye played a part in that is still up for debate, but there is no doubt an effective river bailiff force was required in the face of some fearless, highly efficient and, in some cases at least, professional poachers on the River Wye. The problem reached its height in the late 1970s through to the early 1990s.

GEORGE SMITH, 70

George Smith enjoys a round of golf in his retirement near his Kington home. It's a far cry from the rough and tumble of his working life as a river bailiff. But he loved every minute of his job. In the late 1970s he was appointed the first-ever dog-handling bailiff on the Wye, and his role was to enforce all the legislation on the river. As a new bailiff, his training for the job was, at best, minimal or laughable, depending on your point of view:

George Smith, river bailiff (photo: George Smith)

> I got the job and I was told to meet a chap on the bridge in Kington, at a certain time on a certain day. So, I arrived there and I met this man there and he gave me four things: a truncheon, a pair of handcuffs, a torch, and a map with a big circle on it and he said, "right, that's your area, now get on with it!"

– And that was it and he was gone.

Undaunted, George started in earnest. He had his work cut out though in the face of unprecedented levels of poaching on the Wye, and against sometimes shambolic and other times ruthless professional poachers.

> When we went out anti-poaching, and when we were such a small number, we were watching, say, just one mile of river at night, and the poachers would have thousands and thousands of fish out of the river. It was more lucrative than robbing banks. I worked for 35 years and it's really changed in that time. When I started, there were 12 bailiffs on the whole stretch of the River Wye and 12 on the River Usk. We had an office in Hereford, in St John Street, and a boss and two fishery officers and a secretary. But when I finished in 2012 there were just two of us for the whole of the Wye and the Usk and half of Wales; only two of us doing enforcement work.

The Wye River Authority office was on the top floor in St John Street. It was occasionally noisy when the Cathedral bells rang. Out in the back yard was a building which housed the old records and where copies of letters and documents were stored, written in beautiful copperplate writing. It was here that the beaks of cormorants were handed in for reward. Cormorants, with their habit of taking salmon, were considered a nuisance, and a bounty system had been put in place. There is no record of what happened to the beaks.

George and his river bailiff colleagues were needed direly. Poaching was getting out of control and attracting attention from the national media, including *Newsnight, The Observer* and *The Independent.* Journalists inveigled themselves in pubs with locals where drinks were plied. There was much bragging of alleged poaching exploits and successes. There would have been little need to stretch the truth, however. The numbers of fish lost to poaching is mind-boggling. And it's easy to see the temptation: there was a lot of money to be made. The figures involved stretch the realms of belief: tales of houses being built on the profits are not just apocryphal. George puts it into some sort of perspective:

> The most we ever got out of one net in one evening was 86 fish, worth about £8,000. That was just one pool on one night. It was really big business. In the 1970s, fresh salmon was about £5 per pound, you can buy it now for about £2 per pound, but because there was no farmed salmon then, each fish was worth about £100. Well, if you had ten in a net that's thousands of pounds worth of fish. And one year we had 276 nets out of the Wye and I suppose they averaged ten or twenty fish in each net and that is the ones we got. There must have been many more up and down the Wye.

MORE LUCRATIVE THAN ROBBING BANKS

In the 1980s and 1990s, poaching intensified, with opportunists arriving from as far away as Birmingham and Devon, hopeful to catch some of the spoils. The river bailiffs faced an unrelenting stream of poachers wanting to make big money. Some were highly professional, earning some grudging respect. It was also a hugely risky business. Several poachers drowned in the river they were poaching. It is reported that at least one poacher returned to the river with nets the day after his father drowned doing the same thing.

'I loved every bloody minute of it,' said George Woodward, who gave up ghillying to become a full-time river bailiff.

It was absolutely marvellous. I used to walk down the High Street in Monmouth or Ross and you'd get, "bastard bailiff!" It was good fun. At that time, the nylon mono filament gill net had become popular among poachers. Prior to that, most of the nets were made out of hemp or cotton. The nylon net was a lot finer, a lot easier to carry and transport about. You could put it in your pocket. It wasn't long before people realised, "If we put a net across that river at certain times of year we're going to get quite a lot of salmon in it." And I suppose if you go back to the late 1970s, early 1980s the 1990s, at £2.50 a lb, average weight 10 pounds, a couple of people working together, inflatable dinghies, six or seven nets in the river, it was not impossible for them catching in the region of 30 to a 100 salmon in a night. It doesn't take a mathematician to work out just how much some of them made.

The more proficient poacher may never have got caught, but the bailiffs knew who they were. George Woodward:

There's an old adage isn't there? If you want to keep a secret, then keep it to yourself. And there's a few of those people working together who never boasted, never said anything, just quietly went about what they were doing. They became very, very proficient. They were very, very professional. And there were a few people that made an awful lot of money out of poached salmon. There is a Monmouth chappie, I'm not going to say 100% of his house was built on the back of salmon poaching, but a very large percentage of it was. And that was basically done on a bartering system: x number of poached salmon for x building blocks, x number of poached salmon for x cement. Him being quite a good builder, built his own house. Even if you took a little bit of it away for a bit of boasting and bravado, there was some of them that made an awful lot of money out of it.

It wasn't just men who poached. 'Oh God no. We had one woman. She was known to us. She once rented a cottage in Ballingham for a week, just to poach the Wye.' Such gall wasn't unusual. It demanded a new breed of bailiff. Call in the ghillies.
Lyn Cobley was one of the new ghillie bailiff brigade:

Poaching on the Wye was a major problem in the 1970s, 1980s and 1990s. You'd have peg nets, and the poachers had dinghies and they would put them across or even swim across the river to put them across. They'd paddle across to put one net in, then go down 50 or 60 yards and then put another in, and three or four nets like that. This would be at night; they'd never do it in the day. What we used to do to try and find them was get a dinghy out and drift down-river with a silent engine. They were netting virtually from Builth Wells down. One night we done a drift and we put on the river at Glasbury and between Hay-on-Wye and Whitney Toll Bridge, in that little short spell, we lifted 16 nets.

At one time in his career, George Smith had made the most arrests for poaching on the Wye. He's softly spoken, but it wasn't a job for the tender-hearted. It's tough and it can be very rough:

I was always in the rough spot. I've apprehended hundreds. I've had some nasty ones too. About 25% of people on the river are armed with knives or guns, so there was no pussy-footing around; you went in hard straight away.

The sums of money involved, at least for a few poachers, were dizzying. George Smith again:

A lot of people made a lot of money. There were repeat offenders all the time. They'd be out all night poaching and then sleep all day. We turned one place over in Usk, and my colleagues went down there, searched the house and in the freezer they found £60,000 to £70,000 in notes. The guy didn't know what to do with it. All from salmon poaching. We had our hands full. People don't realise how big a business it was. We had 276 nets out one year and that's just watching a mile of river, so you just imagine how many actual nets there were in the Wye. And they are all taking thousands of pounds a time.

The bailiffs were good, but they had to be because the poachers were very, very good. While some of them wasted their proceeds, others took their 'business' extremely seriously.

Les Moses was one of these. During the drinking and bragging in local pubs, Les kept silent, listening, picking up information, quietly going about his 'business'. He was super-organised, and demonstrated business savvy in his dealings. But the first time he saw the Wye was in very different circumstances at Whitney when he was about seven. Someone gave him a big rod and he sat on the bank all day, wanting to catch something. This is when he says he got the bug. He started again when he was 11. The river bank became his education, and he was late for school most days and wouldn't go in on other days. 'I was mad for it. There was no one about, just by yourself.' His poaching life started in earnest in the roasting summer of 1976, when salmon were dying in their hundreds, as the river dried up and the fish starved of oxygen.

> I came home in the summer 1976, the drought year, and the talk of the town in Monmouth was the amount of salmon dying in the river. People were giving jobs up to have salmon. It was so shallow at the side and you could take the salmon just like that. Nobody took any notice before then. That's when I first got to hear about it. It was always a gentry fish. Two or four salmon was a week's wage. It opened the eyes of a lot of people to the potential.
>
> It all started basically for me when I was caught rabbiting on a road near my house when I was 17 or 18. I was walking down the road with rabbits after lamping them and the police decided to arrest us. There was an old school friend of mine. He was a judge or magistrate, and he turned around and said to me – and it's these words that really made me stick at it – he said, "You will never ever be able to live off the land by catching rabbits or anything else." He should never have said that to me. I'm still bloody doing it! That's the thing that really put the bug in me. I was going to prove him wrong.
>
> And then I got to hear about netting salmon from some Bridport boys in 1976. There were two or three gangs of them in Monmouth then, working away quietly. They were just walking up the river and taking fish out. Nobody knew they were coming up here to do netting. They would stretch a net from one bank to the other. That's how the netting side of things got out. And then I bumped into a mate one evening and he couldn't wait to show me. He said, "Put your hand on the net." It was full of salmon. I wanted to be part of it, not for the money, it was something different, the netting.

But Les' first attempt at netting wasn't successful. He improvised, using a net taken from Monmouth tennis courts. He didn't catch any that night, but it started to become serious when he followed the Bridport boys who had quietly been poaching the river for some time. Working in the evening or the early hours of the morning, Les and his team were soon putting multiple nets across multiple pools. In the beginning, they would swim the pools, later graduating to dinghies:

We used plastic dinghies to begin with, the cheap shop stuff, no life jackets or anything. We had a few close calls mind and we learnt to swim for our lives, because if the current took you down then you were tangled in the net. So, you started spending a bit of what you earned to look after your health, getting proper rubber dinghies. I never got actually tangled in the net, but a lad called Terry drowned ten feet from the bank. He couldn't swim and he jumped out of the boat, but couldn't make it to the bank. Another old man, he drowned swimming the net out. This was years and years ago. I was about 20. I knew them. I used to fish with them. Didn't put me off though but made you think a bit differently. But you're young; you're invincible, aren't you?

Once we knew what we was doing, I organised a group of four lads: we had a driver, a look-out and two of us working the boat, and we would average £4,000 to £5,000 a week back then. And it was good. We was out all the time. We were dedicated and stuck together for eight years. We was a team. We knew what we was doing.

We used to fish eight to twelve nets. Instead of putting one net in and waiting for it to fill up, in the end we worked out the bailiffs would go at four or five in the morning and that's when we would go in. And we would go in to one pool with 12 nets, half hour before the fishing men would turn up with their rods just after light. The bailiffs would be gone and we went to the pool we wanted and watched it fill up with salmon. We emptied the pool. We done that all over the river for years. You'd put one net in straight across, come back for another – back, back, back, ten-yard intervals. Empty the pool completely. And we got away with that for eight years.

In the end, you could row that river in 30 seconds or less. Just lean on the front and just go for it and that was it. At that time in the morning nobody's about; everybody's asleep. We would blow up the dinghies by mouth. Then we would be dropped off to put them in; the driver would go off; we would phone him when we were ready to be picked up and he would literally drive down, reverse to the bank and be gone. Much easier than carrying stuff. We've had to go hire transit vans to pick the fish up! If we knew a pool and estimated what was in there, I'd do it and sit and watch and estimate by how many fish you'd seen jump out, and then we would move in on that pool. We was doing three to four pools every week. I would be in at first light and see if anyone was about, and the fish were gone within an hour before fishermen turned up. I did that for years. That's when we had a lot of fish. No one knows that.

But the arrival on the river bank of ghillies-turned-bailiffs changed the life of the poacher:

> We ended up losing five or six thousand pounds a week in the end, cars, nets, dinghies. And that was regular. Like I say, when they got the likes of the ghillies involved, when they started being bailiffs, they knew what they was doing, and we started to get chased off a lot more. They started to bring in security. Old bailiffs went and they brought in new ones – the ghillies this time. George Woodward got a crew, and he was feared. He knew what he was doing. Like me against the salmon, he was dedicated.
>
> But a lot more boys started doing it because of the *Newsnight* thing. They was coming from Birmingham – everywhere they was coming. A lot of bragging in the pubs and a lot of the others wanted in on it. They didn't have a clue. Just turn up on the side of the river, buying nets and trying it. So, it increased and got bigger, and we should just have kept quiet. And then they started to get security firms. There was even a rumour, can never be proved, that the SAS trained on us.
>
> We had to get a bit more wise. People were getting caught and losing nets and the odd car. We would do a different pool every night. It was like Russian roulette. I would put cotton across just to see if somebody had gone by. Lots of people getting caught.

But Les is unapologetic:

> You can't experience what it's like until you do it. Wasn't illegal to me. When I look at something, I look into it proper, right into the finest detail. Did it with pigeon racing. I don't cause any unnecessary suffering. I am a professional poacher. I've done nothing wrong, kept the family well, with good food and I didn't know nothing else. Glad I done it.

Like it, admire it, loathe it, it happened. The debate is out on the cause behind the salmon decline. But you'll hear no apologies from the poaching brigade.

Just one example of a poachers' hoard, seized by river bailiffs in the 1980s (photo: George Woodward)

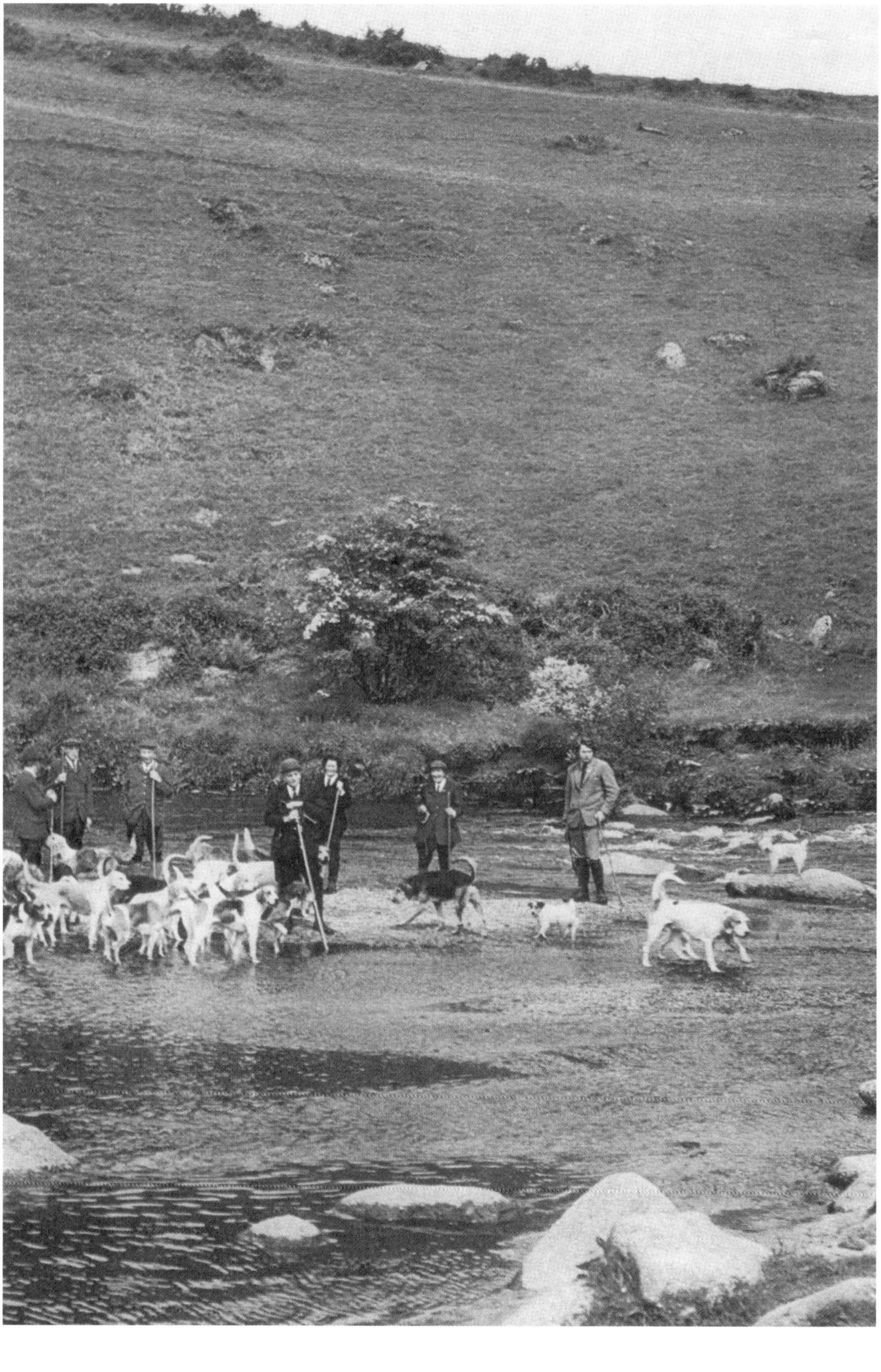

4 Wye Valley Otter Hounds

If not hunting, Ray was adept at wading out of the river, smack in front of an inn, dead on opening time

OTTERS WERE ONCE widespread on the Wye, but populations declined sharply during the 1960s and 1970s due to pollution and persistent pesticides, exacerbated by hunting and habitat loss. However, recent surveys suggest that the otter population is recovering well. It's a delight to see them splashing around in the Wye. It may concern some readers that we have a chapter on otter hunting. But in another 20 or 30 years most people involved in this 'sport' will have passed away. So, it is important that this divisive yet ancient tradition of hunting the poor old otter is recorded.

Otter hunting may be repellent to some, but, before it ended, it was as much a feature of the Wye Valley landscape as the salmon fisherman. One character stands out from all the rest, a legend in hunting circles and one who is still talked about now with reverence and awe. He was Ray Thompson, a gentleman of leisure, a *bon viveur*, generous, and renowned Master of the Wye Valley Otter Hounds, which were based near his home in Goodrich. He was never known to swear, at least not in front of ladies, and was never pompous. He was, above all, a huge and uncompromising character. At the outbreak of the First World War, he signed up as an infantryman and joined the Camel Corps. He might have been an officer, but when his horses were taken away for the war effort, he declared that he had no intention of walking, so plumped for the next best option, camels. Posted to Egypt, he is said to have encountered T.E. Lawrence, Lawrence of Arabia.

Otter hunter, Ray Thompson (photo: N. Frost, R. Davies and E. Everall)

Ray started otter hunting in 1909 as a whipper-in for the Wye Valley Otter Hounds. But by the 1920s he had become its Master, and remained with the Wye Valley for over 40 years. He was as charming as anybody outside the hunting world, but as a huntsman he had one aim and one only and that was to kill the unfortunate otter, and nothing would get in the way of that goal. The hounds' numbers were extremely low at that time, but he continued hunting throughout the Second World War. And he would stop at nothing to get out and hunt. Even if the river was in flood he would make it possible to walk across. If anybody was talking during the hunt he would tell them in no uncertain terms to be quiet. And people respected him for that. The Wye Valley Otter Hounds ceased in 1958 when old age finally caught up with Ray. In its place stepped in the Hawkstone Hunt that continued until they placed a voluntary ban on killing the creatures. Hunting otters ceased in 1978.

Hunt meet at the Cross Keys, Goodrich, late 1950s (photo: N. Frost, R. Davies and E. Everall)

Thompson was heir to a brewing business in Burton-on-Trent, but he was very generous with his money. Wherever he went hunting he would find a public house or an inn, and he would place cheques on the bar and insist, 'Anybody could have drink'. Hunting always started early in the morning and nobody was allowed to go 'thirsty'. Lunch would last for over an hour and, as these were liquid lunches, most people thoroughly enjoyed themselves – and so did a fair few hangers-on, attracted to the free-flowing alcohol. Clues to his seemingly bottomless expense account were given at the inquest of the untimely and tragic death of his beloved daughter, killed in a car accident on the way back from a day's hunting. When asked in court his occupation, Thompson, standing bolt upright, replied, 'I'm of independent means!' And that was that, no more questions asked.

Dylan Jones has devoted some of his professional life to recording the social history of the Wye Valley Otter Hounds. While working at the St Fagans Museum in Wales, he was responsible for the fishing, hunting and sporting collections, including otter hunting. He decided it was about time the artefacts and memories regarding this sporting tradition were collected:

Left: three otter hunters, including Wing Commander Frost (centre)
Right: Gathering at Colgarron (photos: N. Frost, R. Davies and E. Everall)

The otter hunting tradition in England and Wales was basically open for everybody and anybody interested in the countryside. Anyone who was interested in the sport would follow the hounds. There are various photos from the 1880s onwards of whole villages following the Hawkstone and the Wye Valley. You can see young children, boys and girls, solicitors, inn-keepers; anybody would go along for the spectacle.

It was said the scent of the otter was better early in the morning, so some would start hunting at four or five o'clock in the morning, many making their way to the meets the night before. The hunters would go in trains and the packs would be put on wagons and sent off to the meets and then they would all get up early and start the hunting day.

Whereas everybody else would have had a couple of bottles of alcohol for dinner or a couple of pints, they would lunch on champagne on occasions. It was a huge social event for everybody really because there was a subscription pack for both the Wye Valley Otter Hounds and the Hawkstone too. A lot of the taverns and inns on the Marches would open early for the hunters. The Master was well aware that he had to find an otter for the people to be happy, really. It's a bit like football and rugby today. It was entertainment and the Hunt had to go out of its way to get as much fun as possible for the people involved. But on the other hand, they had to be professional as well.

The prodigious drinking involved is amply illustrated in a hilarious account written in 1951 by E. Gethin Davey, who describes a Wye Valley opening meet at the Raglan Arms in Llandenny, and his first meeting with the great man, Ray Thompson. There was a lot of alcohol consumed:

> It was a bitterly cold April morning and as I approached the inn, out of the door came Thompson. "Come and have some coffee," he said. Coffee! That was about 11 a.m. and we didn't leave until one the following morning. I made a brave effort to cross the flagstone kitchen floor after lunchtime, but the landlady caught me and gently persuaded me back. When we did leave, the body was eased gently into the driving seat, and the car's head pointed towards home. One elderly gent, with his back to the driver's door, was trying to get an ignition key into a tree trunk. We turned him about, but he was most irate when offered a lift.

Tom Henderson of Brilley was one of those young boys eagerly anticipating the arrival of the hounds at the Boat Inn, Whitney-on-Wye just after the Second World War:

> It would be 1946 or 1948. I do remember the boys in the village got pretty excited as the otter hounds were arriving at The Boat Inn, and we used to get on our bicycles and go down the hill there from Brilley. It was quite a spectacle really. There was a beat-up old cattle lorry and they used to drop the tailgate and out would come all these hounds. What amused us was the uniform the people wore, a royal blue colour and they had red stockings and red piping and they wore a grey hat and had WVOH on their brass buttons. The men had these tunics and waistcoats and the ladies had big woollen skirts, and to prevent their skirts floating up in the water, they had lead weights sewn into the hems. On their feet, they wore quite strong boots as they had to get into the river a lot. They were all on foot – not a horse in sight. They would do a stretch of the river as far as The Rhydspence, maybe further.

The principal meets in Herefordshire included Kentchurch, Kerne Bridge, the Wye Bridge at Hereford, Fawley and Wilton Bridge, Ross-on-Wye. Mike Whittingham was brought up in Goodrich, and he has vivid memories of Charlie Bundy, WVOH whipper-in at the hunt meet:

> I can see Charlie Bundy now just walking out into the river. Some used to wear waders but Charlie just went straight out into the river. Once one of the hounds had spotted something they would go into this terrific shrill noise because they had picked up the scent. I remember dad was home one day because the river was in flood and they were meeting and dad had to take the boat out for them. Ray Thompson was master of the Otter Hunt then and they used to gather at the Hostelrie in Goodrich and have their ritual tipple. The WVOH and the Hawkstone used to have different uniforms. The Wye Valley Otter Hunt wore blue and Hawkstone wore red [caps]. I used to see all the hounds running around the bottom of the village meadow, as we called it, and over the other side was what we called the withy beds. There were masses of willow trees, but they were dense and I think the otters used them for protection. The hunters used to ask our dad if he had seen any otters on the river.

In Maurice A. Lulham's account of the Wye Valley Otter Hounds, he records a 1930 marathon hunting day that exhausted the hunters, the hounds and the poor old otter:

> The hounds met at the Wilton Bridge in Ross. An otter was found, showing himself among the boats, he moved downstream with the pack screaming after him at a good pace and swimming at great speed. At Weirend he showed himself, slipping past the whip. The hounds continued to push him with tremendous cry in spite of the fact there was a strong wind blowing against the current and waves breaking in the hounds' faces. The huntsman followed behind in a borrowed boat, the otter sometimes breaking the surface, but he kept ahead and the last that was seen of him was just above the withy bed opposite Goodrich Castle. From start to finish, the hunt covered six miles in six and a half hours. A prodigious swim!

Adrian Howard's childhood home was within shouting distance of the Wye Valley Otter Hunt kennels at Colgarron in Goodrich. As we have seen, these men and women hunted hard and drank even harder:

> There was a chap called Redwood. He lived in the flat at Colgarron and all he did was hunt. He even walked around with his hunting uniform on. I can remember going otter hunting with them up the River Garron once, right at the end of the otter hunting time. The hunters used to get into the water up to waist level and they had poles. The poles were these

Otter hunters in the river during a meet (photo: N. Frost, R. Davies and E. Everall)

big stave things, like Robin Hood would have had, and they were just prodding them into the banks, because these otters would get up under the roots and the hunters would try and get them moving and hopefully the hounds would get them up the river. As a teenager, I can remember old Garnet Williams threatening to throw 'Jack' Frost, Captain Frost (of the Hawkstone Hunt), into the river.

At Colgarron, before a hunt, there was an urn in the passageway and everyone would have a tot of something, and if you had anything left it was just tipped back in there and the lid put back on. Colgarron was quite famous for that.

Tony Norman of Pembridge, keen fisherman and country farmer, still has his father-in-law's mounted otter's head and silver-mounted otter's pad, etched with, 'F.I.S. the otter hunt took place at The Leen, September 24th 1923'.

Tony:

> These were presented to my father-in-law. I know he got blooded [an informal initiation ceremony in which the face of a novice is smeared with the blood of the first otter that the person has seen killed] on that occasion and was then presented with one of the paws, which was mounted. Otter hunting was a real social occasion. Different people ran it and different people would follow it.

Otter hunt meet at Colgarron (photo: N. Frost, R. Davies and E. Everall)

And, last word on the otter from Maurice Hudson:

> I was bought up on Cadora [a pleasant fishery on the left-hand bank of the river, at the bottom end of the river between Bigsweir and Redbrook, which has been in Maurice's family for decades] on the River Wye. As a kid, I sort of kept or looked after it. Cadora belonged to the Crown then and The Beaufort at Tintern had a 99-year lease on it. When I was a youngster at Monmouth Boys School I used to cycle there, getting up at five o'clock in the morning and putting eel traps in the river and night lines down. A chap came to The Beaufort called Bill Graham, who was in the Scots Guards during the war. Bill was a super chap and his staff worshipped him. He was a very good manager and I remember some of his guests, including Neville Chamberlain, before the war. In fact, before Bill Graham became the manager, it was run by a chap called Captain Sharpe, who kept pet otters and he used to take these otters around Monmouth on a lead and collar. My father used to catch eels to feed the otters, because they loved eels.

5 Boat-Building & other River Craft

THE ADVENT OF the railway in the mid nineteenth century signalled the death of the River Wye as a trading passage. For hundreds of years, barges, boats and trows had traded along the river, supporting a host of industries including pubs, rope makers, coal merchants, sail makers, fishermen, basket makers and, of course, boatbuilders. Boat-building was a thriving industry. There was Jordan's of course, whose boat-yard was where the car park for Asda is today in Hereford. Other less familiar boat-building names included Richard Lewis, Thomas Maund, John Easton, and William Radford. In April 1834, Radford had the distinction of launching the Water Witch at Hereford. It was the largest vessel built above the Wye bridge, and at 80 feet long it would have been an impressive sight. There are some indications (but yet to be verified) that the Water Witch ended its service days in South Africa. The Wye Tour in the mid nineteenth century created a mini boat-building boom, as demand for spaces on boats outstripped supply. But today, in the early part of the twenty-first century, boat-building on the river passes with barely a mention. In fact, there would be surprise that it happens at all. But boats have been built – some ordinary, others extraordinary.

JOHN FISHPOOL, 72
It would seat three or four people at a push, if they weren't too heavy. Even with me in, it didn't sink!

John married his wife Chris in 1968 and moved close to Ross where he worked. He began his working life as an apprentice Engineer at Haigh Engineering in the town before moving to Woodville. He finished his working career as Engineering

Director at Watts Industrial Wheels and Tyres in Lydney. Today, he lives high above the Wye on Coppett Hill. As a boy, he lived in Brampton Abbotts. His father was a wheelwright and a coffin maker, whose workshop supplied the raw material for John's boat.

John Fishpool's rowing boat (photo: John Fishpool)

> In 1960, I was 15 and decided I would make a boat in father's carpentry shop. I made it out of ply and glued and screwed it together with hundreds of brass screws, all put in by hand. I made the oars as well. When it was finished it could seat three or four people at a push, if they weren't too heavy. Even with me in, it didn't sink! I launched it at Foy because it was fairly close to Brampton Abbotts. My father had a Morris 1000 and we tied it onto the roof rack, but it was almost bigger than the car and it was difficult to see the road at times. We parked at Foy Bridge and launched it and rowed up and down the river. I had it a couple of years and then sold it to the landlord of the Kerne Bridge Inn. I don't know what happened to it after that.

A decade later and up-stream in Breinton, Bruce Wallace was faced with the same question: whatever happened to his boat? The punt, painted bright blue, was quite distinctive. It was built in the orchard at Bruce's home overlooking the Wye, opposite the now closed Camp Inn:

> My wife's stepfather-in-law, Boyser, had his eyes on a "pointy-nosed" boat that had been moored for years near the Hunderton Ferry steps. He always knew somebody who knew somebody else, and eventually bought it and we had a lot of fun in it. But then our neighbour, Eddie Hull, decided he wanted a boat too, so he decided to build one. He was the most fantastic engineer you could ever wish to come across.
>
> Eddie built four boats altogether using a Robin Reliant engine with a marine adaptation. When Boyser died I took one on and used to go up and down the river in it and we had great fun. We kept that boat moored down on the river and then it was taken by a flood one year. We were really disappointed and put letters in the *Hereford Times* in an attempt to find it, but we never did.

Top: Bruce Wallace's 'pointy-nosed' boat. Middle and bottom: one of the punts made by Eddie Hull, and lost in a flood, despite appeals in the *Hereford Times* (photo: Bruce Wallace)

Charles Lyster, 58, lives in Llangrove in a restored cottage with attached barn containing his workshop. He is an adventurer and sailor, smokes a pipe and does snow-holing in the Scottish mountains in the winter, just for fun. He runs Royal Yachting Association RYA courses on Driac, his 1930 classic yacht. In 2002, he built a replica Norwegian longboat, christened Yggdrasil. However, it is not strictly a longboat, but more correctly a Faering, the smallest traditional working boat from the fjords. It was launched on the Wye at Ross in 2002.

> I wanted a boat that would row and sail. In this country boats have specialised over a long period of time. A boat is either a specialist rowing boat or a sailing dinghy, and it is impossible to move between the two. But a Faering is just that, in between the two; it rows and sails. I saw one when we were on holiday in Norway in 2000 and was struck by how beautiful and simply built it was, very much a folk artisan construction, done with simple tools with ordinary people, not finely finished or beautifully varnished.

Maybe he follows in the footsteps/ boat's draught of Eric Blood Axe, whose marauding expedition found its way down the Wye in 911 AD, taking up a position at Symonds Yat. From his small 'Viking' outpost in the Wye Valley, Charles has played his role in rescuing a traditional Norwegian 'folk' craft from obscurity. The Faering nearly died out in the early twentieth century in Norway, and it was thanks to Øystein Faerøyvik, who travelled the length of Norway, photographing and measuring remaining models, that ensured the methods in construction were recorded for posterity. After a visit to the Viking Museum in Oslo, these are the designs Charles used and they have barely changed from 800 AD. He used wood from the Doward, selecting each piece, chopping it down and bringing it home to his workshop. After many months in the making, Yggdrasil was launched at Ross Rowing Club. The four-person crew enjoyed a summer's day cruise up to Backney, drawing some intrigued onlookers.

> People were curious about it. It was good to launch it on the Wye. We eventually took it back to Norway. They couldn't quite understand why an Englishman would want to make a traditional Norwegian boat, and why it was built in the UK and not Norway. We even had the local paper come out and photograph us!'

Opposite: Charles Lyster and his 'Faering' boat Yggdrasil (photo: Charles Lyster)

BOAT-BUILDING & OTHER RIVER CRAFT 107

But that's not the end of the story. Yggdrasil was in demand and even reached the silver screen:

> I was asked to rent Yggdrasil to Marine Film Services for the Russell Crowe Robin Hood film. And then they asked me to build a second Faering (with only oars, no sails) for them, which I did and one of them has appeared a number of times in *Game of Thrones*.

THE HEREFORD BULL

2012 was a golden year. The Olympics came to a buoyant London, the sun shone (most of the time) and the Queen celebrated her Diamond anniversary with year-long celebrations. Twelve months before, in a quiet corner of Herefordshire, an idea was being hatched that would result in the commissioning of a craft for the Queen's Diamond Jubilee Pageant on the Thames. Bob Tabor, then Deputy Lieutenant, was thrown the gauntlet by Lord Lieutenant Lady Darnley. Bob's excellent organisational skills saw him pull together a crack team of maritime people, among them Rear Admiral Philip Wilcocks, from the Golden Valley, Ray Hunter of Ledbury and Tommy Neilsen and his team of traditional boat-builders from Gloucester.

The Hereford Bull being built by T. Neilson & Co., Gloucester (photo: Andrew Wynn)

REAR ADMIRAL PHILIP WILCOCKS, 64
I've spent a lot of time driving ships, especially very fast ships.

In 2007, Philip's last job before retirement was Chief of Staff to the Commander-in-Chief Fleet, so he was a most suitably qualified team member. He went to the Falklands War in 1982 on board the frigate HMS Ambuscade, was Commander of the destroyer HMS Gloucester and took her to the first Gulf War in 1990–91, which involved the operations Desert Shield and Desert Storm. He then did a

Left: the newly built Hereford Bull at Gloucester Docks. Right: the trow on the Wye in Hereford, with the Victoria Bridge in the background (photos: Andrew Wynn)

tour in the Ministry of Defence as the Director of Naval Operations. On promotion to Admiral, he was the Deputy Chief of UK Operations Overseas. Finally, as well as being Chief of Staff to The Commander-in-Chief Fleet, Philip was the 'Tribal Chief' of the Surface Flotilla; that is all surface ships from patrol vessels to aircraft carriers:

> At our first or second meeting about Herefordshire's contribution to the Diamond Thames Pageant, I had my iPad with me and started Googling River Wye/ Hereford/ boats and came up with the trow, the boats which used to ply between Chepstow, Brockweir and Hereford. At that stage, we didn't know what we were going to do, whether we would charter or build something. Once we started looking at the River Wye trow, one of us went down to Monmouth Museum, where there's an old replica. It became clear that if we could get the money together to fund the project, then building a replica trow to represent the county would be something that would link the River Wye, the county and its heritage. At the same time, it was clear that the pageant sequence of boats meant that any vessel driven by oar would be right at the front, so we thought let's build something that could be rowed.

It was an ambitious plan, but with no funding available, there was no guarantee it was going to happen. However, the appearance of a mysterious benefactor gave the project the green light. and traditional boatbuilders in Gloucester, T. Neilson & Co., were commissioned.

Philip:

> It was clear that it was a type of boat-building which is not done these days. The bow and the stern were particularly challenging and it's to Tommy Neilson and his team's credit that they managed to design the boat as well they did. I mean, she is a beautiful boat. They sourced wood and some came by Ray Hunter and some wood was actually provided from landowners in Herefordshire, which was again very generous of them.

A chilly day on a sailing vessel in the open air is business as usual for ex-naval man, Philip:

> It was cold; the wind was from the east and you can imagine the number of boats that were involved in the Queen's Pageant. Some people stayed in hotels or camped and we manned the boat from about 9 a.m., then we had to make our way down towards Putney to hold there. That was quite interesting as we were probably one of the largest boats in that front part of the pageant and we ended up with a lot of boats mooring up alongside us.
>
> On smaller rowing boats one of the things they didn't have is a loo (or 'heads' to use the naval expression) but we did. Among the things that we planned was a toilet plus a canopy to provide a degree of privacy. As we were all rafted up waiting to get into position, a lot of people on the other rowing boats and skiffs and others, suddenly realised that we had this loo. We found that we were being inundated by people to come and use the toilet!
>
> Then we had lunch and in the early afternoon we started making our way towards Westminster where the Queen was. We got ourselves up towards the front. We had a challenge as we had a pageant mast and every time we went under the bridges we had to take that down and put it back up again, but Lady Darnley and Bob Tabor took charge of that. We also had to fly the Blue Ensign as we had a naval officer on board, the only boat in the oared class that could do that. The other boats flew the Red Ensign, the identifying flag flown to designate a British ship. And then we went past the Queen which was great fun, but by then the weather was pretty nasty.

The Hereford Bull – designated a Man-Powered Craft in the Pageant Order – had a crew of eight oarsmen and -women. Commanded by Rear Admiral Philip Wilcocks, it carried Herefordshire's Lord Lieutenant, Lady Darnley, attended by Bob Tabor. On 3 June 2012 the Bull, in the company of 670 other craft of all shapes and sizes, left its moorings at Putney Bridge and followed the Royal Barge down-river to Tower Bridge (photo: Andrew Wynn)

Ray Hunter, 69

Ray Hunter is a retired Royal Navy Submarine Commander who now lives near Ledbury. Between 1969 and 1974 his submarine appointments included HMS/M Aeneas (in command), and between 1974 and 1984 his surface ship and staff appointments included British Forces Falkland Islands 1983. He worked as a farmer until his retirement in 2016 and was former chairman of the Herefordshire Community Foundation. He was responsible for drawing up the specification of the Hereford Bull, as the trow became named.

> The trow was built in Nielson's Shipyard in Gloucester docks. Tommy Nielson and his team of shipwrights, riggers and engineers are one of the most skilled and experienced wooden ship builders and repairers in the world, with whom it was a great privilege to work. I was also responsible for procuring the timber for the 'Bull'. The Foxley Estate at Mansell Lacy gave larch for the planking, oak for the frames and douglas fir for the mast, whilst Ty'r Olchon, Longtown supplied oak for the decking.

Nielsen's set to work in the autumn of 2011 and were faced with the formidable task of designing and building the Bull by the end of the following March. They achieved this and the Hereford Bull was launched as planned, and conducted successful sea trials in Gloucester Docks Basin and the Sharpness Canal. With the Jubilee only seven weeks away, time was short to train the crew, learn how to navigate the Bull, and prove that the skilfully hidden outboard motor, a safety requirement for the Pageant, performed as designed. The oarsmen and -women, drawn mainly from Ross-on-Wye Rowing Club, were provided with specially designed oars and they embarked on Pageant training with much enthusiasm and skill.

Ray:

> When building the Bull, we had learnt that the Hereford Sea Cadet Unit was planning to build a jetty at their new unit on the Wye up-stream of Hereford City. And so it was planned that the Sea Cadets should moor the Bull at the jetty after the Pageant. Unfortunately, the funding for this ambitious project was not forthcoming and so the Bull was secured to a temporary mooring laid in the Bishop's Pool just down-stream from the Old Bridge, a mooring known not to be heavy enough to withstand the river's winter floods. So, in September 2012 the Bull was lifted out of the river and returned to Gloucester for the winter, during which plans were prepared for the following year's deployment. In spring 2013, the Bull was moved from Gloucester to Drummonds Dub, a 12-acre lake below Upton Bishop, then used for outward bound water training. The Bull spent the summer taking parties of school children sailing on Drummonds Dub. After it returned to Neilson's Yard in Gloucester, where the craft remains whilst searching for a permanent "dry" home.

THE WYE CORACLE

William Dew of Kerne Bridge (*see frontispiece, ii*) is described as the last recorded coracle user on the River Wye; although, with the growth in this small craft's popularity, this claim could be contested. Following Dew's death in 1931, his coracle was donated to Hereford Museum. It's a pretty sorry sight today, variously described as 'a pickled prune' and 'a badly crashed raven's nest'. It is still worth taking a moment to remember Dew's skill in a coracle. In her memoirs, Dew's granddaughter, Nancy Howell, remembers him:

> It was a curious sight to see grandfather looking like a giant tortoise, returning home in the evening across the meadows, his truckle on his back secured by a wide strap attached to the seat. He would fish for salmon with a rod and reel, and walk to Ross market, where he sold it for 6p a pound. He often went out on the river in his coracle for the sheer joy of it, even when it was in flood. He was quite fearless!

In the early 1960s coracle races on the Wye took place at Hereford Rowing Club's annual regatta. One of their members, Bruce Wallace, took part:

> The club had two coracles that they had made from new. I was never really very good paddling them. At the Regatta, we would have a coracle race across the river and back.

Coracle racing in front of Hereford Rowing Club (photo: Derek Foxton)

While William Dew is widely regarded as the last coracle user on the Wye, Pete Redding's distinctive figure is often seen sauntering down to the Wye, coracle strapped to his back. He's a convert.

Pete Redding, 50

Pete is originally from Pershore and has been living in Hereford for seven years, with lengthy excursions to Australia (canoeing Catherine Gorge, bypassing some impressive canyons and a few crocodiles along the way), France and Poland. He and his family chose Hereford as their home because of its closeness to the Welsh hills and the River Wye. He works in social housing as a learning and development officer. Two years ago, he swapped canoes for coracles, introducing the Coracle Regatta to the resurrected River Carnival.

Pete Redding in his coracle
(photo: Emma Drabble)

> It was through the River Carnival that I first came across coracles. I'd seen them, I knew what they were, but I'd never got close to one or had a chance to paddle one. But then I had a go, which very quickly led to the coracle being left at my house, which is where it sits today. It was made by a Polish lady, Monica. She was a web designer, but when she was living over here, she integrated beautifully and joined in with lots of our community projects. She went away, booked herself onto a little week course, built a coracle and brought it back to Hereford.
>
> One of the beauties of the coracle for me is that I can walk to Victoria Bridge in less than ten minutes and launch it there and I might paddle up-stream, towards Hunderton, under the Great Western Bridge, and I tend to float back. I'm hoping to start a coracle-building course and I've recently found a lady who weaves willow and is keen to make coracle frames. My dream is to have a flotilla of coracles go down at the front of the River Carnival. Last year, we nailed a baton to the back of one with two flaming torches, and spun the coracle down in darkness, which was quite a magical experience.

Ex-Metropolitan police officer and coracle maker Karl Chattington, from Cardiff, has constructed the only working Wye coracle still in existence. He was so inspired by the work of coracle makers, that he now follows that pursuit full-time. He has studied the art of its construction at length and is now widely regarded as one of the pre-eminent experts of the craft in the country:

There is a coracle specific to each river, including the Wye. The nature of each river, the speed, flow, and conditions, dictates the style and construction of each coracle.

The Wye coracle was traditionally built from ash and it would have been locked in place with a hazel gunwale. You need sixty-seven hazel logs of approximately nine feet in length and the thickness of a good pencil. The Wye coracle originates from the Towy coracle and yet the rivers are miles apart. It's always been my contention that somebody either went down to west Wales, saw the coracle and took it up and started to use it on the Wye, or somebody took specifically a Towy coracle up to fish on the Wye. But the Wye coracle, if you look at it, is almost certainly originally a Towy construction.

The last time a Wye Coracle was built was between 100 and 120 years ago. Karl had always intended to make one and was eventually inspired by a meeting with Geoffrey Grevell, a fellow Wye coracle fan. Regrettably, Geoffrey died and his widow asked Karl to build a Wye coracle in memory of her husband. Today, it hangs on the wall of St Arvans Church near Chepstow. It's such an appropriate home and no coincidence either.

Karl again:

Karl Chattington and his coracle
(photo: Bill Laws)

> St Arvan was a ninth-century hermit that lived basically on the River Wye. He had his roving community, but he sustained himself by fishing for salmon. He drowned when he was into a big salmon, which pulled him over the side of the boat. It capsized and in he went!
>
> Very kindly, Hereford Museum gave us access to William Dew's coracle. I went up with Dylan Jones and measured it. It was very difficult to get an accurate measurement because with age it's spread out. So, the only way I could do this was to get black and white photographic plates. The coracle seat was still remaining and some of the paddles, and I could work out, from the actual paddles and the seat, the dimensions and I could scale them against the photographs. So, once I done that I looked into the nuances of the Wye coracle and how different it was to the Towy coracle. There are only two bands that lock the coracle together: on the

BOAT-BUILDING & OTHER RIVER CRAFT

Towy, you got usually one below and two above the seat. But the Wye coracle is unique because traditionally there's one band below the seat and one band above the seat.

Now if you look at later photographs of the Wye coracle they got a planked gunwale where there's no weave involved; it's just the frame is brought up, on all sides to pull it all together. So that's one of the unique features again of the Wye coracle.

Dylan Jones, 49

Another Welshman and Wye coracle aficionado, Dylan Jones, is secretary of the Coracle Society and a keen exponent of the coracle craft. Formerly of St Fagans Museum of Wales, Dylan was responsible for the Museum's fishing, hunting and sporting collection. The 'silent', half-walnut shaped vessel has been a feature of the nation's rivers for hundreds if not thousands of years, and Dylan is on a mission to keep it that way.

> The coracle is a silent vessel and you can go to parts of the river inaccessible to anybody else really. Basically, you can see parts of the rivers that are quiet, and have good fun. You can feel yourself going back to hundreds, centuries, even thousands of years, because the coracle hasn't changed in that time at all.
>
> On both sections of the River Wye, the Welsh and the English sections, coracles would have been used primarily to fish for salmon really, but there are instances as well, documented by travellers from the seventeenth century onwards, that the coracles were used for racing as well, racing coracles. From the seventeenth and eighteenth centuries, there are various reports of coracles going from Ross to Chepstow, and of going over to Bristol as well.
>
> An average Wye coracle would look something similar to a River Teifi or a River Towy coracle. Again, a typical description of a coracle from the seventeenth or eighteenth century would have been a walnut shell. Basically, that would have been something like the Wye coracle. There is still only one Wye coracle in existence and thankfully that's in Hereford Museum.
>
> The Wye coracle is quite unique because apparently for the nineteenth century for a while it was covered in zinc and that is the only mention of zinc being used in a coracle. Because with most coracles, the material is locally sourced. There were, at a time, aluminium laths used up in Llangollen, but not anymore. They went back to the materials sourced locally. As you know it's a silent craft so an ideal poaching craft.

RIVER CARNIVAL

All the boats were decorated. One year I entered as Miss Muffet and the boat was decorated as a web with a very large spider that had eyes on it.

After lying dormant for a few decades, the Wye River Carnival was resurrected in 2014 by a group of volunteers. In 2018, it entered its fourth year, freshly invigorated, with the River Wye slap-bang in the middle of celebrations. In the heady days of the River Carnival in the late 1960s and mid 1970s, over 8,000 spectators hugged the banks of the Wye watching the stream of floats, followed by spectacular firework displays. Companies, clubs and associations would all have a float. In 1973, Hereford City Young Conservative Club won with 'Old Woman Who Lived in a Shoe', and Denco Sports and Social Club came second. The Burma Star Association even had an entry.

The Denco entry, 'Disney Fair', in the Wye River Carnival, 1970s (photo: John Baker)

In 1966, England were the football World Cup holders for the last and only time. Meanwhile, the same year, there were antics at the River Carnival as Keith Morgan remembers:

BOAT-BUILDING & OTHER RIVER CRAFT 117

A float being decorated for the 1964 carnival (photo: Derek Foxton Collection)

Despite being a poor swimmer I was fascinated with anything on the water, and in 1966 we started a Bulmers' crew with me as cox, Bill Walker stroke and Tony Clements, Chris Williams and John Tedstone. Our entry, inspired by North Sea Gas, was South Sea Gas featuring a manned drilling rig and two grass-skirted maidens, Gail Carpenter and Margaret Harris with Alec Cook and yours truly and Chris Ellison rowing. Sadly, we couldn't make headway against the current and when I pulled the plug on our electrics there were cries of "They've sunk!" We were eventually landed on the Rowing Club steps.

Their next effort, 'Rub-a-Dub-Dub, Three Men in a Tub', fared little better and prompted Keith's girlfriend (now wife) to veto plans to take a raft across the English Channel and deliver a new-season cask of cider to the French in response to their bringing over Beaujolais Nouveau.

Gary McLeod was a young carnival spectator, and later on a competitor:

> As a kid, we lived up the College and I always remember the old man used to bring me down once a year to the River Carnival and it was a hell of a big thing. All the firms had their floats on the river and there were some fantastic boats, with big batteries for the lights. There were different categories, so Bulmers and Painters would be in 'A' category for example and others would be in 'B'.

Wye River Carnival, 1973: the Hereford City Young Conservative Club's winning float, 'Old Woman Who Lived in a Shoe' (photo: John Baker)

BOAT-BUILDING & OTHER RIVER CRAFT   119

> We launched one float at Hunderton Ferry and by the time we got to the Great Western Bridge the battery had run out, and this thing went down the river just as a silver calico thing; people couldn't make out what we were. And then there was Ikie. He was the last person I know who entered because no one was entering at the end; it had sort of dwindled off, but there were some smaller entries and I always remember they said all the entrants would get £10. Well, Ikie got his canoe and he got a mini car battery, some leads, and he put some wire going over, and he had one light bulb on a hook and he called himself 'Wee Willie Winkie'. All you could see was this one bulb and a bloody canoe coming down. He had his number on his back. And everyone was laughing when he was doing this. But when he came in The Vaga with a tenner – a lot of money in those days – well, the last laugh was on him.

Ron Hodges

Ron Hodges was working for Edis Swan in the early 1970s and helped build a float with multi carnival usage:

> We were at Edis Swan then, and we had a big swan in the carnival that I helped build. We made a structure of wire netting and then it was covered in white flowers. The first time we used it we plastered it and painted it for the River Carnival. Then the Road Carnival followed that so we drilled it all over and covered it with flowers and entered it for the Road Carnival.

In 1964, Christine MacIntyre helped her brother, Roger Searle's entry, by making hundreds of crêpe paper flowers.

RIVER CARNIVAL ENTERS NEW AGE

In 2017 the River Carnival was nominated for Outstanding Contribution to the City. It was a huge boost for organisers of this community event. Director Jo Henshaw has been there from the beginning:

> We were chuffed to bits. It was really important for the event to have that kind of recognition, to be taken seriously in such a short time. And it's bigger than the people who work to make it happen. It's not ours, it's this thing that people seem to have taken to their hearts.

Rebecca Huggett is Artistic Director of the present incarnation of the festival:

It's a big community celebration, with the River Wye in Hereford at the centre of that celebration. Well, there used to be a River Carnival in Hereford in the 1950s, 1960s and early 1970s and we have some people on our team, such as Tricia Hales, whose family were involved in that event. So, in 2014 when we had an opportunity to put on an event on the river, it seemed like a really good idea to bring back the River Carnival. It was great to find out about the history of the event – lots of local people remember it.

At the end of 2013 I saw an article in the *Hereford Times* about the Wye Valley Area of Outstanding Natural Beauty wanting to put on a river festival, and their idea initially was that it would start in Hay and go all the way down the River Wye and down to Chepstow so I got in touch with them and I was really excited. I'd mentioned it to Jo, Catherine Gilling and Rob Strawson and I organised an open meeting, which the Friends of Castle Green hosted at the Pavilion and lots of people came to that including Tricia Hales. I realised, really quickly, this is a woman I really need to get to know, because she obviously has a big history with the river, actively uses the river with the raft race, but also, she was really into this idea of bringing the Carnival back. So that's really where it all started and then various other people heard about what we were doing and wanted to get involved.

But we have an amazing team from CHAR (Committee of Hereford Amateur Rafters) led by Tricia Hales, who take a lead as they have a unique knowledge of the river. The Street Carnival is really important too because it's more accessible to some people than maybe getting onto a float on the river, so we make lots of costumes and carnival structures for that.

The all-new River Carnival has probably had to negotiate some labyrinthine rules, laws and regulations before even getting close to the river's edge. But there was a time when some wood, canvas and a can-do attitude was enough to provide a vessel for all sorts of water-bound adventures.

CLOG MAKING

Boat- and raft-building are not the only crafts found along the river. The sole remaining hand-carver of bespoke clogs in England is Jeremy Atkinson of Kington. But at the start of the Second World War there were others like him at 'clogging' camps in Preston-on-Wye, where teams of cloggers gathered for the 'clogging' season each year. They camped in the woods, cutting down the alder trees, later to be carved into wooden clog soles. The cut shapes of the wooden shoes were stacked in a circle to dry and the cloggers moved on to the next tree.

The stumps of the trees were left to grow again for the next cutting for another 'clogging' season. (*Herefordshire Within Living Memory*). This was one use of wood growing on the riverside, but there were others.

The late John Brookes lived in Strangford for all of his 85 years. He never ventured far, living all his life in the house he was born in and spending his working days on the farm next door. He was a contented man. When he was a boy he remembered his mother buying pegs from gypsies:

> They made them out of sally wood, wood you'd get near the river. They used to gather it down by the river here and split it with a knife and get a very thin pin and wrap around the end. They'd sell perhaps a dozen or two dozen, and walk all over the village carrying their basket of pegs. Mother used to buy some.

Adrian Howard

Adrian has worked in woodland management for years with the Woodland Trust, particularly on the Doward. Thousands of poplar trees were planted in the area when the Moreland Brothers, of England's Glory matchbox fame, lived nearby on the Foy peninsula. The great number of poplar trees growing in the area is no coincidence, the poplar being the basic raw ingredient for the match stick.

Adrian:

> The Moreland Brothers owned all the farms around there and people would grow poplars because they knew they could sell them easily and make some money. That's the reason all the estates around here grew poplar because there was a market for it. But of course, by the time these trees had grown to maturity, Moreland's had packed up. They've just got too big now and are a bit of a problem.

Another crop and another tree was the oak, planted in nearby Forest of Dean by request of the British Navy during the Napoleonic Wars in preparation to build the fleet of the mid-twentieth century. The ash and the elm were also in demand for the solid clinker-style boats once a common sight on the Wye. These heavy boats were used as practice boats for novice rowers, and also rented out to groups for the once-popular pleasure boat businesses on the river. Canoes, however, before they became more widely available, were cruder in construction and material. Not that that mattered too much to those keen to get out and navigate the Wye.

6 Navigating the Wye

> I seem to remember Derek Jones hunting in Herefordshire in the 1930s, and going to one of the tributaries of the Wye River and seeing a canoeist for the first time. He just couldn't believe it. He thought they were like Indians! He had never seen anything like it before. Dylan Jones

Scottish explorer John MacGregor was introduced to the canoe on a trip to North America in the 1850s. On his return to Britain he designed a 4.6 metre craft based on the Native American canoes he had paddled on his travels. Constructed from oak planking and covered with rubberised canvas, the boat had an open cockpit and was powered with a double-bladed oar. His book, *A Thousand Miles in the Rob Roy Canoe*, brought the craft, and the activity, to a European audience. Fast forward 150 years and canoeing on the Wye has really taken off. Not everyone is happy about it and there continues to be tension between users of the Wye's navigational rights and those enjoying its riparian rights. Mostly, however, they rub alongside each other quite well.

One of the early canoeing holiday pioneers was Peter Gordon Lawrence (died 2004). An experienced canoeist, he had negotiated many European rivers in the 1950s before settling on the Wye as the base for his holiday idea; its navigational rights and the sublime countryside were bonuses. The brochure at the time promised punters 'anorak waterproof top jackets, dining marquee, and hutted ablutions!' From its former base in sleepy Hole in the Wall, outside Ross-on-Wye, Peter built PGL into a huge international organisation. Kenneth Johnson, a friend of Peter's, was on one of their maiden Wye voyages. He wrote in his diaries:

Maybe you have never experienced the thrill of canoeing down the Wye through the peaceful English countryside. I could tell you about the stormy night at Symonds Yat and waking in the morning to watch the opposite bank creeping upwards into the sunlight; or of paddling across the river to fetch the morning milk at Weir End. Or I could tell you about the various short, steep excursions to shops and a castle and Yats. I could tell you so much.

PETER DAINES, 82

These days, a canoe trip for Peter Daines involves a walk to the end of his garden, lifting a canoe off its rack, and then sliding it into the river. It's that easy. For a life-long canoeist, his home is in the most perfect spot on the river at Fownhope. He has canoed since the age of ten and between the 1960s and 1990s he ran canoeing holidays along the Wye, often encountering Peter Gordon Lawrence. These days, access to the river is far easier than when he started in the 1940s and lived in Tupsley.

Peter Daines and his wife Marjorie set up canoeing holidays on the Wye in the 1960s
(photo: Peter Daines)

Peter:

> I was born in 1935 and lived in Hampton Dene Road. We used to roam the local quarry and thought it was ours. It was an idyllic place in which to live. Fields all around and a quarry and brickyard buildings in which we used to play, but weren't supposed to really.
>
> We used to wander on both the Lugg and the Wye. My earliest memory of canoeing is on the Wye at Litley Orchard with an older cousin, who lived just down the bottom of Hampton Dene Road. We also used to get on the river at the bottom of Old Eign Hill, opposite the present veterinary practice, but was then the Whalebone public house. To transport our canoes, we made a trolley out of a couple of old pram wheels and used it to trolley the canoe down; or you found someone to carry the other end. When a friend built a canoe, I decided I wanted to build one too, so I just did. In those days, you would get some plans and build the canoe making the frame out of wood and then you covered it with canvas. Over the years I have made lots of canoes this way.

Canvas canoes, of course, could damage easily, so it was important that repair kits were carried.

Peter again:

> You would need to waterproof the canvas by painting it, firstly with an undercoat then with at least one coat of paint. Because of rocks in the river, canvas canoes were easily holed so you always carried a repair kit on board.

Camping today is so easy: you buy a tent in a bag, shake it out, and hey presto! you have overnight accommodation. It wasn't quite as quick in Vic Gammage's day.

Vic Gammage, 71

A Herefordian born and bred, Vic is the stalwart behind the Hereford Canoe Centre on Castle Green. He is passionate that this youth club continues: 'You need places like this to pass the knowledge on to young people.' He worked at the General Hospital as an engineer for 42 years before his retirement:

> I've spent my life on the river. My house was by Hunderton Youth Club and you could be in the river in three minutes. We all used to swim in

it as kids. Our parents never warned us; there was no health and safety then. The river was your playground. You'd either go up to the woods, or you'd swim in the river in the summer, or you'd camp out by the river at Belmont. We would just go home after a week. You'd go up there, pitch your tent and just get on with it. Either fish, swim, or canoe, it was your life then.

In 1958, I was at Hunderton Youth Club and we started to make canvas boats. It was cheaper to make one than buy one then and there were fewer canoes on the river in those days. There was a guy called Percy Blandford who drew up the drawings of the skeletons of the boat and we made them up with plywood. And then you wrapped them in canvas and held that down with copper tacks.

We launched just by Hunderton ferry. We would do just the Belmont stretch at first and then we started to get a bit more adventurous when I was 15 or 16 and we started to go up to Glasbury and stop at Preston-on-Wye overnight, and stick the tents up.

We used to make the tents too. Because there was a lady with the Education Authority in those days and she used to go around all the clubs and say, "What would you like to make?" And we said, "Well, we want to make a tent". So she came to the Youth Club and we made the tents up ourselves.

We first tried them at Preston-on-Wye at the campsite. Basically, you got out of your kayak, got on top of the bank, put your tent up, which was excellent, a form of a bell tent and could sleep four or six easily. Then we would get the timber and start a fire and cook over the fire. There was no gas fires then; you just did the best you could. We could get quite a bit of kit in our canoes. We built four of them in the end. In those days, you would pack your kayak and off you'd go and if you forgot something that was it for the next few days: you couldn't do anything about it. And we would have just one adult with us, Bruce Ruderford. But it's all changed these days.

Ron Shoesmith, 82
I think I've sold more River Wye canoeing guides than anything else.

Ron Shoesmith is the author of many books, including the first-ever canoeing guide to the Wye, printed in 1964, which was inspired by his new role as manager at Staunton-on-Wye YHA (Youth Hostel Association). He arrived in the arctic winter of 1962/ 63.

> I came out that winter and shivered my way through until March, when it finally started to warm up and the hostel opened. It was basically a

summer hostel, so it didn't pay me very well, but it was good fun. Within 12 months I had helped to organise the YHA canoeing holidays, which were to be based at Staunton and involved tours down the Wye. At the beginning, we had an antique ambulance for transport, but we got rid of that within the first year and replaced it with a 15-seater minibus and canoe trailer. Apart from running the youth hostel, I was chasing around after the canoeists, and collecting them from Chepstow at the end of the week, so it was a hectic time.

People had boats, but in 1963 canoeing really was in its infancy. There were pleasure boats in places like Symonds Yat and Hereford, and even ferry boats, including the one at Hunderton. But when I started the canoe holidays at Staunton, we needed something to get the hostel on its feet, because we were only getting some 2,000 bed nights a year and that was not enough to keep it running.

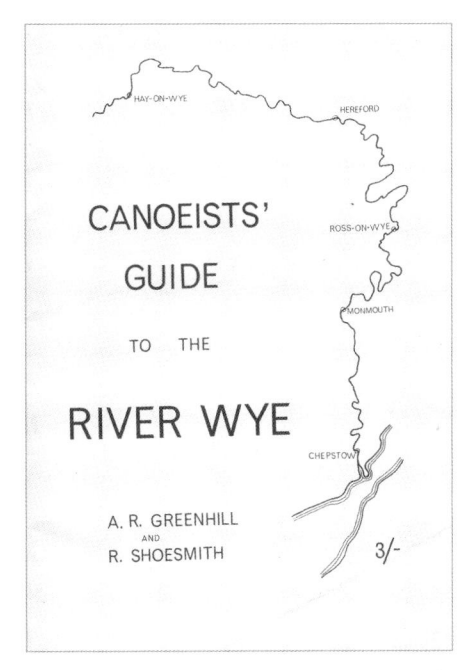

The first River Wye canoeing guide (Ron Shoesmith)

So the canoeing holidays started to get publicity as well. To begin with we did tours down the river, starting at Glasbury and going down to Brockweir or Chepstow, depending on the tide. Eventually, we did a second holiday, which was canoe training, where we took canoeists to various parts of the river where there were rapids such as Monnington Falls or Symonds Yat.

There was always a problem of where you could launch and where you couldn't, and I found that, if I went around and had a chat with people beforehand, I could get it all nicely organised. As a result, I wrote the *Canoeists' Guide to the River Wye*, which gave people ideas where launching was permissible and where you didn't get into any problems.

I must have written the first guide in 1964, very early really. I had to get all the information properly organised and it was my first attempt at writing anything good enough to print. I was quite pleased with that. I've written a lot of books since then, but I think I've sold more River Wye canoeing guides than anything else.

Butts Camp (photo: Doris Kershaw)

BUTTS CAMP

In the 1940s and 1950s, there was an encampment up-stream from Hereford at Warham, which was occupied from Easter through to winter and known as 'Butts Camp'. There was swimming, fishing, sleeping under canvas and cooking over fires. But a day's work still beckoned for some, and these campers made their daily trek to the work place, either on foot or even by canoe.

Frank Ford:

> The Butts was on the river bank just beyond the milepost above Warham, and people used to camp out there from Easter – a whole crowd of them. Dad always used to say their first swim was Easter Sunday and when he was a bachelor he used to live there right through until about Christmas time. My mother was a Sister at the County Hospital. They weren't married then, but she used to go up to the Camp and Dad would take her back to work at the General Hospital by canoe.

Another Butts camper was Frank Williams:

> For two years, I camped there with Leslie 'Bunnie' Harris, Fred Nichols and Leslie Beason, all in one bell tent. The following year I moved across the river, where there were many more tents. We had to walk to and from work

Butts Camp (photo: Doris Kershaw)

every day, a distance of two miles. Swimming in the river was a favourite pastime, especially diving off the tree branches. One summer there was a drought and the river was low and I went for a swim, dived in the usual place and hit the bottom, badly cutting my head. I still have the scar.

Hereford Rowing club regular Bruce Wallace:

Back in the 1930s and 1940s, my wife Jane's uncle and his friends used to have boats on the river and they would camp up at the old Butts, the old rifle range up there. They had great fun swimming in the river and messing about. I mean going back to that era, they were all fighters of the Second World War and they did their training as boys in the trees on the Wye.

ROWING

British success on the water at the Olympics has made rowing hugely popular in recent years, which is good news for our local rowing clubs, Hereford and Ross. There have been lean times and buoyant ones too, but they thrive today, with active junior and veteran sections and an impressive collection of 'pots' between them. The clubs attract rowers, crews and spectators locally and from across the country to their annual Regattas. But in the pre-Second World War years, club

The old Hereford Rowing Clubhouse, c.1920 (photo: Hammonds Family)

members were exclusively white collar, professional people, and the artisans – in crude terms, men who worked with their hands – were excluded for fear that their 'brute' strength might make them fearsome competitors on the water.

It wasn't all plain sailing for women either, who had to fight for their places on the water too. At the end of the 1931 season, it was decided that ladies,

> could be invited to form a Ladies Club with headquarters at the Boathouse, and with rights of using the Hereford Rowing Club Pleasure Boats on terms to be decided by the Hereford Rowing Club Committee.

However, in 1951, the entry of a woman, a Miss B. Jones, in the scratch fours caused great consternation among the older rowing members. Nonetheless, she performed so well as cox and inspired her crew to such good effect, that they won the final by one length, despite her being a woman!

HEREFORD ROWING CLUB

In 1949 Hereford Rowing Club's clubhouse and boathouse were crumbling wooden buildings and their racing fleet modest. The balance sheet at the AGM

The new Hereford Rowing Clubhouse, c.1958 (photo: Hammonds Family)

that year showed just £270 in the bank. The future wasn't looking good for the club. However, in 1952, a remarkable stroke of good fortune lead to dramatic change at the club. Five club members were travelling to Birmingham to attend a divisional meeting of the Amateur Rowing Association. They were: Geoff Hammonds, Harry Pressey, Norman Groom, Fred Lee and Malcolm Startin. At Kidderminster, a large number of Harriers football fans got on to watch their team play at Birmingham in a round of the FA cup. One of the fans started to chat about a successful lottery being run locally by the Catholic church and he promised to send the Hereford Rowing Club members details. And true to his word, he did. It seemed a lottery might just be the club's salvation.

After careful consideration, at the club's extraordinary general meeting that year, it was agreed they would start their own lottery on the same lines, called the River Wye Guild, and it was to be managed by the directors, including Geoff Hammonds, Harry Pressey and Tommy Dawes. Tickets were sold through individual agents, clubs and societies, with large sales across the area, including south Wales. Sales grew very quickly and within a year it was possible to start buying new boats, and by 1954 there was enough money to build a new boathouse and in 1958 new premises opened with a unique indoor rowing tank.

Among the illustrious roll-call of club members were some colourful characters. Frank Owen was one. Former Vice President of the club, he was a British journalist and radical Liberal Member of Parliament. He was Liberal MP for Hereford between 1929 and 1931 and later editor of the *Evening Standard* and the *Daily Mail*. He was awarded the OBE in 1946. Then there was F.E. Hayter, a prominent oarsman in his day, he went on to be a hunter and collector of wild animals in Northern Africa. He had been on friendly terms with Ras Tafari, the Emperor of Abyssinia, and had explored the country for many years, becoming a Fellow of the Zoological Society. He died in February 1936 in Abyssinia in a plane crash. The following year, news reached the club of the death of Clive Lewis 'having occurred in action in Spain during the Civil War.'

At its height, 200,000 Wye Valley Pool tickets were being sold each week, with many community groups also benefiting, including other rowing clubs, like Ross-on-Wye. Malcolm Startin was one of the original committee that started the River Wye Guild. In 2008, he talked about the scheme's huge success:

> By 1960, my final year of Captaincy, over 200,000 tickets were being sold each week by the Wye Valley Pools. More than £4,500 was paid out in prizes – first prize being £3,000 – and £1,250 was going into the "Charity Pot". Around £300,000 was distributed in Herefordshire to other good causes and charities.

Hammonds Family

Herefordians will be familiar with the Hammonds family through their photographic business in the city in the last century, which continues today. Certainly, for many years Geoffrey Hammonds, commonly known as Geoff (died 1983), was Hereford Cathedral School's official photographer – and the Rowing Club's too. The family's links with the club go back to the 1880s, when Henry John Hammonds (Geoff's father) started at the club in 1886 as coxswain and steered the club to victory in the race for the Wye Vase. He was Captain of the club for over 25 years. In 1896, he received a bravery award when he rescued a woman from a sinking boat. In the report of the day, Henry,

> without divesting himself of his clothes, at once dived under and succeeded in bringing Miss Dallow to the surface in an unconscious condition but he had the great difficulty in getting her through the weeds.

In 1949 Geoff was elected captain of the club and, in the minutes of the day, he reminded the club that, 'he was following in the footsteps of his father, H.J. Hammonds, who had been captain from 1901 to 1924, and he hoped his sons would one day be elected to the same office.' Geoff Hammonds was president at Hereford Rowing Club for 25 years. Malcolm Startin, who did most of the organising of the Regattas during Geoff's presidency, was known to be one of the best organisers and he once stopped Worcester Rowing Club (one of the best teams at the time) from entering for being late back in the day!

Marie and Geoffrey Hammonds
(photo: Hammonds Family)

Henry John Hammonds (whose nickname was 'Skip') standing second from right, with friends, picnicking at 'The Jackdaws', which is past Breinton (photo: Hammonds Family)

Hereford Regatta in 1950 – a dead heat (photo: Hammonds Family)

FRANK FORD

Frank Ford has been a member of Hereford Rowing Club for 60 years, taking up the sport in the 1950s. Before him, his father Arthur Ford was involved with the Club all the way through the war years. Arthur was managing director of Bevan and Hodges building contractors, but the Club's Artisans' Rule at that time excluded him from competing:

Frank:

> They used to have all the Welsh miners and Welsh valleys contribute to the Pool and it made a lot of money. That's really what built the new clubhouse. Dad was in the Reserved Occupation for the early part of the Second World War, and at that time he was a Rowing Club member, but was barred by the Artisans' Rule then. He wasn't allowed to compete, but he was involved in the club with pleasure boating.
>
> I think his interest in the Rowing Club really was from the Butts and seeing other boats on the river. And then during the war years, of course, he and another man, Walter Palfrey, used to do a lot of maintenance work down at the Club. Dad was eventually called up into the Royal

A crew watches on at the Hereford Regatta (photo: Hammonds Family)

Engineers and served in Italy, where he contracted TB and was invalided out to Newport House in Almeley. When he recovered he was back at the Rowing Club doing repair and maintenance work.

In the early days, the club would normally close down during the winter months. Bert Crissall was the boatman and he would be down there servicing all the boats. In those days, the boats were wooden and needed a lot of maintenance and re-varnishing every year.

In October, 1939, Bert Crissall's 36 years of service with the Hereford Rowing Club were recognised by members when, on their behalf, he was presented with a cheque and a plaque inscribed with the names of the subscribers by the Mayor of Hereford, Mr H.P. Barnsley. The Mayor's son Mr P.E. Barnsley recalled Crissall's 30 years' association with the Club and paid strong tribute to his skill as a boatbuilder, saying that, 'it was due to Mr. Crissall's industry that some of the boats which were as much as 40 years old were still on the water and giving pleasure to members'.

Frank again:

> When I was 11, Paul Miller taught me to scull, then I sculled on a family membership ticket right the way through the school years. When I left school in 1964 I joined the Rowing Club as a senior member and started training quite hard and I won my first 'pot' in 1965, at Bridgnorth Regatta. The Club started to be very successful, and by the late 1960s I was training seven times a week. There would have been 16 or 17 of us training, and every Saturday we used to race from the Rowing Club up to Warham Steps and back.
>
> When I first joined the Club in 1964 there were many schools rowing: there was the Cathedral School, Whitecross School, High School, Belmont Abbey and the RAF camp at Credenhill. So, there were all of these feeders to the Rowing Club. At that time, it was a male-dominated club. In fact, I don't think there was a women's senior rowing category until the mid 1970s; I think it was 1975, 1976 before women were allowed to row down there, but they were allowed to use pleasure boats on Sundays.
>
> The new club was built in 1960 and the Wye Guild bought us a complete shed of new boats and I think there was about a quarter of a million pounds cash donated to the club, so it set us off on a very good footing. And we had an excellent coaching team. Harry Pressey was one and he used to say to us: "Time is everything. You scull up to Warham Head and back and you'll soon learn to scull; you'll learn the easiest way of doing it."

Bruce Wallace

Bruce Wallace was 13 years old when he first rowed at Hereford Regatta in 1952. He served on the committee for several years under the presidency of Geoff Hammonds. 'I had won so many 'pots' at one time that yet another photograph became quite old hat!'

'Eights' from Hereford Rowing Club on the Wye, 1970s (photo: Frank Ford)

We had an eight, which of course belonged to the rowing club, and we started off in tubs, rather like sea cadet whaler boats. I rowed until I left school in 1958 and then I went straight into a four for Hereford Rowing Club and my last competitive regatta was at Ross Regatta in August 1968. I won so many pots that in the end having my photo seemed a bit naff. It was very much a team; we were a club. I joined the committee in 1963 and the other members of the committee included Richard Barton, Malcolm Startin, Bill Socket, Geoff Hammonds, Frank Bevan, Tommy Dawes and John Hartland, who was the games master who started me rowing. He was replaced by Malcolm Startin, who was the managing director of Painter Bros., the construction company. In fact there were a lot of Painters at the Rowing Club. Hereford was the top provincial regatta in those days, and it was run primarily by Richard Barton and Malcolm Startin, and they ran it like a military exercise. If you were late on the start you were scratched. Everybody knew that if you were going to row at Hereford you had to be on time. It was one of the few regattas that finished on time.

Bruce, his winning team and trophies
(photo: Bruce Wallace)

These rowers had to turn out smart and the blazer and club badge were an important part of the uniform. King Street tailor Terence Agate was the man responsible for turning out the presentable rowers.

Bruce again:

> When it was Regatta time we would dress up in our blazers. If you were an older member and you weren't rowing, you could still wear your blazer. My wife Jane bought me my first proper rowing club blazer the year we got engaged in 1959, and it was hand-made by Terence Agate, a little Jewish tailor next door to the Orange Tree on King Street. He made all the blazers for the Rowing Club, and the Rugby Club. They were all hand-measured and fitted. The club badge was very distinctive and very expensive. It cost more than the blazer, all gold and silver and interwoven, and that was made by Terence too.

Visit of Princess Alexandra to Hereford Rowing Club, and crowds at a regatta, early 1960s
(photos: Derek Evans Studio Archive/ HLTAL/ HARC/ Hereford Libraries)

ROSS ROWING CLUB

Ross Rowing Club – also known as the 'Henley of the West' – was established in 1870. Old photographs show the distinctive wooden boat-house on brick stilts. William Butcher was one of a number of townspeople who helped build it and form the Athletic and Rowing Club. Regatta programmes from the late nineteenth and early twentieth centuries illustrate the multi-disciplinary activities that included sports other than just rowing. There were swimming and diving competitions (in the river), jousting (in the river!) canoe races, and a multitude of cycling events.

William's grandson, Brian Butcher, 89, the youngest of five boys and two sisters, remembers his early days at the Club:

> My grandfather founded Butchers Garage. He was always involved with the Club. So was my father, Allan, and all my brothers, Ivor, John, Tibs and Dennis. My sister Vera also rowed. I remember, on regatta day, grandfather was judge and we used to have to catch the ferry across to the judging stage on the Benhall side of the river. I was bored to death of course. I also used to row a lot and coxed for my brothers, bored to death. I was told I had to do it.

Left to right: brothers Ivor, Brian, John and 'Tibs' (William) at Ross
(photo: Brian Butcher)

Ross Rowing Club, boathouse (photo: *Ross Gazette*)

Brian again:

> I was too young to sign up to the forces during the war, but all my brothers did, to the RAF and the Royal Navy, and they all came home. Amazing really. The club lost a few boys during the war. One of them was Dixie Dean. I knew him of course; he went to the Grammar School. He was killed on a bombing raid right at the beginning of the war. I remember his father used to come down to the boathouse with terriers.

The Second World War claimed other club members: Cyril Babbage, who was awarded the DFM; Tom Wright, killed flying a bomber; and Wilf Phillips, killed in the Commandos.

The wooden boathouse had other uses too during the pre-Second World War years. Brian again:

> The boathouse was used as a roller-skating venue. It was very popular but it stopped in the end because the club wasn't felt to be very suitable, so the skaters came up to our paint shop in town instead and did it in there.

The river bank at Ross, prior to steps being added for the Rowing Club (photo: Brian Butcher)

The Benhall Pontoon at Ross (photo: Brian Butcher)

The Butcher family also enjoyed summer Sundays out in the Rowing Club's 'boats for hire':

> All the boats had names. I think one was called Alice. You didn't have to pay if you were a Club member, but you did have to book. We would go up to Backney for a picnic or even down to Symonds Yat and we would hire Cuthbert Harker's furniture van to come and pick us all up and bring the boats back to Ross. He used to tie the oars on the side so you couldn't open the doors on the driver's side!

In 1949 and 1950 there were a couple of new recruits, and they remain members to this day: Howard Copping, 91, who rowed at Henley in the summer of 2017, joined in 1949; and Brian Dean, 82 (Dixie Dean's cousin), in 1950. Between them they have over 100 rowing trophies.

Howard was born in Folkestone, but arrived in the area to attend Forestry School at Parkend, Forest of Dean, in 1949. It was nothing for him to hop on his bike at the end of a day's work and cycle to Ross Rowing Club, row for an hour, and then cycle back, a round trip of 26 miles: 'I was very fit,' he says.

Brian was born on Bulls Hill outside Ross and was introduced to the Rowing Club by two well-known local characters: Tony 'Atlas' Jewson and Ken Bundy.

> I was on the juniors' side of the Youth Club one night and they said to me, "Oh, you are the right size for a cox, come on down". So that's when I started coxing the crews. I was just a little boy then and coxes used to address crews as Mister. We had pontoons in those days to get in the boats and I had to be there before the crew arrived to bale the pontoons out because they were full of water. And woe betide you if you hadn't done that or you'd end up in the river yourself! Happened to me many a time.

Today, the Club has steps leading down from the boathouse to the river, but it wasn't always like that. It used to be a precarious process launching boats from often unstable pontoons. It had to change as the Club grew, so a fund raising campaign to pay for the steps started, but it was a long and slow process, until the Wye Guild stepped in. Brian Dean:

> The Club has gone from strength to strength, but there were days in the 1950s when we didn't think we would exist because we were so short of

money we had to think of ways of raising money. If you wanted a salmon for a draw, Pashley would get you one. When Pashley died, his housekeeper advertised his punt and I went to purchase that punt for the rowing club. What happened was I said I would pick it up on the Friday evening at six but I didn't have anything to carry it on so I asked someone to collect it and he was several minutes late leaving the Club and when we got down there we said sorry for being late, and she said if you can't be bothered getting here on time then you're not going to have the punt, and wouldn't sell it to me! And that punt would have been worth some money mind.

I remember a well-known benefactor of the Club who owned the Central Café in Ross. He decided to hold a whist drive and he reported to one committee that it had bought in 12 shillings and six pence profit! At that rate we were never going to achieve much. So in the end I met Geoff Hammonds, who was President of Hereford Rowing Club and of the Wye Guild, and appealed to him, saying, "Can you help us out? We want to build some steps, but we haven't got the money?" And Geoff said, "I think we can," and they did.

Howard: 'The older members of Hereford Rowing Club, like Geoff Hammonds, used to look kindly at Ross. There was a bit of camaraderie. Competition was only on the water.'

Getting to boat races was unorthodox compared to today. Brian again:

> We never had any transport in those days, in the fifties, and so we put our blades on the train at Ross Railway station, travelled up to Hereford on the train and walked through Hereford with them, all the way to Hereford Regatta on the Wye Bridge. There was no other way of getting there. And in 1950/ 51, we borrowed Hereford's boat to train in, but we wouldn't use it until after two o'clock on the Sunday afternoon because they were using it.

Both Howard and Brian remember one formidable character and rowing coach, Jack Farmer. Howard again:

> Jack was a painter and decorator in Ross and he was a well-known coach too. His first words to you when you were in your boat was, "Backney!" So you would row all the way up to Backney, just to get warmed up, two-and-a-half miles, and he would pick you up somewhere along the river on his bike. There were no coaching boats in those days. But his coaching worked though.

Jousting at the annual Ross Athletic and Rowing Club sports day, 1905 (photo: Brian Butcher)

Mrs Trafford of Goodrich Court presenting Regatta prizes (photo: Brian Butcher)

Brian Dean:

> I see the Rowing Club as being the greater part of my education. You'd see people and think, "I want to be like that". So you would strive to do it. There were some really lovely, gentle people in the Club. My grandfather, Albert Dean was a wagoner. People like him weren't Club members, but they were always welcome because they would help out. They were looked after and allowed to fish off the clubhouse steps. And there was Joe Griffiths. He was the full-time boatman who did all the boat repairs in and around the Club. He was known as Boathouse Joe. All these old characters are gone now.

PEN PUSHERS VS TRADESMEN: THE BELMONT PLATE

The Belmont Plate was a hotly contested boat race that pitched club rowers against their less likely competitors, pub and work crews. Many of these 'once a year rowers' were, by their own admission, more familiar with a pint of ale and a pack of cigarettes than with competitive rowing. But that didn't mean they weren't up for a fight to cross the finishing line first. For a fortnight every year, pub teams entered into a regime of training that was a shock to the system for many, with men bent over gasping for air and retching after a training session. But something was clearly working for The Vaga Tavern team at Hunderton. They became the team to beat, with some of them, including Roy Williams, Geoff Edwards, Trevor Whitefoot, Keith Scott and Terry 'Tug' Bullock, achieving legendary status in 'Shanghai'. Serious rivals to The Vaga during the 1970s included the Moon at Mordiford, The Strongbow from Bulmers and the Orange Tree's Motor Cycle Club. Over the years the Bullock family, 'Tug' and his brother Les, put their names on the Plate as winners no fewer than 28 times.

Ron Hodges won the Belmont Plate in 1952 – but not for The Vaga. His wife, Kit, cheered him on while she was pregnant with their daughter, Tricia Hailes.

Ron:

> We beat the Vaga in the final. I was working at Smart & Brown at Rotherwas then and we entered a team because of my experience with Jordan's boatyard and I was in the crew for several years. I will always remember that year because some of the lads who drank at The Vaga also worked at Smart & Brown and so we were up against them in the final. The Vaga were the great team; they were "the boys". I suppose being up at Hunderton, most of them were on the river at various times.

THE VAGA, THE TEAM TO BEAT

The glory days of the Belmont Plate brought The Vaga, and Hunderton, centre-stage. Their prowess in the competition became the stuff of local legend. In crude terms, these were strong, physical, hard-working men pitched against pen-pushers!

There were plenty of celebrations and the odd pint downed at The Vaga after another Belmont Plate victory. Gary McLeod's dad was landlord during some of the winning years:

> The Vaga were very successful in it. Charlie Trier, the Hankins and all those, they used to row for the Booth Hall. And then, of course, they moved back up here, and they started rowing for The Vaga and they won the most shields on the Plate. Every time they won, my old man would put a new shield on. He must have put on eight or nine I expect, and they are the only shields on there that are solid silver. He used to go to Oswins and get a proper silver shield. Of course, all the other pubs used to get an old tin shield, didn't they.
>
> People used to say that the Rowing Club's biggest earner was their Regatta. But the second biggest one-take was the final of the Belmont Plate. The Vaga would be empty and everyone would be across watching because The Vaga team was always in the final. And they would be there going bananas, doing somersaults. All the big firms had teams in there, like Wiggins, Bulmers – everyone would have a crew. This wasn't a small event. The Vaga team was so good. And there were big celebrations in the pub after; it would be an all-day event. They'd be down there 12 o'clock; they might start to row at one or two; and then, of course, the beer starts to flow, and they'd all come back to The Vaga for a few more beers after.
>
> The boats were owned by the Rowing Club, but they weren't the actual racing boats. They were four-man tubs and they used to have a week or two week's training. It was comical. A lot of the crew probably hadn't rowed a boat before. They would go, "right, you can go down on Monday night and you can have an hour's training". I mean for 50 bloody weeks of the year they are guzzling beer every day of the week, and then suddenly, "Oh, we have to go training tonight." They were on the side of the bank throwing up, knackered. Of course, they started the heats during the week, but the semi-final and the final used to be on the Sunday. But a lot of these lads didn't get halfway down the river: they were knackered. Of course, you had to have your own cox and he had to come from the pub. I mean some of the lads coxing, well, some went into the bridge!

Belmont Plate winners, The Vaga, with Walter Preedy seated at right (photo: Janet Preedy)

Rowing Club member Bruce Wallace recalls the atmosphere of the Belmont Plate:

> The crowds were all congregated on the Belmont side, the pen-pushers sort and the artisans sort. All the pubs used to put in a crew and The Vaga used to be the team to beat, and they invariably won. I remember Derek Hankins, big fellow with a bald head, a builder. Goodness me, it was a big event. It was in the old tug boats, not the clinker built, racing boats, but very heavy boats that belonged to the Rowing Club. The Wye Guild sponsored it and all through the week there would be heats and then on the Saturday or the Sunday, there would be the final and of course there was always a party afterwards.

Deborah Hill (seated second from left) and her team from South Hereford District Council competing in the Belmont Plate. Despite a lot of training they only won one of their heats
(photo: Hammonds)

After all that competitive, testosterone-driven sport, time for something with a slower pace ...

PLEASURE BOATS

There were loads of boats on the river in the summer. You could get pleasure boats every day and people used to have the time of their lives.

Pleasure boat cruising on the Wye was a popular day out for many families up until the early 1960s. Motorised trips still continue in Symonds Yat, but the days of oar-driven, clinker built vessels are long gone. Ross Rowing Club, like the Hereford Club, rented out pleasure boats to its members – but you had to book. Once on board, picnic baskets would be safely stowed away, children were told to sit still, fishing nets at the ready, while dad took up the oars.

KIT HODGES, 91

Kit used to help out with the pleasure boats hired from Jordan's boat-yard alongside her husband, Ron. Welsh day-trippers could be relied upon to provide quite a bit of entertainment in those days:

> Wednesday market day and the weekends in Hereford were really popular with Welsh people. I was rowing a few of them up the river one day and this quite large Welsh lady wanted to row as well. So she started with the oars, and they'd all had a few drinks of course, and then she suddenly fell backwards and her legs were in the air and her bloomers were all on show. People on the old Wye Bridge were watching and you could hear roars of laughter.

Doris Kershaw, née Townsend, painted a blissful image of languid summer days in the 1930s of boating up the river, straight out of an E.M. Forster novel:

> My mother, Gladys Ruby, brothers, Norman and John, and I lived with my grandparents, John and Rosetta Kate Marshall, in St Nicholas Street, after my father died. Grandfather John, a piano tuner and church organist at St Peter's and St Paul's in Tupsley, ran the family music shop next door. The Marshalls were members of Hereford Rowing Club for over 50 years and many hours were spent on the Wye. My friend, Barbara Jordan (of Jordan boats), and I spent lots of time messing about in boats and were brought up to respect the river's dangers.
>
> The most memorable fortnight of the year was when my relations came from Bradford for their summer holiday. The Great Western Railway ran their trunk in advance and they followed by train. Each day we packed

Boating up to Breinton (photo: Doris Kershaw)

an enormous picnic and rowed up-stream in two of Mr Crissall's largest boats, The Comet and The Randan. Grandma steered and we rowed sometimes as far as to Bridge Sollars and Monnington Falls, but more often to magical Breinton, where, from the shingle beach below Belmont Abbey, we could moor our boats and swim.

On August Bank Holiday the Windsor family would join us, making up a party of 16. Wilson, the grocer opposite our house, delivered food while Gardiners the fishmonger provided fruit, veg and fresh salad. I remember buying 17 loaves for sandwiches, cutlery, crockery, milk in terracotta coolers and swimwear. Once moored, we lit a driftwood fire and boiled a kettle for tea. Lunch was a major operation; my mother and aunts sitting in a row, conveyor-belt style, slicing and buttering bread, adding salad, then meat. Grandfather always carved. Adults drank cider and we were treated to Corona. Afterwards, grandmother made daisy chains or balsam leaf hats trimmed with buttercups. There were nature walks to learn the names of wild flowers. After a game of cricket or rounders, we returned to the boats and set off down-stream, racing the Hammond family if we encountered them. A pennyworth of chips from Elcox rounded off the idyllic childhood Bank Holiday with the tantalising possibility of a scoop of free batter bits.

Boating up to Breinton, cooking on the beach and washing up (photos: Doris Kershaw)

While Doris Kershaw's boating afternoons were sedate, the Hereford Rowing Club Captain's day out was a riotous affair, with an inordinate amount of drinking and eating that tested even the strongest of these young and fit men.

Bruce Wallace:

> The Captain's event always took place in September and the pleasure boats would be taken by road to The Boat at Whitney-on-Wye and left there overnight. We would all go up by bus on the Sunday morning and have rum and coffee for breakfast. After that we would all pile into the pleasure boats and row to Hereford. We always had a break at lunchtime and stopped in

NAVIGATING THE WYE   151

Bredwardine where the landlord of the Red Lion had duly prepared the bar for us with a red canvas on the floor, because we would be very wet, and there would be a nice roaring fire. Of course, we would consume vast quantities of ale. We were eventually barred in the end for being too rowdy. After the Lion, we would row down to Red Rocks, where there was another beach and we would have a barbeque and a snooze and then we would have a race back down to Hereford. The bar used to open at the Club at 7pm on a Sunday and we would try and get back there in time for a shower, change into proper clothes and be in the bar for first orders.

Another Hereford Rowing Club stalwart, Frank Ford, joined the pleasure boat exodus on Sunday mornings. There was no other place to be.
Frank Ford:

On a Sunday morning we would go down to the club, load the boat up at about ten o'clock and scull all the way up to the Camp Inn. Usually my dad and another guy, Paul Muller, would be on oars. Paul was Hungarian and had lost his whole family during the war. He was a very keen sculler in his own country and he taught me. There would be a procession of boats going up the river all trying to arrive at the Camp Inn first, just before opening time at twelve. You'd have to run up the bank to get a drink, and as soon as the Camp closed we'd all go back down, get into our boats and cross the river and onto the other bank where there was a shingle beach and we would light fires, cook steaks, and spend the day there. It was a beautiful day out. Every day was sunny. What I love about the river is that as soon as you're past Hunderton you're in open countryside, not a person around. The kingfishers, the water voles in those days, the herons – oh it was just fabulous! But there was a Club rule and I suppose it was a safety rule really. If you knew that everybody had gone up-stream and somebody hadn't returned you knew that you only had to look up-stream. If somebody had capsized they were going to drift back past the Club.

Despite the hardship of war, there was an enormous amount of fun to be had too. Joan Lloyd and her friend, also a Joan, met a couple of RAF men and, with the permission of Joan's uncle, they hired a boat to go up the river:

We had been to the Camp Inn and, after we left, we came back down the bank, got in the boat, and, for some reason or another, we went too far over the right-hand side and hit a rock and damaged the boat. So we had to get

Boating up to the Camp Inn (photo: Hammonds family)

out and walk home and gather up all our stuff: we had frying pans and saucepans because we were going to cook our food on the bank. We got to a field and we could hear German planes going over, and we hid down by some haystacks and had to wait until they had gone. Anyway, we never got back home 'til about two or three in the morning and the officer of these boys from Credenhill wouldn't believe why they were late so he went down to see my uncle who told him the Air Force were "a bloody nuisance!"

RAFTING THE WYE

In January 1967, two young men, P. Hughes and C.A. Herbert, both 18, ill-equipped and with little experience, decided to embark on an adventure, 'without further delay'. Both men have since passed away, but their charming account, *A Voyage by Raft on the River Wye in January 1967* survives. They built their raft – 'we found twenty, five-gallon oil drums from a disused quarry' – at the river's edge in Hay, and their paddles were 'fashioned from broom handles'. They launched in a snow storm, sustained by a breakfast of 'bread and margarine'. Mooring at Bycross Ferry on their second night in sleet and rain, cold, wet and hungry, the pair snuck into a barn, sleeping on dry and warm hay bales. What an adventure it was. How we wish we could talk to them today. It was all a far cry from the modern raft race.

RAFT RACE

My first husband and I sponsored a raft in the first race in 1978. In those early days crews had to carry all their equipment for the trip. Our raft had a coffin in the middle with all the gear stored inside! Race organiser, Tricia Hales.

In 1977, a poster appeared in a number of Herefordshire pubs challenging customers with the question: 'Have you the guts to compete?' Curiosity piqued, some intrepid locals were to become the prototype rafters in 1978 for the first 100-mile River Wye charity raft race. This first race saw ten ill-assorted homemade craft make their way down the river from Hay to Chepstow. The race was designated 'self-sufficient', i.e. rafts carried not only the crew, but also tents, clothing, bedding, food and all other essentials, including the most important cargo for some: beer and/ or cider. The winning time in 1978 was 28 hours over a four-day period.

David Joyce and his wife Ethel live in Winforton. He trained in Manchester as an optician and practised for most of his professional career in Kington. He grew up on a farm on Brilley Mountain, and it was his close links with other young farmers that led to his participation – and victory – in the 1979 raft race.

The winning raft of David Joyce, seated third from left (photo: David Joyce)

The first raft race was in 1978, but we went in the 1979 event. There were between 30 and 40 teams and there was a draw for the start position. We set off from Hay around 9 a.m. and had eight teams to overtake to get to Hereford first. Whoever came in first was last to leave the next day, so it gave us a real challenge. There was a good deal of banter amongst us on board and there were lots of people on the bridges supporting us. It was great to win and a great experience, but never again.

A lot of my friends were fit young farmers in the Kington area and I was fairly fit at the time and so joined the group. There were eight of us in total and we built our raft together at Kington. One of the farmers had a barn where we were able to do the welding and constructing and we met there on regular occasions to assist with it. The raft was made of five-gallon drums fixed together in a steel frame. It was quite long – it had to be to have enough room to accommodate the plastic chairs, which were okay until you got wet. We had the use of a pool out at Titley where we could go and practise, but we were all pretty strong anyway and it was just a case of getting on the river in the end. I've still got my paddle and estimated it took about 85,000 strokes to get to Chepstow. And even though we had a sail we never used it because there was never enough wind to take advantage of it.

Despite the discomfort of it all, a friend and I took part in the two-man race from Monnington to Hereford in 1983. That race was very successful, but we were accused of cheating and using the wrong paddles. The rules didn't specify that you had to use single paddles and we had used double-sided paddles and, because of that, we just powered our way through everyone and came in first. We even made our own paddles. It was part of the challenge and I've still got mine. It was an amazing race, apart from second day, when it rained most of the day from Hereford to Ross, and we got very tired. We had no choice, but to keep pulling and we got there first in the end. When we arrived, I called my wife who drove over 40 miles to bring us anoraks and dry clothes.

The raft race continues to run each year raising funds for the Plynlimon Trust, altogether pulling in an amazing £2,000,000 since the beginning. At the forefront, and the energy behind the raft race, is Tricia Hales, 66. She's a second-generation raft race organiser. Her parents, Ron and Kit Hodges, came before her, and Tricia's sons may yet continue this particular river 'dynasty'. She organises everything that takes place on the river during the raft race.

Tricia:

> The first ladies' race took place in 1979 and I entered my own raft called Hare Razor, because I owned a hair salon at the time. I think we finished fourth. During one of our training sessions we saved a calf from drowning and the *Hereford Times* got wind of the story and came and took our photos. Later that week the article was pinned to the notice board at the Crown and Anchor with a photo of us and the calf, and somebody had put a caption on it saying, 'Spot the cow!' It made me laugh.
>
> But in the 1979 race I criticised the organisation because I was unhappy that people had alcohol on the raft and there was no health and safety. I just didn't like the way it was being done, and because I've got a big mouth I said something! Apparently, the organisers had a meeting after the race and it was decided that the event needed a proper committee. And I understand that one of the girls there said, "Get Tricia Hales. She's the one that criticised it; let her organise it!" So, I did.

The riparian owners were unhappy with the raft race and that was a big area of concern for the race's future. But they hadn't figured on a woman like Tricia:

> My ex-husband owned a construction company and I had spent time on these sites dealing with a lot of men. But at my first meetings with fishery users and owners I faced downright hostility from some of their members. The chair of one of the Hereford salmon and trout associations would trade insults across the table at me, and I remember saying once, "Do you realise I am the only person around this table who doesn't have a title after their name, but I do know many of you have given me one!" These men sat back and that's when they started to thaw because, although I wanted to get something, I knew I would have to negotiate for it. And I also had to use a little bit of femininity. I think that's an awful thing to say but it's true. You see, everybody is so passionate about their sport that they will all fight their own corner. But I wasn't going to be put off, because we raised £10,000 the first year and we got to a stage around 1984 when we were raising around £100,000 a year. Well, that was an awful lot of money.

Tirelessly energetic, Tricia and her team continue the raft race. It's become a Herefordshire/ River Wye institution. In the summer of 2018 Tricia retired after nearly four decades at the helm as chair of the raft race. The end of an era.

HOVERCRAFT 'INVASION'

Riparian owners had a lot more to worry about in the spring of 1985 when the Hovercraft Club of Great Britain decided the Wye was fair game, with an 'invasion' of these vessels on the river as far up as Goodrich. At a meeting of Ross Town Council in April the same year, Mrs Mary Dew thought them harmless and couldn't understand what all the fuss was about: 'I've never heard so much nonsense in my life. They are only a few feet long and will only visit a couple of times a year'. The 'invasion' did have the effect, however, of mobilising a number of like-minded individuals into taking action and forming the River Wye Preservation Trust. There at the start was Simon Dereham, who retired from the role of chairman in 2017 after 27 years in post.

> There was an invasion of hovercraft on the river and there's a right of navigation and you can't stop them. They had one convoy and the uproar that created was such that a group of people with a common interest got together at the Royal Hotel in Ross and we founded the River Wye Preservation Trust. Most of them are dead now!

This watchdog group still continues its work and is now chaired by Major Patrick Darling.

Hovercraft no longer come up the river, but the canoe is a firm fixture.

CANOE RALLY

In 1975, agricultural lecturer Fred Carpenter and his wife Hilary launched the River Wye Canoe Rally. Over the next 21 years, every midsummer Sunday, hundreds of people, many of whom had never canoed in their life, made the arduous, 27-mile journey. With the support of organisations such as PGL and the SAS, and money raised through individual sponsorship, the rally brought in sufficient funds to buy a house for a group of young people with learning disabilities.

Fred:

> It all started when I joined Hereford MENCAP and, like all societies, they wanted to raise money and I came up with the idea, because I was a canoeist, why don't we do a fund-raising event on the River Wye? I thought it's quite a mammoth trip to paddle from Hereford to Ross on a fairly safe stretch of river – 27 miles. Obviously, the people who were going to take

part were the people who supported MENCAP and they were inexperienced so it had to be a safe stretch of water. And that's how it started. We raised money by sponsoring people to paddle from Hereford to Ross. Me and my wife Hilary got involved because of our daughter, Hannah, who is handicapped. The first rally raised about a thousand pounds in 1975 and we did it for 21 years.

One of our biggest supporters was PGL Holidays and they regularly, throughout the 21 years, lent us quite a lot of boats and their big trailer. But we used to get canoes from all over the place: from youth groups and schools and everywhere. Peter Lawrence was quite a modest fellow. We used to do a presentation at the end of the rally with the fastest and the slowest, and the one who raised the most money and stuff. And he came one year and presented those awards, and in the early years the SAS used to support us by giving us one of their landing craft and crew as a backup on the river. At its peak, over 500 took part and I still meet people today who say: "You're Fred aren't you, from the canoe rally."

We only mislaid a canoeist once and that was rather unusual. He started canoeing from Hereford in one of our canoes and decided before he got to the first check point that it wasn't for him and he got out of the river and left the canoe in somebody's garden and went off! I forget how we got it back, but somebody must have phoned us up and said there was a canoe in their garden and was it anything to do with us!

SCHOOL BOYS TO THE 'RESCUE'

There was navigating of the Wye of a different sort for Richard Shaw, 73, in 1959, when, as a 14-year-old, he was involved in a 'rescue':

> I was at the High School for Boys then, and to get out of rugby I volunteered for rowing. I was in a little boat with two others, when a policeman, PC Tumper, standing on the Rowing Club steps, shouted at us to come over. He said to the boy in the back to get out. He got in and told us to row up the river towards the Hunderton Bridge. He had a rope and grappling hook with him. When we got there, he fished around in the water for a bit with the hook and then ordered us to row back. We realised then that it was a woman's body. Can you imagine a policeman asking schoolboys to do that today?

7 Ferries across the Wye

Foy. This parish is made a peninsula by the abrupt sweep of the river, valuable as a salmon fishery. There is a ferry near the churchyard. At Weirend, the road to Monmouth is carried alongside the river to Glewstone Ferry.

Handbook for Travellers, 1872

THE WYE TOUR, a two-day boat trip along the river from Ross to Chepstow, became popularised in the late eighteenth century amongst the well-heeled; the landscape inspiring painting, writing and sketching, thus sparking the birth of British tourism. But the Wye as a trading route reaches even further back and has been well documented by writers and historians. In the pre-railway days, barges and bargees (those men and women who were in charge of, or working on, a barge) worked the river, bringing coal, flour, wood and other goods to communities along the river's route.

The Great Western Railway reached Hereford from Ross by 1855 and continued on to Hay in 1865. In a few short years, this would inevitably result in the end to trading on the river by boat. And, with increasing wealth, growth in car ownership, and the closure of these two lines, there was a further move away from the river. And yet, even during these times of revolutionary change, some forms of river transport continued, quietly plying their trade. As recently as 1975, ferries on the Wye at Hereford were carrying people, goods, bikes and prams across the river, and in the early part of the twentieth century, there were three river crossings in Ross-on-Wye alone. And of course, in that tourist beauty spot of Symonds Yat, old habits have continued with little change.

Chain ferries still cross the river and motorised boats take tourists up and down short stretches of water. The men and women continuing the tradition are still known today as 'boatmen'. In their time, they could be rabble rousers when their ancient work practices were threatened, and in September 1971 they made headline news when they 'invoked a 1696 statute to fight a by-law' that threatened their livelihoods.

The boatmen are still there of course and work the river at Symonds Yat, but their numbers are a far cry from the heyday when the likes of the Williams, Pughs, Arscotts, Jenkins, Hattendorfs, Thornes and Robins worked the river in their war-vintage boats, with names like Indian Princess, Princess Pat, Imjin River, and Aboukir Bay.

Boats at Symonds Yat (photo: *Ross Gazette*)

HUNDERTON FERRY

Today, if you stand in Hunderton at the bottom of Vaga Street at its junction with Villa Street, you will struggle to see the river. Two newish buildings straddle an overgrown gap of vicious brambles. There is no trace of the once-busy Hunderton ferry crossing. Some have argued it should have a blue plaque, 'hereby marking the spot of the last Hereford river crossing'. If you dare, and no one is around, close your eyes and imagine the scene. One can almost hear the sploshing of oars, the soft thud of boots against the wood of the boat.

In the late nineteenth century, Hereford City had two ferries: a rowing service at the Castle Green and further up-stream at Hunderton, a rope ferry. With the erection of the Victoria footbridge in the 1890s, the rowing ferry was moved up-stream to replace the old rope ferry at Hunderton. The ferry, the Princess Mary, was re-sited by the Villa Hotel in Hunderton, and was run by a Mr Desmond. His 'ferry' was painted cream on the outside and green on the inside, was 27 feet long, flat bottomed with a 4-inch draft. She weighed around one tonne and could carry up to ten passengers. 'Captain' Desmond charged passengers a penny to cross the river each way. Gas lamps along the riverside allowed children to play marbles under the lights.

The Hunderton Ferry (photo: Janet Preedy)

On Mr Desmond's retirement in the early 1920s, a Hunderton man took on the business. Tom Preedy lived a few short strides from the ferry steps. No matter what the weather was like or the conditions of the river, he always turned out smartly for his river crossing job, usually in a three-piece woollen suit and always with a hat, wearing heavy leather boots, no neoprene or hi-vis jacket in sight. In quiet moments or slack times, he kept himself busy: he wasn't just a boatman, he was also a shoemaker, and was often seen making shoes on the river bank while waiting for customers.

The ferry crossing quickly became a family affair. Tom's son, Walter, trained alongside his father from an early age, taking over the business in 1940, soon after his father retired. Walter kept the business running in the post-war period, renting the boats from the council for 2/6 a week. It was a busy period for the river crossing. Workers from the Hunderton area commuted to work at Bulmers or Barton yard sidings via the ferry, or walkers spending the day ambling up to Breinton and back, would take advantage of the crossing. It would be another 20 years before Greyfriars Bridge opened and the old railway bridge became available for walkers. The fare was one penny for adults, half penny for children and two pennies for a bike or pram.

Ken Preedy rowing the Hunderton Ferry (photo: Terry Preedy)

A young Janet Preedy, daughter of Walter, looked forward to spring and the return of boats back on the river. Janet:

> The ferry belonged to the Council and we used to rent it off them. They used to take the boat off the river in the autumn and any repairs had to be done and then it was repainted for the new season, and they used to bring it back ready for Easter. They used to put it on the back of these long lorries and drag it up the steps. I used to be stood up the road going to work, waiting for the bus and watch the boat come under the bridge and around and I used to feel that proud. I used to think, "I can't wait to get home from work and get on that boat."

But it wasn't an occupation for the idle either. You went where the money was, and that often meant working ungodly hours. There were challenging customers and some unwelcome ones too. Janet again:

> They worked all hours during the War and through all the summer months. There were some men who used to work at the Water Works and my Dad used to get up really early in the morning to take them over the river to work, 'cause all they had to do once they were across, was walk up the hill. And Dad used to fetch them home too.

During Walter's tenure on the river, rival boat business (in the hire of pleasure boats) Jordan's, continued their boat trade down-stream close to the old bridge (and closer to where the Greyfriars Bridge was built in 1967), but in 1950 it closed down. With the council deciding it no longer wanted the expense of a ferry boat, Walter took the decision to take on the ferry as a private concern in 1952/ 53. This proved to be popular and the family business continued. With his death in 1961, it fell to Ken, one of his eight children, to take over the business. Perhaps the writing was on the wall even then. The world was changing, and Hereford was developing. Ken was to be the last Preedy to run a river crossing in Hereford.

Ken Preedy (holding oars)
(photo: Terry Preedy)

Ken died on 12 March 2013. At St Martin's churchyard in Hereford his headstone bears the remarkable epitaph, 'the last ferryman in Hereford'. It is a title he would have wanted and it was what his widow insisted upon. This well-liked man was the third and last generation of his family to operate the city's ferry crossing at Hunderton, and his death brought to an end the City's only remaining river boat crossing.

The third eldest of Walter's eight children, and older brother to Janet, Ken learnt the 'trade' from his father and grandfather before him. Siblings, Terry and Lynn Preedy are Ken's children. As youngsters, they used to play on the ferry steps – though they were warned never to go near the water – and remember their skilled father with great fondness.

Terry:

> He was always with his dad, Walter, and they were very close. I always remember him making things. He was very good with his hands and in quiet moments on the bank he would whittle whistles out of bits of wood. He used to make kites too using just reed and string.

FERRIES ACROSS THE WYE

Tom Preedy on the ferry steps and in his boat (photos: Janet Preedy)

The opening of the Greyfriars Bridge in 1967 and the increase in car ownership had a knock-on effect on Ken's business. Reluctantly, he increased the fare to sixpence per child and one shilling per adult to cover rising expenses. However, there was one passenger who never paid – a cat that travelled across the water daily and would reappear on the south bank some hours later ready for its journey home!

Lynn:

> I used to go to work with dad. He would take a load of passengers across and while I was waiting I would make daisy chains! I was down at the ferry steps all the time. I remember there were two sheds there, both very narrow, and that's where they used to keep the oars, but there was also ropes and fishing rods.

Terry:

> There were two big green gates at the top of the steps and I would unchain them in the mornings and open them up ready for business. I would also help wash the boat out and help un-padlock the boats. When I was there I used to go minnow hunting with a jam jar with bread. I used to row the

> ferry across many times too, I was about 11 or 12. Dad would be on the front with the rope, near the Water Museum. I was always in the boat, but he wouldn't let you go in on your own. He would take ten in a boat but wouldn't take that many if he could help it.

Lynn and Terry had the honour of having a boat named after them by their father. Lynn:

> Dad made the boat from scratch – it was nothing for him, he was really good with his hands – and he called it Terlyn. He kept his boats spotless and he was always dressed in his Sunday best – you can see that in the photographs. He always had a big grin on his face and would talk to anyone. He loved what he did, loved being around the water and being his own boss.

In an attempt to boost a flagging income, Ken invested in six rowing boats to hire to the public. This had some modest success, with weekends being the busiest with up to 200 customers attracted to a lazy day boating on the river. Even so, it was a struggle to make it a sustainable business, with stiff competition from other pleasure boat hirers at Campions and the Rowing Club. Every minute mattered and if hirers were late returning with the boat, Ken would shout 'clocks' up the river and if that still didn't prompt a return, he would jump in his boat with a small outboard motor and head up river to fetch them himself explaining, 'I've got people waiting for this boat'.

Winter meant time for the annual maintenance of the boats.

Terry:

> It would take between five or six men to take the boats out of the water. Storage was in Stonebow Road then. All of this waterproofing of the boats was completed at the ferry steps. Once there, they would scrape the old pitch off and then re-coat them to keep them waterproofed. They used to have a brazier, with pitch on top of it. It used to stink. I remember they had big blocks of pitch in paper sacks and they used to break it down. Dad also was responsible for the piers, on both sides of the river, and would do repairs and maintenance on them too.

In 1974 a distressing event brought to an end a business that had been trading on the Wye at Hereford for nearly a hundred years. In October of that year, one of the boats was knocked off her trestle and broken in two. Two of Ken's rowing boats that were on the bank were also smashed to pieces in an act of vandalism and another two went missing. It was devastating for Ken. There was no hope of compensation, and because the boats were not in a boathouse an insurance claim was out of the question. In those days a new ferry could cost up to £7,000, an astronomical amount of money then.

Ken was left with no alternative but to call it a day. He went through the transition away from the river business with fortitude – he had a family to support after all – but it broke his heart having to give up working on the Wye. He found work at Walter Danks, and later he worked as a caretaker at Hunderton Infant School, a job he loved. It made up for not being on the river. While there is no plaque at the former ferry steps in Hunderton, the last ferryman will always be remembered at St Martin's churchyard. A little piece of history.

Peter Davies, 96

Peter Davies lives in a remote spot in Orcop. Born in Wales, he's lived almost all his life in Herefordshire yet his Welsh lilt remains. He was a tank commander during the Second World War, liberating a Dutch village. He is invited to their liberation celebrations every year and has even had Dutch babies named after him. In 1938/39, he was employed at the Water Works in Hereford:

> Before the war, in 1938/39 the camp at Bradbury Lines opened and Credenhill RAF camp opened too, which meant the demand for water was going to increase tremendously. I was only a 16-year-old lad working with the men. Somebody referred to me as the runner one day because I had to run between the river and the pumping station and to the Water Works. To make room for the extra demand for water, an extra reservoir was built and a new pumping station alongside the old one on the river. I was there for nine months before joining the army. My bit on the river was checking every morning, weekdays and on Saturday and Sunday mornings, just to see that everything was all right, and satisfy myself. Workers did fall in occasionally but fortunately I didn't.

Peter spent six months on the job and never missed out on the opportunity for a bit of poaching:

> My secret joy was tying fishing lines onto the piles every night and going in the morning to check and pick any trout up that I'd caught in the river. Every evening before I went home I'd tie the lines again and every morning I would dash up first thing and check. I caught quite a few trout from the river – illegal activities of course.

Hunderton ferries were big, heavy boats, but under the skilled oarsmanship of their 'captains', they glided beautifully. Forgotten film footage of the River Wye Regatta shows just how adept the Preedys were, moving swiftly across the river, effortlessly moving around the speeding racing boats. The Regatta is on, but the ferry dodges the fast moving vessels with ease, which was just as well, as Janet explains:

> I can remember once when a load of women came down and my Dad said, "Are you going to take these, or shall I?" And I said, "Oh you take 'em." So, they all got on the boat and all of a sudden, these women started screaming. And I looked over and there was my father and all these women stood up, holding on to their skirts and my Dad had the paddle and he was batting something and the screaming was terrible.
>
> When he come back I said, "What the hell was going on, Dad?" He said, "Next time there's women you take 'em, I'm not! When the back of the boat hit the bank, a water rat jumped in and that's when the screaming started. I had to stun it."

Walter Preedy, Janet's dad
(photo: Janet Preedy)

Janet and her eight siblings were brought up by their parents in their two-up, two-down cottage in Villa Street. She still lives there today. Janet was a water baby, picking up rowing almost as soon as she could walk. The river was on her doorstep and, from an early age, she watched her father and grandfather handle boats skilfully, manoeuvring these heavy vessels with just a few short, imperceptible movements of the oar. She followed the family tradition and became an accomplished rower herself:

Janet Preedy (standing) and two of her sisters, Barbara and Molly (photo: Janet Preedy)

> I could row really well, but I don't remember being taught how to. But I do remember, when I was really small, putting the paddles in the river and I had to stand up. I used to go forward and then pull them back, but I was so tiny my feet didn't touch the boards.

THE WELSH ARE COMING!

> On a Sunday, our Dad used to say, "I should undo the boat if I were you because here's the Welsh people coming!" And they were because they used to come up from the Valleys on market day and hire the boats from Jordan's down near the Wye Bridge and come up here and the oars used to be right up in the air and their hands used to go around in one big circle. And our Dad used to say, "in a minute that boat's going to turn over", and he was always right because nine out of ten times we were pulling them out.
>
> Just before my father died, we started doing leisure trips up river. So we bought a little motor to go on the back of the boat. It was all right for a time and then that seemed to dwindle out because people didn't want to go anymore.

Yet Janet still paints a beautiful picture of days out on the water with her father: lazy summer mornings, oars dipping in a languid river, spotting wildlife, picnics, singing:

> On a Sunday morning, Dad used to knock on my door about half past four or five o'clock in the morning, "I'm going up the river. You coming?" And we used to go as far as Sandy Bay and anchor the boat there and then we used to lie back and listen. You could hear the foxes barking, the cows in the distance going to be milked; the snakes used to swim across the river back to the Rough as we used to call it; and now and again you'd see a splash of fish jumping in the water. You could be miles down the river and it used to be really peaceful. We would see kingfishers and moorhens. And then my Dad used to look at his watch and say, "We'll go for breakfast now." I used to row back down and Dad used to say, "Look at 'em, still in bed on a beautiful morning like this!" We used to be very naughty and sing our heads off, 'When It's Springtime in the Rockies', I can hear him singing now.

I know we should all be looking forward, but doesn't that make you yearn for the old days?

SHANGHAI HEIGHTS

You are unlikely to see Shanghai Heights on any Hereford map, but, for reasons best known to themselves, that is how residents of Hunderton know their patch – at least according to one long-time resident, Gary McLeod. Gary has lived in Hunderton since the early 1960s. His father, Gordon, was landlord of The Vaga, a pub that has seen its fair share of river commuters in its time. A police sentry box, useful for the local bobby to check in before pushing off on his bike, was in front of the Preedy kiosk, at the ferry landing stage. Around the kiosk, rose bushes and flowers grew, pretty as a chocolate box, and old Mr Preedy sold sweets and his home-made iced lollipops. There were a lot of salmon in the river in those days – so many in fact that at least one fisherman swore he could 'cross from one bank to the other walking on the backs of salmon' – apocryphal maybe, but a nice image. The lollipops may have lacked flavour, but Mr Preedy knew how to steer a boat.

Gary:

> It was weird, but you would sit in the boat, a penny to go over, and tuppence for your bike, and Mr Preedy would aim for the steps on the other side. He would sort of just push the boat, but he hardly rowed at all, he would go up and the flow would bring him down. I don't know how he did it, but it got us across each time.

Salmon was out of reach for many working class families, but sometimes the river could deliver the odd bounty. Always expect the unexpected. Gary:

> I was in The Vaga one morning helping my old man do the bottling, and there was a knock on the door, and it was Tom Preedy just up from the landing stage. He said, "Where's your dad? Go and get him. I've got a salmon!" He had a huge salmon in his hand and I asked him where he got it from? "I went down to my boat this morning and it was in the boat! It just jumped in." In the end, he had half and we had half. I expect we had to give him a few pints for it.

JORDAN'S FERRY

Jordan's were builders and hirers of pleasure boats on the Wye for over 200 years from their base on the south bank opposite Greyfriars. The boats were hired by the hour, and there were few creature-comforts: the seats were hard

Tom Preedy (photo: Janet Preedy)

Jordan's boat-yard, where Greyfriars Bridge is now (photo: Derek Foxton Collection)

and unforgiving, metal rests supported your back. Jordan's was the boat operator of choice for four university students travelling down the Wye in 1892 from Whitney to Chepstow (*Camping on the Wye*). There was some preparation for their expedition – number one on their list, a boat:

> Jordan, boatbuilder of Hereford, supplied a Salter's Randan [a boat rowed by three people; the middle rower pulls two short oars while the bow and stroke pull one oar each], and after much labour, a Bell tent was secured. Morning was spent visiting the Cathedral, buying stores and meeting trains for tidings and baggage. This eventually turned up and we decided to lose no time in getting to Whitney. Two porters conveyed our luggage across the city to another station, where we found the boat duly packed on a couple of trucks, our luggage filling a van and, after some useful hints from Jordan, we arrived in due course at Whitney. At the end of the trip and at the last camp, Chepstow, waited for the cart to take the baggage to the station. The boat was left at the landing stage in charge of Jordan's men and the remains of the stores handed over to some cottagers.

The scene at Jordan's former landing stage is a very different one today. The tramway buildings of the former Hereford to Abergavenny tramline – the backdrop to Jordan's landing stage and boat-yard – were demolished to make way for the new Greyfriars Bridge in the early 1960s. Where once there were orchards and grass tennis courts, today traffic thunders overhead and shoppers cram into supermarkets, yards from the river. At Jordan's, boats were hired out by the hour or the day. There was no risk assessment. Money was exchanged and customers were sent out in command of a craft and told to get on with it. They would have had little knowledge of the various hazards on the river, of the rocks and the sandbanks. Members of the Jordan family certainly had their work cut out, as Richard Shaw of Hereford remembers:

> At the end of the day, it wasn't uncommon for Mr Jordan to go in search for some boat that had failed to return to base and recover the wreck from wherever it had been abandoned!

JOAN LLOYD, 95

Joan Lloyd is the last surviving member of the extended Jordan family. The river

Boats moored up near to Jordan's boat-yard (photo: Derek Foxton Collection)

path to Hunderton was called Jordan's Walk and there was an appeal once to the Council for a blue plaque to mark the spot, but it came to nothing. At one time the family operated between 30 and 40 boats, and was also the hirer and supplier of choice for boats to Hereford Cathedral School for rowing, training and coaching. Joan:

> When I was a teenager they said Jordan's had been in the business for over a hundred years. So that was when you had barges coming up. My aunt Dorothy Faulkner (née Jordan) was the daughter of William Halford Jordan of the Saracen's Head, near the bridge, a son of Richard Rivers Felix Jordan. William Jordan knew the bridge was to come over the Wye eventually and he closed the business in the late 1940s. He died in 1948 aged 79. His brother, Jack Jordan, a partner, died in the First World War.

The boat-yard by the Wye Bridge came into the Jordan family through Richard Rivers Felix Jordan, who was linked with the river all his life, first with his father in the days when the river was alive with barges, then as an assistant to

Jeffries, the Hereford boatbuilder. His obituary in *The Herefordian* of February 1888 described him as 'an excellent waterman and a bold swimmer. Many a life he saved on the river'. By the late nineteenth century, Richard and his sons took over what had been the Hereford to Abergavenny tram terminus, and started a boat building business there that continued until the late 1940s. One of their first jobs was to break up one of the last barges that had been used to carry coal down the Wye.

In her later life, Joan's aunt Dorothy lived at the Wharf House in Leominster, once a lodging house for bargees who used to work on the canal. In the grounds of Dorothy's home stood an old gas street lamp. This was no ordinary interloper; it was all that was left of her family's boat business. In its previous location near to Greyfriars in Hereford at the Jordan's boat-yard, the lamp helped light the boat-building workshops, where every member of the family assisted. When she was six years old, Dorothy and her father sailed past the lamp in a six-foot flood, travelling from Hay all the way to the Aust ferry. A few years later, in the flood of 1908, she climbed up the same lamp when the river reached nearly to the top of its standard.

You can see why Dorothy formed an attachment to this gas lamp. When an opportunity came to buy it, she jumped at the chance. Joan:

> When the old boat-yard ceased to function, Dorothy didn't want the lamp to go to anyone else who didn't know of its associations, so she asked the mayor of Hereford, an old friend, if it was possible for her to buy it. And she did!

In 2005, the *Hereford Times* reported the same lamp to be in a Bircher garden, belonging to a great grandchild of Richard Rivers.

Ron Hodges, 91

Ron was born in West Ham, London. When he was 12 he was evacuated with his two sisters away from the relentless bombing of the capital. They were sent to Paddington Station with labels pinned to their coats and gas masks hanging by their sides. When they arrived at their destination, Ron's sisters were put into one group while he walked through the streets of Wantage with one of the organisers. Increasingly desperate, they eventually stopped at a house and knocked on the door: 'Right, here's your evacuee,' the householder was told and pushed Ron in. Within time he returned home to London only to be evacuated a second time. Little did he know then that he would never return to London, and moved away permanently, settling in Chepstow. But when he was 16 years old, he found himself in Hereford, working at Jordan's boat-yard:

> When I came from Chepstow to Hereford, I got friendly with a bloke of my own age, Terry Hughes, and he used to do some part-time work at Jordan's boat-house. And he said, "Do you want to come and give us a hand, Ron?" So I did. We used to go down there of an evening or on a Saturday or a Sunday and we used to repair the boats for Miss Jordan. So she used to give us the occasional couple of bob and we'd repair the boats for her. We had 18 boats there at one time.

Visitors enjoying boat rides up-river
(photo: Doris Kershaw)

The weekly invasion of Welsh visitors, attracted to Wednesday market day and pub opening hours on Sundays (they were closed in Wales on the Sabbath), came by the coach-load. They were a welcome sight, bringing much-needed money to the local economy, but they could be a handful. Ron encountered some memorable, and wet, customers:

> It got to the point where we used to row Saturday and Sunday all day, letting out to day-trippers. They couldn't drink in Wales in those days because the pubs were closed on Sundays, so they used to have coach trips up from, say, Merthyr to Hereford. The Saracen's Head was a very popular pub with them then. They could park round the back there and all get in the Sag's Head and by closing time – two o'clock I think it was in those days – they were all pissed-up!
>
> And they used to come along the path, over the Wye Bridge, down to Jordan's boathouse and we'd put them in the boats and take them up the river. Some of them would row themselves and this one woman, she was a bit plump, about 35 I expect, and I was helping her into the boat.

"Be careful now, love," I said and she said, "I'll be all right." And all of a sudden, plonk, straight into the river! So I had to jump in and get her out because we had these steps down. I brought her up on to the towpath and she had that kind of material, like a crêpe dress. If crêpe gets wet it shrinks. And she stood on the path and said, "Oh no, I'm pissing myself!" It was such a sight; the crêpe rose up and she had old-fashioned knickers on and it looked like she had wet herself! She thought it was highly amusing.

SYMONDS YAT BOAT PEOPLE

Of all the places along the Wye, Symonds Yat holds on to its identity as a site of river crossings and a population proudly known as 'boat people', with some businesses running in the same families for decades. Their vessels' repute goes beyond the waters of the Wye, with at least one ferry that belonged to the Williams brothers, 'The Yat', being employed during the evacuation of Dunkirk.

The Williams brothers, Trevor and Harry, lived at Coppett Hill. From their cottage, the river is just about visible in the valley below, with Goodrich Castle in the near distance. They lived with Edie, Trevor's wife, and their other brother, Ivor, a ghillie. It's a steep, long haul up from the river below. When they retired

View from Coppet Hill (photo: *Ross Gazette*)

from their boating business in the mid 1970s, the boats were dragged up the vertiginous slope by winch (another Second World War gunship veteran, purchased in Bishopswood after the war) one last time and stored in a stone shed next to their cottage. And that's where the boats have stayed ever since, untouched and in perfect condition, a forgotten piece of history.

Trevor's grandson, Robin Hulse, 51, is the keeper of these important boats and a shed bursting with river miscellanea unseen for decades. It's going to be a lifetime's work for him and his wife, Caroline. They now live in the cottage. The fruit trees that once supplied the apples for their legendary lethal cider are gone, and so is the rhubarb that was turned into equally strong wine. However, it remains a perfect scene, with deer nibbling grass all around the house.

Ivor Williams in his boat
(photo: Margaret Morgans)

Central TV's Tony Francis was one famous victim of Edie's wine. Over the years, she had gently steered many a wine drinker in the right direction of home after several glasses of her deadly brew. Francis was no different. After a couple of sips, Francis announced it to be 'not too bad' to camera. The effects of the wine manifested themselves moments later when the swaying TV reporter slipped into the river, watched by a bemused, and unmoved, Ivor. He'd probably seen it all before, many, many times.

Robin Hulse:

> My grandfather Trevor and great uncle Harry, were boatmen. They worked the boat originally from Symonds Yat Station, on the Saracen's Head side, for pleasure trips, but they would also take passengers all the way to Monmouth. In the early days they rowed them there and then rowed them back all the way to Symonds Yat. It was motor a bit later. I think the small boats took four passengers, but there were bigger boats as well. I have those two still in the shed now. They haven't moved since they retired in the 1970s. One of the boats in the shed was delivered by train to Kerne Bridge station. Once it arrived there, they were probably taken to Symonds Yat by river.

The shed containing the boats appears as if untouched from the day the brothers closed the doors on their final day of working the river. In some ways, you wish it could always stay like this. Inside, there are the boats of course, more than one, beautiful, clinker built types, 12 to 14 feet long. On the wall hang the metal back rests for passengers. There are vintage brass life rings, dozens of cider flagons (their cider mill could start pressing again tomorrow; it's in mint condition), oars, seats and much more. The shed is dry, the collection is safe.

Kerne Bridge with Jarrot's House in the background (photo: Margaret Morgans)

Robin:

> At the end of each season they were brought back up the river and taken out opposite Bishopswood Village Hall for maintenance. The big one was left on the river bank and the small ones were carried back up here, either dragged by the family horse or much later a winch was also used. The boats were stored in the shed and worked on in the winter, to preserve them and they would strip the tar off and then varnish them again. I do know when they motorised them with an outboard motor, they had to increase the height of the sides of the boats, and put two planks on to make it a deeper boat. One of them was made in Caerleon in 1933 I think and built to order. Trevor and Harry would take the train to get to their boats moored at Symonds Yat. All they had to do was go down the hill from their cottage to the river and then cross the railway bridge to Kerne Bridge Station on the other side. It was just a five-minute train journey then to Symonds Yat.

Swimming, canoeing, and yes, even snorkelling, is harder when you're heading up-stream with the full flow of the river against you. Imagine doing that with a boatload of paying passengers on board, negotiating trees, rocks, and unruly guests. This is exactly what the Williams brothers, and other boatmen like them, did for decades. Oh, the joy of drifting dreamily down-river, dipping manicured hands into the gently passing water, laughing gaily with fellow passengers.

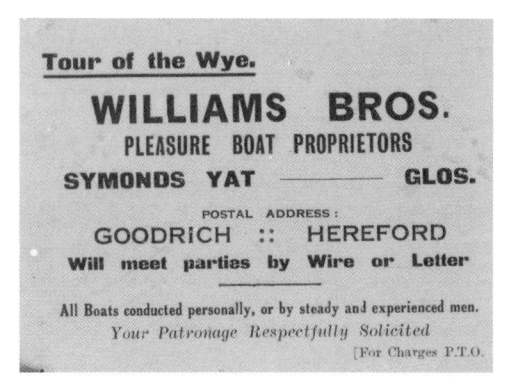

A Williams Brothers business card, showing fares for boat hire (photo: Robin Hulse)

What about the boatman? How did he cope? These men and women were highly skilled, wizards with oars. As a boy, Robert Davies of Monmouth watched one boatman with awe:

> He had a Wye skiff and he could row up against the current; he knew exactly where the slack water was. I've been up there with a power boat and watched him manoeuvre his wooden skiff so easily and expertly, just pulling a bit on one side, then to the other, holding the boat in position, just with the paddles. A boat with a motor wouldn't stay still in the water like that.

And so it was with the Williams brothers and their fellow boat people.
Robin:

> In the summer, the boats were rowed from Symonds Yat over the rapids to Monmouth from where the passengers were either transported back by train or by horse-drawn coach. The boat would then be punted or rowed back by one man. This journey was often being done twice a day.
>
> Neither of my uncles could swim but they never lost anyone. They worked all through the season, from Easter up to September. It was the family's main income. They would certainly do Monmouth and back once a day, seven days a week, because they made their money in the season and not much money in the winter. Apparently, the tips were very good.

During the off-season, the brothers would sustain themselves by cutting logs and managing their huge garden, while Edie would gather large quantities of fern (not bracken), which would be put into large bundles, bound in sacking with twine and taken down to Kerne Bridge station in the late afternoon, to catch the early morning train. The bundles were sold on Birmingham market to florists. And of course, she was always busy making her home-made wine from the produce that grew in her garden. As we have already seen, many a visitor to their cottage would leave a lesser man after sampling her lethal concoctions.

Robin:

> They grew their own vegetables and fruit to supplement their income through the winter. From their apple orchard, they made cider. We still have the press out there and they made it up until the late '80s. Initially they used a pony. But you could use the press by hand. I've done it. The cider was very, very strong and the longer it was left the stronger it got. Many of my grandfather's friends and working colleagues were from Symonds Yat and they would come and drink cider and fail to go home sometimes!

In Symonds Yat, there was an ever-ready stream of tourists and therefore plenty of competition and money to be made.

Robin again:

> I can remember in the 1970s and 1980s, Symonds Yat was very popular with day-trippers in cars and coaches, especially at weekends. There would be 20 to 30 coaches at the Paddocks Hotel, on the west side. On the Saracen's Head side, because of the access after the railway closed, only cars could park there. So, I think that's what possibly stopped the trade there.
>
> My grandfather and uncle did talk of competition from other boatmen. When coach parties were coming, each team of boatmen would have their own motorcyclists to go and meet the coaches some distance away and secure the business prior to the coach getting to Symonds Yat, and pre-book the passengers. Skirmishes would take place apparently. In the later stages of their business before they retired, there were probably about a dozen or thirteen different men wanting the trade. With all the people getting off the trains as well, I imagine there was a lot of competition.

The arrival of the railway at Symonds Yat in 1873 brought a surge of visitors to the area, eager to take part in all there was to offer. There were, of course, the boat trips; there was even butterfly collecting. Amongst Victorian butterfly collectors, the Doward was a destination of choice, and special excursion trains were chartered to the riverside beauty spot. Enterprising local boys collected rare Purple Emperors and other butterflies to sell to keen lepidopterists waiting at the station, eager to get back home and pin even more to their growing collection. But it was the river's fame for salmon that was the real draw and saw the arrival at stations up and down the Wye Valley of an endless line-up of 'fishy' types all casting out with the promise of 'the big one'.

Top: **Symonds Yat** (photo: Derek Foxton Collection)
Bottom: **the Purple Emperor butterfly sought by Victorian lepidopterists** (photo: R. Wheeler)

8 Bridges & Trains

IN 1969 A headline in the *Ross Gazette* announced,

> Women not allowed on bridge. There is a sex ban on the Stowfield Viaduct at Lydbrook, which spans the River Wye, between Gloucestershire and Herefordshire. Women are not allowed to cross it. Mr Winston Whittington told the Gloucestershire Highways Committee that six men have permission to cross the bridge to their work, but many other people used it too. Ald. Leslie Tily, chairman of the committee said: "I had not realised there was a sex ban on the bridge!"

The sex ban didn't continue, of course, and by 2016 Stowfield Viaduct was closed to all because of its poor state of repair. There was a similar fate for Moccas Bridge too. Erected in 1867 to replace the existing ferry, it connected two sides of the Cornewall family estate. The Bridge, already in need of repair, was damaged by the great flood of 1960/ 61 and it was eventually demolished in 1963, bringing to an end the river crossing connecting Moccas and Preston-on-Wye.

Moccas Bridge coming down, with Ken Pickford in foreground (head forester on Sir Richard Cotterell's Garnons estate 1959–75) (photo: John and Hannah Pickford)

Miss Hereford crossing the Wye in a novel way in August 1945 – by zip-rope!
(photo: Derek Foxton Collection)

Fawley Station (photo: Derek Foxton Collection)

David Joyce's childhood vantage point from the family farm on Brilley Mountain was perfect for spotting trains along the Hereford to Brecon line:

> From high on the ridge, we had the whole vista of Herefordshire before us. As children, we used to watch the trains puffing their way along the valley, all the way up to Norton Canon and then to Credenhill and into Hereford. My brother was fascinated by steam and he used to sit in his bedroom window and watch them all day. At that time, we used to use the railway, and when we were older we could cycle down to Whitney and get on the train to Hay or to Hereford. It was like getting a bus; it was normal, nothing special about it. There was a station master there and we could leave the bike and it would still be there when we came back. But it was tough cycling back up the mountain afterwards.

In 1892, during his walk along the Wye, H. Thornhill Timmins wrote in typical hail-fellow language, as he approached Fawley from Caradoc:

> Traversing the water meadows, we strike the river in a few hundred yards; and, after a 'yeo ho!' for the ferry, punt quietly across the full current, and so regain our path to Fawley Station in time for the evening train, which speedily carries us to Ross.

When a young Hugo Mason started his architect's apprenticeship with Mr John Hook, he had first to find his way from his Brockhampton home to the office in Hereford. The train halt at Fawley, down the hill from the village, came in handy:

> Having to travel to Hereford daily was a big thing to me and I took out a hire purchase agreement and bought a brand-new drop handlebar Raleigh bicycle from Hereford. Every morning I would cycle from home to Fawley Station with my sandwich box, often to hear the train coming from Backney Halt, when I was as far away as Fawley Court! Fortunately, it was the downhill part of the journey. When I got to Fawley some two miles from home, rain or shine, I had to leave my bike behind the station and run across the line before the train pulled in on the other side.
>
> Sometimes, in adverse weather conditions, I would be very cold and/or soaking wet and it was some time before I acquired a decent waterproof coat. There would only be a handful of passengers on the train, with plenty of room for us all, including some freight. The return train fare was 17/6d (87.5p) per week, leaving virtually nothing for emergencies.
>
> I made additional money in the evenings and at weekends by carving wooden house signs and doing plans on the side. The train had to travel through Fawley Tunnel immediately after leaving the station. It would soon reach the viaduct on the Aramstone side of the hill. This is a very special and spectacular space. I spent many hours just up-stream at Carey Islands, fishing and wildlife watching. A remarkable, unspoilt corner of England. Just beyond the viaduct was Ballingham Station, and from there to Holme Lacy Station and then Hereford – it was just eight miles from Fawley. I travelled to Hereford in this way for almost three years, by which time I bought an old Vauxhall Wyvern (LAD429) from the local garage, Biggs Motors of Fownhope.

SELLACK BRIDGE

The bridge connecting the parishes of Sellack and Kings Caple was built by public subscription in 1895, thus uniting the two parishes. It was sorely needed. There had been some difficulties at the river crossing. Patrick Darling is church warden at Sellack Church:

> At the time of the bridge's construction, Sellack was quite an old church and Kings Caple a young one. In those days, the vicar of Sellack had a curate at Kings Caple, who looked after the parish there. From time to time the

vicar obviously would need to cross the river to check on the curate. At the time, there was a ford at the crossing point and it required a man in a boat to bring the vicar across. Well the boatman used to often get drunk, which meant the poor old vicar couldn't get across to see his curate. As if that wasn't enough, the boatman would also verbally abuse the vicar. And there was the added nuisance in the summer when the river would become too shallow to use the boat and so it is said people, including the vicar, crossed on stilts – men using stilts would apparently carry passengers on their backs! So the building of a bridge was felt to be a good thing and a lasting unity of the two parishes.

Sellack Bridge (photo: M O'Mahony)

GREYFRIARS BRIDGE

Another 'new' bridge, and this time in Hereford, Greyfriars, opened to great fanfare in the spring of 1967 – a much-needed second river crossing in the City. Hundreds of workers were employed in its construction, and we can rescue the name of at least one from obscurity: Welshman Bryn Jones. Born in Llandudno, he arrived in Hereford after national service in the 1950s and found work in Hereford's tile factories where he eventually met his wife, Patricia. His son Philip describes a man who worked on some major projects in the county. But Greyfriars Bridge was a pretty special one:

> After working in the tile factories, he moved into the building industry in the mid-1950s and over the years he was employed on many Hereford developments, including Greyfriars Bridge, Holme Lacy Bridge, Eign Sewage Treatment Works, Ridgehill reservoir, the SAS camp at Pontrilas, and many more. He was a steel fixer – not a steel erector: it was a skilled job that required working to drawings, and bending and assembling ties in steel bars that were inside reinforced concrete structures. The only tool he ever carried was a pair of NIPS (short for top cutting nippers). He often talked about working on Greyfriars Bridge, especially whenever we drove over it. I'm glad we've got the photos to remember the role he played in it. He passed away in January 2017, six weeks before his 89th birthday.

Early stages in the construction of Greyfriars Bridge (photo: Derek Foxton Collection)

Philip Jones (first left) working on Greyfriars Bridge (photo: Jones family)

FELSTED SCHOOL, ESSEX

Out of this nettle, danger, we pluck this flower, safety. PM Neville Chamberlain in September 1938, on his return from Berchtesgaden with the Munich Agreement.

While PM-in-waiting Winston Churchill described the Agreement as, 'an awful milestone in our history', the teachers of Felsted School in Essex were making plans to evacuate. By 1939, expecting the worst, they moved, lock, stock and barrel, seeking wartime refuge in Herefordshire thanks to the generosity of Mrs Trafford of Goodrich Court. She made her home, and Hill Court house, handsome houses along the river, available to the School. Pencraig Court, another handsome riverside house, was also requisitioned by the school.

The boys' accommodation at Hill Court was situated across the river from their temporary school at Goodrich Court, requiring a circuitous journey either on foot, by bicycle, or bus, along the Walford Road, over Kerne Bridge, under the dry arch, before finally arriving at their destination. But in a fit of derring-do we are unlikely to see from any school now, the school-run was cut short dramatically by the construction of a bridge; and not just any old bridge, but a suspension bridge, which reduced the journey from over three miles to just one.

The Scouts' motto 'be prepared' couldn't be more aptly applied than to the Scout troop of Felsted School. They, with one of their school masters, a Mr Rendall, planned and built their

The suspension bridge at Goodrich
(photo: Felsted School)

'shortcut' suspension bridge. It was a feat of some engineering brilliance and it was estimated to have been crossed 120,000 times. A contemporary account reports:

> The walkers departed at 8.30; the cyclists any time before 8.45. There was always a queue at the bridge, as it was officially crossed in groups of four, and there were at least 20 people waiting to cross. In winter, it was slippery and the water was much nearer! Remarkably, few people or things fell in!

– Which suggests a few did, but no reports of who, when or what!

The Felsted School suspension bridge at Goodrich (photo: Felsted School)

Janet Howard lives in Crokers Ash today, but her late mother came down from Essex with the Auxiliary Territorial Service during the War, later joining Felsted School as a housekeeper. She kept a diary of her war years in Herefordshire, including tales of flirting with soldiers and airmen in down-town Ross-on-Wye. But of her mother's time at the school, Janet remembers:

> Mum said there was something like 500 kids that used to go across that bridge every day and I think she must have used the bridge. Kenneth Kendall, the BBC broadcaster, was one of the boys there then.

Graham Andrews, 87

Graham Andrews comes from a long line of hop farmers in the Bosbury area. It was usual in the 1930s and '40s for farmers to send their sons away to boarding school for a 'good education in order to run the family business'. Graham went to Lucton School initially before starting at Felsted School in Essex prior to the start of the Second World War. It was somewhat of a surprise when the school was evacuated to Graham's home county of Herefordshire – and useful too:

I knew quite a lot of hop farmers' sons at Felsted including Bob Stan and John Parker. I wasn't the only one. When the school was in Essex we had about a week's notice telling us we had to get out of there, and quick. Some Brigadier arranged railway trucks and the whole school – desks, chairs, the lot – were taken away by train and arrived eventually at Kerne Bridge Station. It was all right at Goodrich Court and Hill Court, they were quite close to home, but I never liked using that bridge. Three or four pupils would go across at a time and it was so damn frightening, rocking side to side and up and down. It was quite a long bridge too. And when it flooded it was near in the water. I got scared. If you were lucky you had a bike and cycled round the long way rather than take the short cut over the bridge, because there was no transport in those days to get you around. Once you got across you had to walk over fields to get to Goodrich Court and it was often muddy. We would scramble down to the bridge, cross and then walk up to the school.

After using it for about three or four weeks, I sent an SOS back home to Bosbury saying, "I need a bike!" And my parents brought one to Goodrich for me and I never had to use the bridge again.

From her Coppett Hill home, 93-year-old June Thimblethorpe can, at a stretch, just about see where the bridge once was. June, a historical romance novelist (pen-name, Sylvia Thorpe), once gave short shrift to her contemporary, Barbara Cartland, when the grande dame of fluffy literature arrived late for a meeting of the Historical Romance Writers Association. Cartland, wrapped in white mink and arriving in a white Rolls Royce, cut no mustard with June, who let her know in no uncertain terms that arriving late was impolite. Ms Cartland left soon after. June was one of those who crossed the bridge and it was not something to be forgotten, or tried more than once:

You see Goodrich Court and Hill Court were on opposite sides of the river and it meant going all the way round. So, the scoutmaster organised it and they built a suspension bridge of cables and planks. I went across it once, but I had to come back. With the river flowing beneath and the bridge swaying, I mean in these days of health and safety, it wouldn't be allowed, would it? The boys used to go down through the woods on their bikes and we walked across in the summer. But you wouldn't have got me across it again. I don't think my mother would have crossed it. She had more sense.

Along the former Ross to Hereford railway, there are bridges, and there are tunnels. At least one commuter was left with a rather poor option one evening in the late 1950s when his train stopped short of his destination. Peter Daines remembers:

> I was with a group of friends camping at a farmer friend's farm in Carey. I had come up from Bournemouth to join them and caught the last train from Hereford to Ross, not knowing that it didn't stop at Ballingham, which was my stop. It did, however, stop at the next station, Fawley. The guard let me off there around about 11 p.m. and the station master told me I had two choices: "You can either go through the woods and down the other side (I wouldn't take that one if I was you); or you can go through the tunnel. There's no more trains – you'll be all right." I had a light, so I walked through this tunnel in the middle of the track, because there was water dripping down on either side of it. I walked all the way to the other end and when I got out I was quite relieved.

Headlines in local papers in August 1963 announced 18 November as the date fixed by the British Railways Board for the closing of passenger services on the Hereford–Ross–Gloucester railway line. Any objections were to be 'received by September 28th to the secretary of the West Midland Area Transport Users' Consultative Committee'. But the wheels of motion had already started and this grandly-named committee was powerless to stop it.

Riverside parishes between Hereford and Ross, where once the train had been the chosen and most reliable form of transport, were badly hit. Mrs A. Pember, wife of the licensee of the British Lion at Fawley, told the reporter from the local paper how upset she was: 'We shall miss the train very much in this area. In fact, we shall be completely lost without it.' Meanwhile, Mr J. Terry, sub-postmaster at Carey said,

> Five or six people have travelled from Ballingham to Hereford each day by train. The nearest bus is at Hoarwithy, three miles from the bottom of Ballingham Hill. We badly need a bus service.

Their cries for help came to nothing. Tracks were pulled up and bus services remained minimal.

The last train, crossing Whitney Bridge on the Hereford to Brecon line, 1963
(photo: Tom Henderson)

Tom Henderson of Brilley was born and brought up next door to the Whitney Toll Bridge. In 1963, he was back from his national service and at home working with his father at his riverside engineering business. When the last train passed on the Hereford to Brecon line, he was on hand with his camera. It was the end of an era and the trains were missed:

> You could set your watches by the train. If it was the nine train, or the ten train or whatever, then you knew it was that time when the train passed. I used to catch the train to Hereford or to Hay. A lot of people used to walk through Whitney Wood to the train station, where the saw-yard is now. The footpath came out by the station in those days. I used to catch the eleven train, go to Hereford on a Saturday and mother used to take me to the pictures. It was a shame the trains stopped. We liked the old trains and there were some old characters too.
>
> There was one old boy who used to work at the station and he used to exaggerate his health problems. There was one particular occasion when he was walking on these two sticks and he was laying out rabbit wires. He was hobbling along and he was just about at the gate to go out, when a rabbit got in one of the traps and it started to squeal. He dropped his sticks and ran like hell towards that rabbit! It was the talk of the village.

WHITNEY-ON-WYE TOLL BRIDGE
David Warnes, 73

Nature loving, aging hippy, bibliophile and acclaimed folk musician, Dave has performed all over the county, south Wales and the Midlands as a soloist and part of a duo. He has something of the Cecil Sharpe about him in his collecting and archiving of folk tunes, including those of the gypsy communities working in the county hop fields. He is a prolific book collector and tree planter. For a couple of years in the early 1970s, Dave was toll keeper at Whitney-on-Wye Toll Bridge, providing some local colour, music and a smile.

> My ex-wife and I were living in Llowes at the time, when she saw an advertisement in the paper for a toll bridge keeper at Whitney. It was £20 a week and I thought, "Oh, that sounds like a good crack," so we applied. The owners lived in Australia, so we had an interview with the agent in Kington, who explained that it was very important that the bridge was opened from dawn to dusk, and then he handed over the keys, and that was it. After that he came once a month and took the takings and paid us our wages.

David Warnes at Whitney Toll Bridge (photo: David Warnes)

From the unlikeliest of starts, Dave was made for the job, creating an impressive revenue, the best the bridge had ever seen:

> When cars came through, I would stand in the doorway and sing to the passengers and practise my guitar playing. Sometimes a car would draw up and request a song, and if I knew it then I would sing it. I made so much money from that, more than the toll ever made. In those days, it was a penny for a car to cross and half a penny for each passenger. So a car with two passengers would be two pence. They might give me ten and say, "keep the change". I would put the toll in one jam jar and the rest in another. It was big money to us then. People seemed pleased to have a song sung to them while they were paying the toll, and it was great practise for me too. I also sold books, bric-a-brac, and antique furniture that

> I would put outside the toll booth. And when we weren't there we had an honesty box. But often we used to just wave the locals through anyway.

This was the 1970s after all, and, as toll keeper, Dave met some interesting characters, including Paddy the Irish ghillie from Brilley, and a guru who ran an ashram in Letton, with ten followers locally and another thirty in the USA. Dave himself became something of a draw for fellow musicians, impressed by his vast and eclectic music collection:

> Traffic's Jim Capaldi lived in a house near Hay Bluff and it attracted lots of interesting people and they would often come down here – people like Stevie Winwood and Neil Innes, because I had a varied record collection and we would spend an hour or two listening and chatting about music.

The local fox and otter hunts were not 'just waved through' however. Dave, virulently anti-hunt, made their bridge crossing as challenging as possible:

> They had to cross the bridge and the previous toll keeper just let them through paying the fixed rate. But I insisted on counting them all: I would count all the horses, a penny each, all the hounds, halfpenny each, the followers, another halfpenny each, and I kept the gate closed while I was counting. They used to get really angry. They complained to the agent in the end and eventually they paid in advance.

The otter hounds didn't fare much better:

> The bridge had several hundred yards of river bank and when I heard the otter hounds were coming I put up big signs on either side of the bank saying, 'private land – otter hunters will be shot!' I refused to let them cross the toll bridge and they had to go the long way round.

On the Ross to Monmouth line was Kerne Bridge station. Margaret Morgans' parents were licensees of the Kerne Bridge Inn, situated almost opposite the station. She also used trains for time-keeping:

> I remember we always used to tell the time from the train. They were always so punctual. When it came by at half past eight and it hooted, we knew it was half past eight in the morning.

Kerne Bridge Station (photo: Margaret Morgans)

KERNE TOLL BRIDGE

The War in Europe was hurtling towards its dénouement in March 1945, when a letter appeared in the *Ross Gazette*. The continued toll at Kerne Bridge was causing much vexation for one 'concerned' reader because an appeal to abolish the toll had been rejected by Hereford Council. There was no mincing of words from the correspondent:

> Both the Member of Parliament and the Ministry of War Transport support our request; it is solely the supine indifference of HCC to the financial burden imposed on all those who live in the neighbourhood of Kerne Bridge that prevents something being done to relieve it.

But there was no sympathy from 'gentleman of leisure', Alderman Robert Pashley, the Wizard of the Wye and resident of the area, who believed the removal of the tolls would 'cause traffic problems in Ross!'

And yet, within two years, there was an about-face from the Council and Sam Wooley, the last gate-keeper, closed the gates for the final time. It was a relief for Goodrich pupils and their parents living on the wrong side of the gates. The toll had been 'intolerable for many families, causing undue worry'. Sam Wooley lived

Kerne Bridge Toll House (photo: Margaret Morgans)

with his wife in the Toll House at the end of the bridge, on the Walford side. After the tolls were discontinued, the house was abandoned and slowly slid into the river. Nothing remains of it today.

Bob Duberley's childhood playground was on the banks of the River Wye in Bishopswood. He frequently passed through the nearby toll gates:

> When 10 o'clock at night came, old Sam Wooley would leave the gate open and you wouldn't have to pay at all. There was the big gate for cars and lorries and a foot passenger gate by the side of it. He'd come out and open the gate and you'd pay, and he'd take the money. And that's how it worked.

June Thimblethorpe also knew the gatekeeper:

> I think it was 6p to go across and I think the ticket lasted for the day, and if you were walking it was only a penny or something like that. If you wanted to come back Sam knew you'd been across and wave you through.

After the collection of tolls was finally decommissioned in 1948, Cecil Williams, a Goodrich roadman, was called upon, with several others, to help unhitch the

The late Bob Duberley with the Kerne Bridge toll gate (photo: M. O'Mahony)

deadweight gates – it was time for them to go. What happened to them after that was unknown, until a phone call in August 2017 from the late Bob Duberley. Far from disappearing, they had, all these years, been lovingly cared for by Bob, and before him, his father. They hang proudly at the entrance to Bob's farm in Hope Mansell. When he was alive, Bob religiously repainted the gates – which towered over him – every year. He died in October 2017. In his interview, and over a glass of red wine at eleven in the morning, he told his story of the Kerne Bridge toll gate:

> My father bought the toll gate when the council sold it off in 1948, and he gave them £2.50 for it. It was taken off its hinges and was left in a shed in Bishopswood for 40 years. I had put a metal stanchion to hang it on, built a stone pillar, and my wife got somebody to move it up here to Hope Mansell. So we managed to get it up here after it had been stored for 40 years – when, lo and behold, two days after moving, the shed burnt down! If the gate had been in there it would have been totally wiped out. A stroke of luck really.

Bob's father was an enterprising man by all accounts and often found the most unlikely of work at the beginning of the last century:

> He was a clever man, my father, I tell you. There wasn't much work about then so he got a job on the railway, and they were working on Kerne Bridge, checking the stanchions to see they were all okay. Anyway, there was a diver who used to go over the side and down under the bridge and into the river to check the stanchions. Dad was there, on top of the bridge pumping air for the divers. But there was a chap working with him and he used to go down the line when they weren't doing much, and he'd collect up the snails and cook them and when they had a break they'd eat them up!

The trains were efficient, and items reliably turned up where they should be and on time: ice cream, people, bikes, boats and horses – there seems to have been no limit to what could be transported by train.

Bob again:

> I seem to remember my father buying a horse once up in Hereford at the horse sales, and he had it sent down on the train. Oh, he was really into his horses was my dad. Anyway, he brought her down here, and we collected her from Kerne Bridge Station. She was an honest old horse, we called her Dinah. She was as wicked as a devil, but you could put a child on her back, totally safe.

While Bob's dad collected his horse, Bob was busy sending off his wool from the same station:

> I kept a few sheep and I used to take my wool along to the station in Kerne Bridge. I knew where the key was in the goods yard; we all did in those days. I used to go down, unlock the gates and put the wool in a truck ready to go to Harrison Bowen at Worcester. I had it all ticketed up. I can't think of the station master's name, but he was quite a nice man and he lived in Lydbrook. We used to have day-old chickens come down on the train sometimes, which we had to pick up from the train station. The station master used to cycle past our house on his way home, so he would often drop them off for us.

A goods train crossing Hunderton Bridge (photo: Derek Foxton Collection)

Sometimes, when times are hard, you have to find a way of surviving. The coal wagon that stopped overnight on the Hunderton Bridge in Hereford in the 1960s presented a ripe opportunity to make a few pennies, as Gary McLeod remembered:

> All of a sudden somebody would come around selling coal, "Do you want a sack of coal or a bucket of coal?" They'd come to The Vaga asking for a couple of bob for a sack. And unbeknown to us, the actual coal train would stop on the bridge overnight and, of course, kids would get up on the wagon and they'd be chucking coal all the way down the bank, and there would be somebody at the bottom collecting it in sacks.

BACKNEY HALT

Backney was the last of the four bridges over the Wye on the Hereford to Ross railway. The bridge spans were removed after the closure of the line in 1965. A quiet spot today, Backney Halt was once an industrious place, as the late John Brookes recalled:

Repairs to Strangford Bridge, September 1947 (photo: Derek Foxton Collection)

We used to take our milk churns down to Backney Halt on a motorbike and sidecar. I didn't drive it; I was on the back. All the farmers did it then. We sent our sugar beet from there, and hay and straw – all manner of things. It was only a small station but it was a very busy one and very important for loading stuff and sending it off, on to Gloucester and Hereford.

STRANGFORD BRIDGE

During a stormy night on 1 March 1947, the central pier of Strangford Bridge collapsed and the spans on either side fell into the river. Record floods that winter are thought to have compromised the bridge's foundations. That evening, two poachers are alleged to have run for their lives on hearing the structure's collapse. Jack Alford was returning to his Kings Caple home that evening. His wife Jean recounted:

> Jack was coming home that night with Eddie Davis to Kings Caple when they heard a tremendous crash. Jack, who worked on the family smallholding at Lightfields, went to investigate. They discovered a pier on Strangford railway bridge had collapsed, brought down by the weight of the winter's flood. The station master at Fawley was alerted and the late-night GWR from Gloucester was stopped just in time.

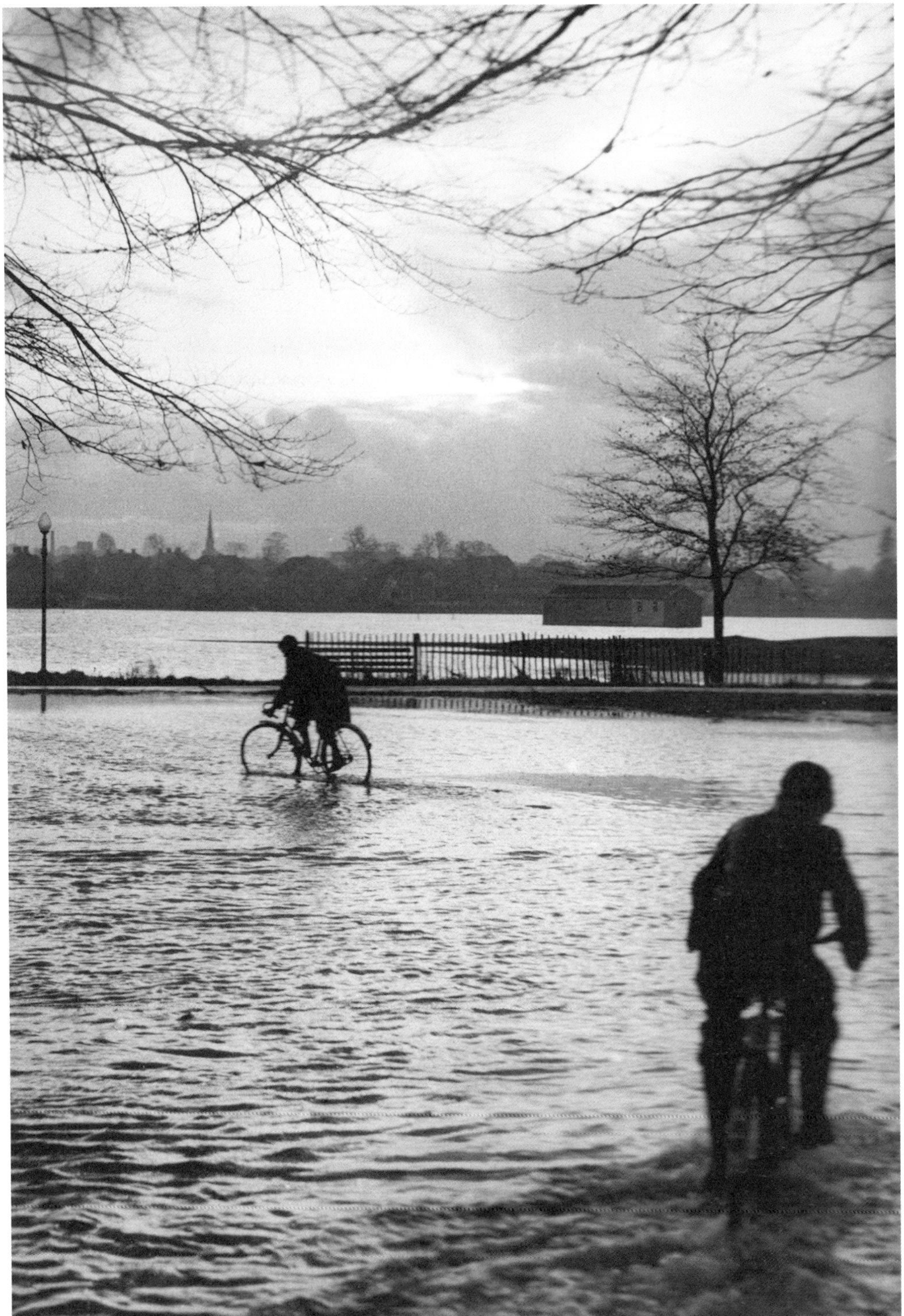

9 Ice Age & Biblical Floods

> Grandfather used to look at the river and always used to turn around and say as we went up towards Sandy Bay, "don't be up there too long; there's a storm coming." Nine out of ten times he was right. He used to go by nature. Even now, before I go out, I usually look down the river and if it is all rippled in the middle and glassy on either side that's a sure sign there's moisture in the air. So, we mightn't get rain, but I always take my pac-a-mac with me. Janet Preedy

The great flood of 1947, the big freeze of 1963, the long drought of 1976: such extreme weather conditions have seared themselves into our collective consciousness. 'Arctic conditions', and 'floods of the century' are gifts from the heavens for local news reporters and the *Hereford Times* squeezed the life out of the opportunity in February 1963 when its headline screamed:

SPECTACLE OF THE CENTURY AS WYE ICE BREAKS UP!

It went on to describe, '18-inch ice floes breaking up in upper river'. It was dramatic, once-in-a-lifetime stuff, and ice fever spread. A householder close to the Victoria Bridge was woken up at 3 a.m., 'by a noise that sounded like a lorry-load of bricks being tipped outside the front door'. This was the ice crashing into the Victoria Bridge. By daylight, spectators had poured onto the bridge to see the freakish weather conditions.

Ice skating on the frozen Wye in Hereford, 1917 (photo: Derek Foxton Collection)

Victorian and Edwardian photos of a frozen Wye demonstrate it wasn't such a rare occurrence after all. A *Hereford Journal* report in 1917 describes the river as 'thronging with hundreds of persons attracted by the splendid piece of ice from the boathouse up'. Wednesday was market day and at Hardings the Ironmongers on Bridge Street it was expected to be busy if there had been a frost for three or four days. If so, down would come the rabbit wires and up would go all the skates. At Ross, Brian Dean's grandmother earnt many a farthing by tying skates on to the gentry's shoes.

Still in Ross in 1963, the river was frozen from bank to bank for a month at the riverside pub, the Hope and Anchor. It was the least likely of places for a spot of soccer but, sure enough, the local paper reported, '20 young men playing football with a beach ball on a pitch stretching right across the river. Others circled the "pitch" on bicycles'. This same stretch of river during the same winter proved the perfect skating spot for Howard Copping, 91, of Ross, who happened to have a pair of skates in his cupboard.

1963 and this time in Whitney-on-Wye, where the ice over the river, at 18-inches thick, was proving difficult to break. Tom Henderson:

Tom Henderson walking on the frozen Wye at Whitney (photo: Tom Henderson)

> Me and father took a sledgehammer to the ice and we couldn't break it. There was a thin layer of snow on it. He said, "Come on Tom, let's go across for a cup of tea". We tested the ice and walked from the factory, down the bank and crossed the river, up the other bank, had a cup of tea with a neighbour and then we went back the way we came. No winter like that since. We were defrosting everything.

Gary McLeod at Hunderton, 'walked on water' in 1963. His father wasn't impressed though:

> I used to drink in the Lichfield Vaults then with Michael Allett and Teddie Skinner, who was the hairdresser. Teddie was telling us some soldiers had just come to the camp and they had moved into Bradbury Lines, and they had said you could drive a four-ton trunk onto the Wye and it wouldn't go down because they had drilled holes to see how thick the ice was. Anyway, we were walking home and Teddie said, "I'm not walking along that bridge. Come on, let's walk across the river." Of course, we had the booze in us, so we went down by the rowing club and got on there. Teddie was in the centre jumping up and down on this ice. We went under the railway bridge and got off at the Hunderton ferry steps. As it happens the old man's lights were

Hereford in the snow, looking towards the Victoria Bridge
(photo: Derek Evans Studio Archive/ HLTAL/ HARC/ Hereford Libraries)

still on in the bar at The Vaga, so we knocked on the door and told him that we had walked across the water, and all he could say was, "You prats!"

Vic Gammage took the same walk that same winter and was upbraided in a similar way:

> I walked across by the Hunderton ferry. It was solid ice. There was a few of us doing it and I can remember the police officer giving us a bit of tongue pie when he saw what we were doing!

The frozen River Arrow in 1963 was solid enough to take the weight of a herd of Hereford cattle belonging to Andrew Powell's father.

> Whether it was a case that they were looking for food or they just enjoyed the freedom of it, but they started to walk on the river and eventually ended up walking several miles down-stream! Another farmer said that a herd of cattle had appeared in his field and dad ended up walking down to fetch them, from Michaelchurch-on-Arrow to Hergest, and then drove them back up the same frozen river to our land again!

After the crippling winter of 1947, the thaw, when it eventually came, was welcome, but could be noisy – as Tom Henderson experienced at his riverside home in Whitney-on-Wye:

> It was a very severe winter during the War and the river froze, and it froze that hard that some actually drove a horse and cart across it, and that was done in more than one place on the river. And then after the thaw came – and it came suddenly – there was a lot of rain and it got very mild quickly and the ice floes broke up. I was sleeping in a little bungalow above the river and during the night I could hear this *doiing, doiing* sound all the time as the ice hit the pillars of the railway viaduct.

Rosemary Brown

Rosemary went to Ross Secondary Modern School in the early 1950s. Her school bus picked up at How Caple, before travelling on to Brockhampton, then Foy, before arriving at its final destination in Ross. It was a bus journey with some adventure and a bus driver with some 'character' as Rosemary was to learn:

> He kept a gun in his cab and regularly bagged a rabbit for his tea during the school run. He would also stop where the sweet chestnuts grew by the river, allowing us children to collect them up. Just up from Foy, *en route* to Ross, was a very steep hill called the Slad. In winter, it was near impossible to negotiate, but the bus driver had a plan. He carried quite a few shovels and he coaxed us pupils to dig the bus out so that it could progress. But on one occasion it refused to budge, even after some frantic digging and pushing. So the bus had to be turned around by all of us pupils pushing. We all pushed at the rear and the bus gently glided round to face the opposite way. We were late for school that day.

FLOODING

Extreme flooding at Preston-on-Wye at the end of the nineteenth century forced one cowman to seek refuge in the church – with his bull. Inside, the cowman found the highest point, the pulpit, and held onto the bull's halter. Both survived the deluge. So did the pulpit.

David Joyce witnessed flooding from Brilley Mountain:

> We were up at the farm on Brilley Mountain during the flood of December 12th, 1960 and we could see that the valley was quite badly flooded. My father said, "Come on, let's go down in the van and have a look at it". All the family bundled in the back and trundled down and we parked just off the main road by the Whitney Toll Bridge and then walked up onto it and we could feel it shaking with water thundering through underneath. We were amazed by the volume, took some photographs and then we went home. The next day the road where we had been parked had been completely washed away, and was later rebuilt further away from the river.

Flooding at Bredwardine, mid 1960s (photo: John and Hannah Pickford)

'Always test your brakes' is the old adage after driving through water. It's sound advice. This is Rosemary Brown's rather carefree school bus driver again, who, doubtless, wouldn't get close to the keys of a school bus in 2018:

The route of the bus took it through Foy, alongside the River Wye. If the river was in flood, the bus had to turn around at Foy village and retrace its route back to Ross via How Caple. On one occasion the driver ignored the deep waters and continued regardless, and at Brampton Abbots it was in a collision with a lorry as the water had got into the brake linings, rendering the brakes useless. All on board were okay, but the driver was pinned in his cab. Some of the bigger lads managed to release him, but I can still hear the screams now!

TRAPPED BY FLOODS

Laconic, wise and beady eyed, there aren't many left who know the river quite as well as Maurice Hudson: 'I am so old I can remember the flood of 1947!'
Maurice:

> There were sash windows and I got one down and I said, "Is there anything you want from that house?" And my neighbour replied, "There are some nice pictures I wouldn't want damaged." I knew the river was still rising, so I canoed through the windows, through the house and it was pitch dark. There was furniture floating around and I couldn't sit upright under the ceiling because I was crouched down tight. But I got his pictures off the wall, put them in the canoe, and just managed to get through the sash windows because the river was still rising.

In an exhaustive history of Hereford Rowing Club, the following account has all the requisite drama so beloved of local newspapers:

> In February 1945, widespread flooding caused havoc along the River and damaged Club property. Rising from winter level to flood level and beyond in a few hours the water swept away the boathouse raft, a fishing boat and one of a pair of mahogany single sculling dinghies. These were serious losses and when the weekend had closed without any news of them the Club Captain W. Palfrey decided it would be possible to take a search party down the river. Four other members and the boatman B. Crissall volunteered for the voyage. By Sunday, the river had thrown off the effects of the thaw, but under the impulse of rain from the Welsh hills, was running at a rising eight feet. The travellers, P. Miller, V. Langford, A. Lane and E. Wright (Captain of the Hereford Cathedral School) set off with Mr. Palfrey and Mr Crissall in one of the Club's big Randans in

expectation of adventure. They got it! Skilfully escaping disaster almost at the start of the trip – the massive pillars of the Wye Bridge are large obstacles on fast flowing water when there is little headroom – they pursued a rapid course downstream. They ran into some islands at Hoarwithy and towards the end nearly hit Bicknor Bridge. The boat was found hitched by its chain to a tree near Rotherwas Island. They did not find the raft or the dinghy. On their return trip – by road – after experiencing generous hospitality from the Ross Rowing Club, they found the Wye had risen to over 12 feet and was still going up! Ross R.C. lent a helping hand later, with the loan of raft and other equipment to replace that which was lost.

Brian Saunders' father, Jack, was a baker through the War years, and in the floods of 1947 he was press-ganged into the rescue efforts:

Rowing boats were commandeered from Jordan's boathouse and used to take supplies to people stranded in their upstairs rooms. I remember a senior police officer asking father to help supply tea and sugar for stranded cottagers. I was dispatched in a police van to bring back from our shop whatever could be spared.

Flooding at Greyfriars, mid 1990s
(photo: Derek Evans Studio Archive/ HLTAL/ HARC/ Hereford Libraries)

Flooded kitchen at Hampton Bishop, 1960s
(photo: Derek Evans Studio Archive/ HLTAL/ HARC/ Hereford Libraries)

Flooding in St Martin's Street, Hereford in 1946 (photo: Derek Foxton Collection)

Flooding near the Ship Inn, Ross Road, Hereford in 1946 (photo: Derek Foxton Collection)

Flood waters near the top of the arches of the Wye Bridge (photo: Derek Foxton Collection)

You would think, wouldn't you, that if there was one place to be in a flood, then a boat club surely would be it? Well, nature is a formidable beast, and the floods unleashed in 1952 tested even Hereford Rowing Club. Member John Slatford was there that fateful October day when their brand new, £300 boat was swept broadside against the Wye Bridge.

> The river was flowing about five feet higher than normal and within seconds the boat broke into three pieces and each was swept through the arches with most of us clinging on for dear life – it was very cold. Robin Hammond and I were in the central section and we landed on the bank opposite the Cathedral. Back at the Club later we were given large brandies. In another section, cox Tommy Dawes was in difficulty because of his heavy clothing, and the stroke, Jim Snead, had to support him. The rest of the crew were stranded up to their waists in water on the apron of one of the bridge pillars. They were rescued by boat and the broken sections were towed back to the landing stage.

Eight years later, and Hereford Rowing club was experiencing another exceptional deluge of water. Club member Frank Ford was there for the record-breaking 21-foot flood of 1960. It's not one he will forget in a hurry:

> I was walking over the Old Bridge and the water was sort of tunnelling through the arches; it was right up above the top voussoirs of the arch. We

really thought the bridge was going to go. Walter Palfrey and a couple of other members managed to get a pleasure boat to the Club because they were concerned about the beer cellar and tethering boats and so forth. And while they were in the Club the water came up to such a dangerous height that they couldn't get back out. Walter and one or two others had to stay in the Club overnight. Of course, the heating had broken down because the boilers were on the ground floor and flooded. It was bitterly cold and they wrapped themselves in carpets to stay warm through the night.

Fellow Rowing Club member Bruce Wallace had a similar experience, a mixture of the amusing and the tragic:

The Rowing Club did a lot of work in 1960, when the big flood came and that was when twenty feet and six inches of water came down the Wye. We all went out on flood rescue with these pleasure boats, going all over the place. I was with a couple of crews out at Letton and it was quite horrific because there were people trapped in their houses on the upper floor and we were rowing up and we'd seen this fella waving. We rowed over to him and as we pulled up at his bedroom window, one of us poked our head in and asked, "Are you all right?". And he said, "Yeh, sure. D'ya know, lads, there's a pig in here in my bedroom. I had to get it upstairs out of the water". We had to say, "We're coming to take you". But he wasn't happy because he said, "Well I'm not leaving the pig". So he stayed with the pig.

In the 1950s, Charlie Amos has help moving his pig during floods in Willersley (photo: Derek Evans Studio Archive/ HLTAL/ HARC/ Hereford Libraries)

10 Pubs, Clubs & Missionaries

> **Many, of course, were decent family men, intent only on making a living, but there was a leavening of vagabonds, who were willing to work hard, but were determined to play hard in their own time.** H.L.V. Fletcher in his *Portrait of the Wye Valley*, (1968) describing the hardworking, hard-drinking, Irish navvies who helped build the dams upstream of the Wye.

In Goodrich and Welsh Bicknor in 1851 there lived 496 people. Of these, 150 were married adults and 113 unmarried adults, and 29 widows or widowers. The parish supported a number of occupations, including agricultural labourers, a ship's carpenter, fishermen, a miller, cordwinder, coachman, housemaid, and wagoners. They must have been thirsty after a day's work, for there were also two innkeepers. There are not many villages that can boast two pubs in the modern era, and many riverside inns have called last orders for the final time. Some we are glad to see the back of, others we wish would open their doors one more time.

THE CAMP INN, EATON BISHOP
As nice as the seaside

Now closed, The Camp Inn, perched high above the Wye, had the most enviable of positions. It's no wonder it was a draw. The pub dated back to the 1830s, when it was a cider house, before becoming a pub in the late nineteenth century. Thirsty customers would arrive by car, on foot, by bike and often by water. In the 1950s, Hereford Rowing Club's John Slatford remembers lazy days, picnics, games, and floating up in time for opening hours:

The Camp Inn, Eaton Bishop, 1950s (photo: Hammonds family)

> As I remember, there were at least four pleasure boats that the Club owned, and they were probably already 50 years old. We got some from Jordan's when they closed down. The largest of these boats, with four pairs of oars, was affectionately known as the Comet, and another with three pairs was called the Randan. We would set off on a Sunday morning with food, ready for a river-bank fry-up, arrive at the Vee stream, disembark and climb up to The Camp in time for midday opening. There we would stay until closing time at two o'clock.

Arriving by river was idyllic, but it was a steep climb up to the Inn. Canoeist Peter Daines did it many times:

> I was with two friends and my wife, Marjorie. We were camping and it was peeing with rain and we ended up at Ruckall by The Camp Inn, down the bottom, and we decided we'd cook the meal. I was frying sausages and I put a plate on a saucepan of water and then another one, and that was my oven. But the pan fell over and the sausages went all the way down and into the river. We were so hungry that we dunked them in the hot water and just put them back in the pan. After that, we walked up all those steps all the way up to the pub, very steep and often muddy.

Ivy Doody spent her childhood summer days in Eaton Bishop:

> In the 1930s, folks used to come up from Hereford in their boats and picnic on the river bank. It was as nice as the seaside. We used to paddle in the river and climb the 38 steps to The Camp Inn, which was run by Anne and Tom Flecknor. We would sometimes walk up to the Laurels nearby, which was owned by Mr and Mrs Cook, and enjoy their tea, homemade cake, sandwiches and marrow jam.

COURTFIELD ARMS, BISHOPSWOOD

The Courtfield Arms was just a short walk from Bob Duberley's Bishopswood childhood home. It was so named because of its proximity to the Courtfield Estate, directly across the river, the ancestral home for nearly 500 years of the Vaughan family. Lately a Bangladeshi restaurant, it was known as a 'good pub' in its day. Bob remembered a couple of larger-than-life characters: the landlord, Old Miller and Courtfield's Laird, Joe Vaughan; 'The Major', who, as a young man, had wagered – and lost – his Daimler in a card game in the south of France:

There was pubs everywhere once. But Old Miller kept the Courtfield Arms, and Joe Vaughan used to come down the hill on the other side and cross the river opposite the pub. When Joe Vaughan arrived, he and Old Miller would have a good session together. There was swords on the wall in those days, and as the evening went on they would both get to the top of the stairs and they'd fight a duel. I've seen them many a time do that. At the end of the night Mr Vaughan would head back home across the river. He wouldn't think twice about it. They said he knew his way back across and I expect he chose where there was not too much water and he would walk across the river and straight back up to Courtfield. Sometimes when it was in flood, you had to hold him back mind!

LAKIN SISTERS' OFF LICENSE

The Lakin sisters' off licence was on Villa Street, Hunderton, a short distance from the Hunderton ferry steps. The veranda that once faced the river indicates that some of the shop's trade once came from the river. Today, a Cheltenham and Hereford Brewery sign is still on the wall. The sisters, Mabel and Gladys, sold penny sweets, bacon and other goods, but their drinks licence kept them busy, serving perry or port from casks. It was eventually taken over by Doug Smith, former landlord of the Anglers Inn in Union Street. Doreen Byrnes was sent down to the Lakin's shop by her mother:

> I can remember the little shop ran by the two ladies, and I was often made to run down there for sugar or five Woodbines. Imagine sending a child to get Woodbines these days?

Janet Preedy:

> The sisters had a brother, Bertie. They used to have a load of sweets in the window and my brother Roy went over and bought some and my mum said, "Oh, what you want to buy those out of the window for? The cats have been lying on them". So Roy, being like he was (he must have been about five), went back over with the sweets, and said: "I don't want these, because the cats have piddled all over them!" Mum was mortified.

And just across the road, the legendary …

THE VAGA TAVERN

The Vaga, a dying breed of a pub. Proper backstreet boozer, it was and is the centre of the community. Gordon McLeod was landlord in the 1960s, and son Gary used to help out:

> There was always someone bringing things into the pub to sell, all sorts of seasonal foods. If you knew someone killing pheasants then they would bring pheasants in and then you would get fed up of pheasants, or you'd get fed up of eels and then people would catch rabbits. Everything in Hunderton revolved around the pub, because it was, well – it was The Vaga. If you were a total stranger and you walked in years ago everyone would just stop and look and think, "Is that a Copper?" Then someone would go and find out, "What do you want pal?" At Christmas and New Year, no one locked their doors. Nothing ever got stolen.
>
> You had two men's quoits teams; you had two lady's quoits teams. Then you had the lady's darts, which used to be on a Wednesday. Then you had the men's 'Fat' (that was cards) on the Tuesday. Then you had the crib on the Tuesday, and the men's darts would be on the Monday. We had two teams – two at home and two away. When they were playing away my old man always used to give the captain beer money for eight pints (that's for the eight in a team). When they were home, naturally they didn't have it, but when they went to play away he made sure they had a pint to go with. Because he used to maintain that probably on a Monday night the lads had spent out, they were skint, they wouldn't go out for a pint, but they would go out for two pints. So, if they've got enough for two then they would have three.

SARACEN'S HEAD, 'SAGS', HEREFORD

This is a riverside public house which has good views over the River Wye and has been a well-used hostelry for over 200 years. During the 1800s, almost all business would have been generated from the local river trade and the ancillary occupations nearby. Long after the loss of the river trade, it continued to prosper from not only normal pub activities, but also football and cricket teams, who used the Sags as their headquarters. It is also the Registered Office of a (dormant) company named Ross Docks Limited, whose business is described as 'Inland Passenger Water Transport' and 'Inland Freight Water Transport', and The Rivers Wye and Lugg Navigation and Horse Towing-path Company Limited.

The Buffs. Wesley Mason's grandfather, Thomas, moved to Herefordshire in 1932. He was manager of the Hampton Park Brickworks and continued to live at Brickworks House until about 1956. He became heavily involved with the Buffs. His grandson, living in Hereford, still has Thomas's Buff's regalia, belts, sashes, buttons and medals (photo: Wesley Mason)

Its other association for many years was with the 'poor man's Freemasons'. Between the 1940s and 1960s, the Saracen's Head was the local lodge of the Royal Antediluvian Order of Buffaloes (RAOB) – or 'Buffs' to most local people. It was a fraternal organisation with origins dating back to 1822 in London. However, their headquarters is the Grand Lodge of England and is based in Harrogate, Yorkshire. It is still an active organisation, and footage shot at the 1948 Remembrance Parade in Hereford shows how popular an organisation it was, with a stream of Buffs members marching down Broad Street, many of them in their later years, with First and Second World War medals jostling for space on their chests.

Gary McLeod:

> The Buffs was always called the 'poor man's Freemasons'. Members would pay a pittance to be part of it, but if you were off work or had hard times, you could go to the local officer and say you've got no work or the kids are ill, and they would give you money. It originally came from all those mining towns up north. It was on par with a trade union, like a private union. You would pay a subscription and you would meet at these public houses, like the Sags, because it was somewhere they could all meet and have a drink. But they had this charitable pot because the things the Buffs did to help people was unbelievable.

The Buffs, while meeting at the Saracen's Head, came up with an inspired fundraising idea in the 1960s.

Gary McLeod:

> They were collecting money for the Buffalos and there was a sign on the wall saying, "Go and see the water otter in the cellar for a thr'pence". Of course, when the river flooded the water used to come up in the cellar at the Sags and they used to get all the barrels up. But people was actually paying thr'pence to go down and see this water otter. But it was just a kettle on a string floating on the water with a brush on it! And of course, the money was going into the landlord's or the Buffalo's pocket!

THE YEW TREE

The Yew Tree – also known as the Wood Inn – occupied an idyllic if remote position near to Brockhampton. There was a winning darts team there in the 1960s. Mains electricity was yet to arrive, so contests were lit by Tilley lamps and 'facilities' were 'anywhere outside'. That didn't mean it was short of customers, however, among passing fishermen and farmers, as lifelong Brockhampton resident and Yew Tree regular Hugo Mason (*see page 65*) recalls:

> Up until I was in my thirties, there were two pubs in the neighbourhood, both of which have now become private homes. There was the Yew Tree Inn at Fawley (known as the Wood Pub, probably because of its close proximity to Capler Woods); and at the road junction with the B4224, there was Gurney's Oak.
>
> Gurney's Oak not only catered for the local community, but was the pub of Brockhampton Cricket Club. The Wood Pub was the most interesting of the two, and probably so in most of Herefordshire. It was one of those fantastic places which sometimes would be empty and sometimes jammed full. It was originally a Victorian cottage which had two small rooms and a beer store in the kitchen; the epitome of spit and sawdust and full of the most basic furnishings, including a piano for party nights. The hosts were Reg and Olive Pritchard. To call them good hosts would be an understatement. They always welcomed you and fortunately did not keep to the statutory opening hours. Reg's Welsh accent will live with me forever. As youngsters, we would often help the Brace Brothers with their harvesting and bale hauling until late on summers' evenings and end up at the Wood well after closing time. And a few pints of Hancock's bitter

later we would be ready to walk the one-and-a-half miles home. The pub was demolished around 1990 to make way for a new house. That was very sad as the other local pub, Gurney's Oak, at the opposite end of the village, also closed about this time.

KERNE BRIDGE INN

As the rail tracks emerge from the tunnel under Coppett Hill, they cross the river on the viaduct, before coming to rest at Kerne Bridge Station. Situated almost opposite the station was the popular Kerne Bridge Inn. It still stands but is now a private residence. It would have welcomed many a thirsty traveller in its time. The family of Margaret Morgans (née Horsley) ran the Inn from 1890 right up to the 1970s. She was born there, as was her mother before her. Today, Margaret lives near Cirencester, and her home is furnished with some of the items that once graced the Kerne Bridge Inn.

The Kerne Bridge Inn (photo: Margaret Morgans)

My family first arrived at the Kerne Bridge Inn in 1890, when it was a hotel. By the time I arrived in 1944, it was a very rural place then and we had a well in our house and most of the little houses around would go there to get their fresh drinking water. I can see them now coming down with their metal pails. They also collected their paraffin as well, which we sold at the

Left: the Morgans behind the bar at the Kerne Bridge Inn.
Right: petrol pumps outside the Inn (photos: Margaret Morgans)

Inn, and newspapers too. We had our petrol pumps outside. You'd have people from all walks of life dropping in. They would come in at lunchtime and there would be this open forum about politics. It was a mixed clientele.

Margaret's father, James Lewis Horsley, was living at a neighbouring inn, the Albion, when he met Margaret's mother, Winifred, and they eventually worked together at the Kerne Bridge Inn.

> Daddy used to let out some of the fields for camping and people used to come from Birmingham and put their tents up. I had a very large chicken hut, which we set up in one of the fields, which was my playhouse, but eventually it went to someone who used it as their holiday place! My mother had all the balls in the air and they never went to bed before 12 or 1 a.m. She was the one that really ran the place, but father would always sort the fires out in the mornings.

The pub was the centre of the community:

> My parents set up a tennis club, a cricket club and a football club. I remember mummy preparing oranges for half-time. She held the Women's Institute in what was also called the Club Room, which was also my wonderful playroom, and the police parties were held there too. They knew they could come and it was a safe place to let their hair down.

At weekends, we had women in the pub and we also had a chap who was a wonderful pianist, and I loved it when he came, because everyone would gather around him as he played, and sang along. And some of the Forest people would come in at the weekend too.

They used to play traditional pub games, table skittles in the pub, dominos and shove ha'penny. I used to sit upstairs and listen through the bannisters. I've got a lot of furniture here in my home that was in the Kerne Bridge Inn. I have a table in my hallway that used to have a cider barrel on it at the pub, with the telephone beside it. I remember a chap called Harry Jarrett who lived alone in the cottage over the railway bridge. He had no water or electricity and drank tea out of jam jars at home. He would come over the bridge and I remember he always wore waders, but he wasn't a mixer. He would come down the corridor and have a glass of whatever it was and stand there, alone all night, not saying a word to anyone.

We used to get salmon fishermen in too, of course, we were so close to the river, and we had so many salmon we didn't know what to do with them. In those days, it was almost sacrilegious to be making fish cakes from salmon. I can see Mum now scaling the salmon. I knew the ghillie Ivor Williams very well. He used to come in the pub a lot and I used to ride about in his boat sometimes. You could do what you liked in those days. Ivor was a nice man.

Dray men used to come every Thursday from Hereford. The grocer would ring up on a Friday morning and ask mummy what she wanted. The owner of Jolley's in Goodrich was a friend of my father's, and Fred Powell, who used to work there, used to ring us on a Friday morning, take our order, and then everything was delivered on a Friday afternoon. And of course, we had the baker delivering twice a week and everything was brought to the door.

And just a stone's throw away was the …

ALBION INN

Long after it closed, this former pub in Bishopswood still has 'Albion' painted on the outside. Emmanuel Husbands, originally from Presteigne and a pit sawyer, took over as publican in 1892, and ran the pub for decades as a tenant of Alton Court Breweries. His daughters, Jane and Sarah Ann, served as barmaids. He is buried in Walford churchyard.

Like its neighbour, the Kerne Bridge Inn, the Albion supported the local football team. Margaret Wilce, now living in Walford, was born in Bishopswood, and remembers her boyfriend, now husband Dennis, playing football:

> He had to go to the Albion on a Monday night to help pick the football team for the following Saturday's match, this would be from 1952/ 53. The Albion was the football headquarters for Bishopswood Football Club in those days and the changing rooms were in the old village hall, which was directly below. The football pitch was on the river bank in front of where the new village hall is now, and the ball often went into the river, so more than one was always available.

The Albion Inn
(photo: Margaret Morgans)

THE SUGWAS BOAT

Another pub placed strategically on the river, ideal for passing river trade and traffic was the Sugwas Boat. Like the Albion, white lettering on the red brick wall still announces the building as a former pub. It's the site of a former ferry crossing too. Ninety-six-year-old Joan Lloyd was one of its former customers and describes a landlord rather lacking in customer care:

> He used to be a bit crabby. The pub got to be so packed that we used to sit on the tables. "Get off the table," he said, "they were made for glasses not asses!" So we would move.

MILL HILL MISSIONARY ORDER

In September 2015, Hereford Baptist Church's Senior Minister Antony Wareham and Youth Pastor Jason Borlase conducted the church's first baptism in the river near the Victoria Bridge on the special request of Ben Menzies and Joseph Meiklejohn. A large group from the church lined the bridge to witness this unique event. Far earlier and further downstream at the Courtfield Estate, the Mill Hill Fathers were conducting their own baptism ceremonies.

While the missionaries were not overtly customers of the local hostelries, there are tales of lore about the parties at Mill Hill, a former missionary training

Left: **Courtfield House**. Right: **The Mill Hill Fathers** (photo: Mill Hill Fathers)

school and, later on, a retreat centre, with sweeping views of the river from the Courtfield Estate, the ancestral home of the Catholic Vaughan family. The Mill Hill Missionaries were originally founded by Cardinal Herbert Vaughan in the mid nineteenth century, and in the early 1960s Courtfield became their home and training centre for Brother candidates, preparing them for missionary work in the developing world. In rocks below the house, looking out towards the river, is a grotto with a statue of Our Lady, her hand outstretched. There couldn't be a more fitting setting for this missionary order.

When the Mill Hill Fathers arrived, workshops were built and machinery was installed, all with the aim of training these young Brothers in the practical skills needed for mission work in remote outposts around the world. At one time, there were 30 Brothers training there. In 1976, local papers announced the opening of their newly-completed residential block, built completely by the Brothers. Juxtaposed against the grand Courtfield house, its construction was rather ugly, but functional. Nonetheless, the Auxiliary Bishop of Cardiff opened the new building with a celebratory Mass and a promise that the buildings would, 'provide the Brothers with practical experience in crafts they will teach in the mission fields'.

Of the 17–20 Brothers who worked on the building, many travelled from their Wye Valley oasis to put into practise their missionary calling, in locations such as the Philippines, Cameroon and the Congo. By the 1970s, the training centre was transferred elsewhere, and the building was turned into a retreat centre. By the time the Order left for the last time in June 2003, there had been a stream of weddings, deaths, confessions, christenings and a passing parade of missionaries. Midnight Mass was a special event, with a glass of sherry and a mince pie enjoyed in the dining room afterwards; and in the summer there were open-air Masses in the grounds, spilling out onto the bank, with tea and cake taken in the courtyard.

Father Christopher Fox worked for over 20 years in Uganda, where he represented the Mill Hill Missionaries. He was administrator at Courtfield from 1996 until its closure in 2003, and was often asked to talk at John Kyrle High School assemblies during his tenure about the Order's work. He is retired now and living back in his native Dublin, but has fond memories of his Herefordshire home.

> Well, I used to like a run alongside the river up towards Symonds Yat. That was one of my favourite pastimes. And, of course, the students and staff alike used to take on other local teams in a game of football on the sloping field near the river. They were not ideal conditions, of course. We used to have teams come up here from different places: Haigh Engineering from Ross was one and there was another from Glewstone.

It's been suggested, although not confirmed, that one of the young missionaries was in fact an ex-Chelsea player, so they were clearly no pushover when it came to soccer.

> Groups of many Faiths used to come and stay, including Russian and Greek Orthodox Churches, Anglicans and Methodists, MPs and the Archbishop of Canterbury on one occasion.

Sunday Mass at the Courtfield estate's chapel was a fixture for many of the Faith, with up to 50 regular worshippers. Fiona Lloyd, who grew up on the Courtfield Estate, was welcomed into Catholic services:

> The priests were lovely. I can clearly see the prayer cave now: it was like a grotto, hundreds of semi-precious stones that they used to kiss for a long, prosperous life. I kissed it many times. It was a sacred place.

In Whitchurch village there used to be the most un-church-like (in appearance at least) Catholic church. It is now a private home, but it was where Lizzie Knock used to go to celebrate Mass and where she first met the Fathers from the Mill Hill Missionaries. One of them, Father Turner, would travel the short distance from the Coppett Hill base to do the service.

In the late 1970s, Lizzie started attending Mass at their Courtfield chapel:

> I absolutely loved it. The Missionary priests and the nuns, from the Missionary Sisters of St Joseph's, were just wonderful people. They were always welcoming and had tea and cake ready at any time we called. Sister Rosina used to keep chickens. I used to go to weekend retreats there too. We would arrive on the Friday night and be shown to our accommodation, built by the missionary students, overlooking the river. It was organised by Father Hurley and Father Frank Thompson and they were such wonderful people, like a double act! And there was Father Turner, who we called Holy Joe. We ran a smallholding in Llangrove then, and Father Turner wanted to have a go at keeping sheep, so we gave him six, but he lost them all the first day. We called him Bo Peep after that. He also used the greenhouses and would leave fruit and veg on our doorstep for us.
>
> It was sad when it closed. I have very special memories of the place and the Fathers there, especially Father Hughes, Father Turner and Father Thompson, all of whom made a great impression on me. I remember clearly sitting on a seat outside the house looking over the river with Father Peter, one retreat weekend. He told me he had just seen a really good film about C.S. Lewis. Of course, he was talking about *Shadowlands*, which had been filmed just along the river from where we were sitting.

The Disabilities Act of 1995 made the cost of updating the Retreat Centre in line with the new legislation impossible, and by 2003 the Mill Hill Missionaries ceased operations after nearly 30 years at Coppett Hill. With only two British students preparing for priesthood, the lack of personnel to administer the centre was another major contributing reason for its closure.

Father Fox was sad to leave his riverside home.

> I spent seven happy years there and made innumerable friends. When I left, there was just Father Louis Purcell and Father Denny O'Connor. I valued their presence and friendship very much indeed. We always tried to make visitors feel welcome and at home. I do hope that memories live on and that Courtfield and its history will continue to inspire.

We've reached the end of the book, but it's not the end of the story. There are many more tales to be told, recorded and discovered and we want to make sure this continues. Many disparate groups have been interviewed for the book, and uniting them all is the glorious and humble River Wye. We are so grateful to all of you who have given your time to us.

This book is a tribute to you.

You can contact Marsha at: riverwyevoices@gmail.com

Voices of the River

1. Dorothy Joyner
2. Tony Norman
3. Major Patrick Darling
4. Robin Hulse
5. Les Moses
6. Brian Dean
7. Lindesay and Ray Norton
8. Dave Warnes
9. Janet Preedy
10. Lyn Cobley
11. George Woodward
12. Lynne Butler, Shona & Cara Palmer & Caroline Hodgeson
13. Lynn Woodward
14. Tom Henderson
15. George Smith
16. Joan Lloyd
17. Ron & Kit Hodges & daughter Tricia Hales
18. David Joyce
19. Nicola Goodwin, Julie Hardman & Ian Rivers
20. Howard Copping
21. Adrian Howard
22. Deborah Hill
23. Hugo Mason
24. Geoff Franks
25. Maurice Hudson
26. Julia Hudson

VOICES OF THE RIVER 231

232 RIVER VOICES

VOICES OF THE RIVER 233

REFERENCES

Barwick, Jennifer, *Parents Get lost! The Man Behind Children's Adventure Holidays*, Streets Publishers, 2013.

Brampton Abbotts Parish, *Our Village within Living Memory*, imprint unknown, 1955.

Butt, Alan, *The River Hobbler's Apprentice: Memories of Working the Severn & Wye*, The History Press, 2010.

Clark, David M., *Fownhope Beyond Memory: Change in a Herefordshire Village 1832–1919*, Fownhope Local History Group, 2016.

Crow, A., *Bridges on the River Wye*, Lapbridge Publications, 1995.

Fletcher, H.L.V., *Portrait of the Wye Valley*, Robert Hale & Co., 1968.

Gilbert, H.A., *The Tale of a Wye Fisherman*, Methuen & Co. Ltd., 1929.

Goffe, M., *Camping on the Wye: The Tale of a Trip along the Wye from Whitney in Herefordshire to Chepstow*, Logaston Press, 2003.

Havergal F.T., *Herefordshire Words, Superstitions and Customs*, Oakmagic Publications, 2001.

Hayman, Richard, *Wye*, Logaston Press, 2016.

Herefordshire Federation of Women's Institutes, *Herefordshire within Living Memory*, Countryside Books, 1993.

Hurley, Heather, *Herefordshire's River Trade: Craft & Cargo on the Wye & Lugg*, Logaston Press, 2013.

— *Landscape Origins of the Wye Valley: Holme Lacy to Bridstow*, Logaston Press, 2008.

— *The Pubs of Ross and South Herefordshire*, Logaston Press, 2001.

Jenkins, J. Geraint, *Nets and Coracles*, David and Charles, 1974.

Kissack, Keith, *The River Wye*, Terence Dalton Ltd., 1978.
Leather, Ella Mary, *The Folk-lore of Herefordshire*, Jakeman & Carver, 1912 (new edition Logaston Press, 2018).
Lulham, Maurice A., *The Wye Valley Otter Hounds 1874–1935*, W Judd.
Morgan, Virginia & Vine, Bridget, *A History of Walford and Bishopswood*, Logaston Press, 2002.
Murray's Handbooks for Travellers, *A Handbook for Travellers in Gloucestershire, Worcestershire, and Herefordshire*, John Murray, 1872.
Shoesmith, Ron & Jennifer (Intro.), *Alfred Watkins' Herefordshire: In his own words and photographs*, Logaston Press, 2012.
Shoesmith, Ron & Eisel, John, *The Pubs of Hereford City*, Logaston Press, 1994.
Stockinger, Victor Richard, *The Rivers Wye and Lugg Navigation: A Documentary History, 1555–1951*, Eyre and Strahan Ltd. and Logaston Press for the Trustees of the Rivers Wye and Lugg Navigation, 1996.
Tabernacle, Bob, *The Junior Guy Fawkes: A History of Goodrich School*, imprint unknown, 2003.
Taylor, Elizabeth, *Kings Caple in Archenfield: Centuries of History in a South Herefordshire Parish*, Logaston Press, 1997.
Thornhill, Timmins H., *Nooks and Corners of Herefordshire*, Elliot Stock, 1892 (reprinted by Lapridge Publications, 1992).
Woolhope Naturalists' Field Club, *Herefordshire: Its Natural History, Archaeology, and History*, The British Publishing Company, 1954.
Wye Valley Area of Outstanding Natural Beauty, Overlooking the Wye website http://www.overlookingthewye.org.uk/

BOLLINGER'S CHAMPAGNE

By special appointment to H.M. the KING.

MENU

Ross Rowing Club

-DINNER,-

FRIDAY, FEBRUARY 9th, 1912.

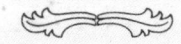

"Cheerful looks make every dish a feast."

SOUP.
Ox Tail.　　　Tomato.

FISH.
Codfish.　　　Sole.

REMOVES.
Saddle Mutton.　　　Sirloin Beef.
Boiled Chicken.　　　Ham.

SWEETS.
Plum Pudding.　　　Apple Tart.
Fruit Salad.　　　Custard.
Cheese.　　　Celery.
Dessert.

"Things sweet to taste prove indigestion sour."

INDEX

Agate, Terence 138
Albion Inn 224, 225, *225*
Alford, Jack 201
Alford, Jean 201
American GIs 4
Amos, Charlie 214
Andrews, Graham 190
Anglers Inn (Union Street) 218
Aramstone 31
Arscotts (boatmen) 160
Arvan, Saint 115
Atkinson, Jeremy 121
Avery, Dave 11

Babbage, Cyril 140
Backney 5
Halt 200, 201
bailiff (river) 22, 67, 85–93, *87*
Ballingham 19, 89
barbel 52
Barnsley, H.P. 136
Barnsley, P.E. 136
Barton, Richard 138
Bartonsham Farm 54
Bartonsham Meadows (*see Bassom*) 13
Bassom, the (*Bartonsham Meadows*) 13–15, *14*, *15*
Beason, Leslie 128
beat map *24*
Beaufort, Duke of 27
Belmont 9
Belmont Plate, the 145–148, *147*, *148*
Benhalls Farm 13
Berkeley Canal 30
Bevan, Frank 138
Bicknor Bridge 210
'Big Boys' (pools) 2, 4
Bigsweir Bridge 63, 74

Bishop's Pool 112
Bishopswood 5, 6, 55, 80, 81, 179, 197, 224, 225
Blandford, Percy 126
bleak (fish) 57
boating 149, 150–153, *150*, *151*, *152*, *153*, *176*
Bone, Diana 11
Borlase, Jason 225
Bradbury Lines 9, 166, 205
Brampton Abbotts 4, 5, 104
Bredwardine 152, *208*
Breinton *3*, 15, 104, *133*, 150, 151, *151*
Brewer's Arms 51
Brewster Cup Wye Swimming Race 16
Bridge Sollars 150
Brilley 99, 185, 208
Brockhampton 27, 41, 221
Brockweir *39*, 62, 109, 127
Brookes, John 122, 200, 201
Brown, Rosemary 207, 208, 209
Bruce-Gardiner, Sir *75*
'Buffs', the 220, *220*
Builth 52, 90
Bullock, Les 145
Bullock, Terry 'Tug' 145
Bundy, Charlie 99, 100
Bundy, Ken 142
Burford, Ron 74
Butcher, Allan 139
Butcher, Brian 139–141
Butcher, Dennis 139
Butcher, Ivor 139
Butcher, John 139
Butcher, Vera 139
Butcher, William ('Tibs') 139
Butler, Doreen 69
Butler, George 68–72

Butler, Lynne 69, *232*
Butt's Camp *128*, 128, 129, *129*
Bycross ferry 153
Byrnes, Doreen 218

Camp Inn, the (Eaton Bishop) 152, 215, *216*, 217
Campions 165
canoeing 123, 124–127, *124*, 217
Capaldi, Jim 195
Capler 28, *45*, 57, 64, *66*
Caradoc 63
Cardora (beat) 48, 102
Carey Islands 186
Carpenter, Fred 157, 158
Carpenter, Gail 118
Carpenter, Hilary 157, 158
Cartland, Barbara 191
Catchpole, Charlie 86, *86*
Catchpole, Jack 50, 51, 86
Chamberlain, Neville (PM) 73, 81, *81*, 82, 102
Chance, Tim 19
Charlton, Jack *25*
Chattington, Karl 114, 115, *115*
Chepstow 19, 38, 40, 60, 109, 115, 116, 159, 173, 176
Cholmondeley-Pennell, H. 63
chubb 52
Clay, Bridget 28
Clay Snr, Peter 27, 28, 41, *41*
Clements, Tony 118
clog making 121, 122
coarse fishing 50, 52
Cobley, Lyn 52, 73, 89, *231*
Coldwell 24
Cook, Alec 118
Coppett Hill 80, 104, 177, 222, 227, 228
Copping, Howard 142, 143, 204, *233*
coracle ii, 20, 112–116, *113*, *114*, *115*

Coracle Society, The 116
Cornwall estate 183
Cotterell, Reg *65*
Cotterell, Sir Richard 183
Courtfield Arms (Bishopswood) 217
Courtfield Estate 23, 74, 217, 227, 228
Courtfield House 226, *226*
Courtfield Water 74
Crissall, Bert 135, 136, 150, 209
Crouch, George 74
Cumper, Caleb 40

dace 57
Daffern, Jack 50
Daines, Marjorie 217
Daines, Peter 124, 125, 192, 217
Darling, Major Patrick 30, 31, 63, 157, 186, *230*
Darnley, Lady 108, 110, 111
Davey, Miss Doreen 31, 80
Davies, Dickie 34
Davies, Peter 166, 167
Davies, Robert 180
Dawes, Tommy 131, 138, 213
Dean, Albert 145
Dean, Brian 13, 142, 145, 204, *231*
Dean, Dixie 140
Della 8
Dereham, Simon 157
Desmond, Mr 160, 161
Devon Minnow, the 28, 44, *44*
Dew, Mrs Mary 157
Dew, William ii, 112
Diffey, Gordon 36
Dinedor Hill 11
Diving Board, the 13
Doody, Ivy 217
Doward, The 106, 122, 181
drowning 1, 2
Duart Smith, F.W. 30

Duberley, Bob 5, 55, 197, 198, *198*, 199, 217, 218

Easton, John 103
Edward VIII 43, 73
Edwards, Geoff 145
Edwards, Margo 13
eel 30, 32, 50, 53–57, *53*, *57*, 59–61, *59*, 102
Eign 50
Eign Railway Bridge *51*
Ellison, Chris 118
elver 53, 61, 62
Evans, Alfred 15, 19

Faering 106, *107*
Farmer, Jack 143
Farm Stream 29
Faulkner, Dorothy 174
Fawley 99, 185, 186, 192, 221
    Station *185*, 192, 201
    Stream 29
Felsted School 1, 189, 190, 191
    suspension bridge 189, *189*, 190, *190*, 191
Ferries 159–182
Fishing Huts 40, *41*, 43
Fishpool, John 4-5, 103, 104
Flecknor, Anne and Tom 217
Fleetwood, Margaret 82, 84
Fletcher, H.L.V. 85, 215
Flooding *202*, *208*, 208–214, *210*, *211*, *212*, *213*, *214*
Ford, Arthur 134
Ford, Frank 128, 134, 152, 213
Fownhope 45, 124
    Forge & Ferry Inn 72
Fox, Father Christopher 227, 228
Foy 29, 104, 122, 159, 207, 209
    suspension bridge 5

Francis, Tony 178
Franks, Geoff 35, 79, *233*
frogmen 20
Frost, Captain 'Jack' 101
Frost, Nicholas 34
Frost, Wing Commander *98*

Gammage, Vic 125, 206
Gardiner, 'Fishy' 35, *35*, 36, 54, 150
Gardiner's Store *35*, 36
Garnons 49, 183
Garron, the 56, *56*
Gaskell, Tom 57
George VI 43
Gethin Davey, E. 99
ghillie 22, 34, 35, 41, 50, 52, 59, *59*, 73–82, *83*, 89, 93, 177
Gibbings, Robert 61, 63
Gilbert, H.A. 81
Gilling, Catherine 121
Glasbury 20, 52, 90, 126, 127
Glewstone 84, 85
Gloucester Docks 112
Golden Valley Fishery 30
Goodrich 1, 23, 38, 74, 82, 99, 189, 215
    Castle 100, 177
    Colgarron *98*, 100, *102*
    Court 189, 191
    Cross Keys 97
    Hill Court 189 191
    Hostelrie 100
Goodwin, Nicola 16–18, *17*, *233*
Golden Valley Fish and Wildlife Association 53
grayling 50
Graham, Bill 102
Green, Mr A. 16
Grevell, Geoffrey 115
Griffiths, Joe 145
Groom, Norman 131

Guest, Keen & Nettlefolds (GKN) 75, 76
Guild of Master Craftsmen 46
Gurney's Oak 221, 222
Guy's Hospital water 32
Gwillam, Ted 74

Hales, Tricia 121, 154–156, *232*
Hammond, Robin 213
Hammonds, Geoff 131–133, *133*, 136, 138, 143
Hammonds, Henry John 132, 133, *133*
Hammonds, Marie *133*
Hampton Bishop 49, *211*
Hampton Park Hill 19
Hancock, C.V. 43
Hardman, Julie 16–19, *17*, *233*
Harris, Leslie 'Bunny' 128
Harris, Margaret 118
Hartland, John 138
Hatton's 26, 38, 43, *46*, 46, 50, 55
Hatton, Herbert Charles *42*, 43–45, *45*, 48
Hatton, John 43, 45
Hatton, Margaret 43, *44*, 45, *45*, 48
Hatton Minnow 29, 44, 45, 47, 48, 49
Hattendorfs (boatmen) 160
Hawkstone Hunt 96, 98, 100, 102
Hay-on-Wye 22, 90
Hayter, F.E. 132
Henderson, Tom 8, 99, 193, 204, 205, *205*, 207, *232*
Henshaw, Jo 120, 121
Herbert, C.A. 153
Hereford 1, *6*, *206*
  Bishop's Palace 1
  Canoe Centre 125
  Eign Bridge 11
  Greyfriars *210*
  Greyfriars Bridge 11, 161, 162, 173, 187, 188, *188*
Hereford and District Angling Association 45
Hereford Beach 7–9, 12
Hereford Bull, The 108–112, *108*, *109*, *111*
Hereford Rowing Club 36, 51, 113, 118, 130–132, *130*, *131*, 134, 136–139, *137*, *139*, 146, 148, 149, 151, 152, 158, 165, 209, 213, 214, 215
  Regatta 113, 134–136 *134*, *135*, 143, 167
Hereford Swimming Club 17
Hereford Triathlon Club 17
Hunderton Farm (*also known as Walls Farm*) 7, 9
King George's Playing Fields 10
Ship Inn 212
Victoria Bridge 9–11, *9*, *10*, *109*, 160, 203, *206*
Wye Bridge 99, 112, 213, *213*
Herefordshire Eel Project 53, 61
Hergest 207
Hill Court Water 82
Hill, Deborah *148*, *233*
Hillman, Jack 74, 75
Hills, Marie 15
Hoarwithy 18, 47, 60, 210
Hodges, Kit 149, 155, *232*
Hodges, Ron 38, 39, 120, 145, 149, 155, 175–177, *232*
Hodgeson, Caroline 67, *68*, 69–71, *71*, *232*
Holme Lacy 70
  Bridge 187
Hook, John 186
Hope, Captain 30
hovercraft 157
Howard, Adrian 16, 56, 100, 122, *233*
Howard, Jane 190

How Caple 29
Howell, Nancy 112
Hudson, Julia *233*
Hudson, Maurice 21, *22*, *26*, 26–27, 102, 209, *233*
Huggett, Rebecca 120
Hughes, Father 228
Hughes, P. 153
Hughes, Terry 176
Hull, Eddie 104, *105*
Hulse, Caroline 178
Hulse, Robin 178, 179, 180, 181, *230*
Hunderton 55, 127, 145, 146, 160, 161, 170, 205, 218
    Bridge 158, 200, *200*
    Ferry 1, 2, 15, 104, 120, 126, 160–167, *161*, *162*, *163*, *167*, 205, 206, 218
    Railway Bridge *20*
    Youth Club 126
Hunter, Ray 108, 110–112
Huntsham Bridge 16
Hurley, Father 228
Husbands, Emmanuel 224
Hutton 49

ice-skating *204*
Ingestone Fishery 29
Ingestone Fishing Log *28*

Jeffries (boatbuilder) 175
Jenkins (boatmen) 160
Jewson, Tony 'Atlas' 142
Johnson, Kenneth 123
Jones, Miss B. 130
Jones, Bryn 187
Jones, Derek 123
Jones, Dylan 116, 123
Jones, Innes 36, 37
Jones, Patricia 187
Jones, Philip 187, *188*

Jordan family 8, 174, 175
Jordan, Jack 174
Jordan, Phil 49
Jordan, Richard Rivers Felix 174, 175
Jordan, William Halford 174
Jordan's (boatyard) 103, 145, 149, 163, 170, *172*, 173, 174, *174*, 176, 210, 217
Joyce, David 154, *154*, 185, 208, *232*
Joyce, Ethel, 154
Joyner, Dorothy 82, 84, *230*

Kentchurch 99
Kerne Bridge 6, 99, 112, *179*, 189, 196, 199
    Inn 104, 195, 222–224, *222*, *223*
    Lodge 38, 59, 82, 84
    Railway Station 5, 80, 151, *151*, 178, 179, 181, 191, 195, *196*, 198, 222
    Toll Gate 198, *198*
    Toll House 197, *197*
Kershaw, Doris 8, 149
Kings Caple 186
Knock, Lizzie 227
Kysow, Meldon 11, 54

Lakin Sisters (Mabel and Gladys) 218
Lamputt, Gordon 14
Lawrence, Peter Gordon 123, 124, 158
Lawrence, T.E. 95
Lee, Fred 131
Letton Court 66
Lewis, C.S. 228
Lewis, Richard 103
Lilley's Lane 28
Lions, the 13
Little Doward 16
Lloyd, Fiona 227
Lloyd, Joan 8, 9, 152, 173–175, 225, *232*
Louis Purcell, Father 228
Lucksall 18

Lugg 12, 20
Lugg and Arrow Fisheries Association 53
Lulham, Maurice A. 100
Lydbrook 74
Lyster, Charles 106, *107*, 108

Mac Fisheries 35, 37, *37*
MacGregor, John 123
MacIntyre, Christine 120
Mansell Lacy 111
Mason, Hugo 27, *27*, 41, 46, 57, *57*, 64, 65, *65*, 186, 221, *233*
Mason, Lucy 64, *64*, *66*
Mason Thomas 220
Mason, Wesley 220
Matthes, Guenter 58, *58*, 74
Matthes, Mandi 59
Maund, Thomas 103
McLeod, Gary 11, 12, 20, 55, 118, 146, 170, 200, 205, 206, 220
McLeod, Gordon 170, 219
Meiklejohn, Joseph 225
Menzies, Ben 225
Michaelchurch-on-Arrow 207
Miller, Paul 136
Mill Hill Fathers 225–228, *226*
minnows, catching of 6, 9–12, *12*
Miss Hereford *184*
Moccas Bridge 183, *183*
Monmouth 32, 62, 89, 91, 109, 180
    School for Boys 26
Monnington Falls 127, 150
Moody, Ron 74
Mordiford 67
    Moon Inn 72, 145
Moreland, Philip 29
Morgan, James Lewis Horsley 223
Morgan, Keith 117
Morgan, Margaret 195, 222
Morgan, Winifred 223

Morgans, Margaret 6
Moses, Les 60–63, 67, 90, 91, 93, *231*
Much Fawley 57

Neilson, Tommy 108, 110–112
Newbridge-on-Wye 52
Newton Brook 7
Nichols, Fred 128
Norman, Tony 30, 36, 48, 53, 58, *230*
Norton, Lindesay and Ray *231*

O'Connor, Father Denny 228
Ogilvie Rennie, Charles 30
Old Miller 217, 218
Otter hunting *94*, 95–102, *96*, *97*, *98*, *101*, 195
Owen, Frank 132
Owen, Norman 26, 38, 43, 45–48, *47*
Owen, Paul *47*
Owen, Simon 47, *47*
Owens, Julian 36

Palfrey, Walter 134, 209, 214
Palmer, Cara 69, 70, *232*
Palmer, Shona 69, 70, *232*
Palmer, Tommy 67–72, *68*, *72*
Pashley, Robert 'Wizard of the Wye' 30, 32, 38, 49, 80–84, *83*, 143, 196
Pearson, General Sir Thomas 58, 59, 73
Pennington, Richard 31, *32*, 66
Perkins (angling shop) 50, 55
Perkins, Fred 50
Peter, Father 228
PGL 123, 157, 158
Phillips, Wilf 140
Pickford, Ken *183*
pike 63–67, *64*, *65*, *66*
Plynlimon 16
    Trust 155
poaching 60, 79, 85–93

Powell, Andrew 207
Powell, Eric 64
Preedy's ferry 55, 161, *161*, 170
Preedy, Janet 1–4, 162, 167, 168, *168*, 203, 218, *231*
Preedy, Ken 162–166, *162*, *163*
Preedy, Lynn 162–165
Preedy, Terry 162–165
Preedy, Tom 161, *163*, *171*
Preedy, Walter 147, 161–163, 167, *167*
Pressey, Harry 131
Preston-on-Wye 121, 126, 183, 208
Pritchard, Reg and Olive 221
Pughs (boatmen) 160
putcher 49

Queen's Diamond Jubilee Pageant 108–111

Radford, William 103
rafting 153
Raft Race 154–156, *154*
Redding, Peter 20, 67, 113, 114, *114*
Rees, Frank 74
River Arrow 86, 207
River Garron 100
River Lugg 67
River Severn 52
River Usk 87
River Wye Canoe Rally 157
River Wye Guild 131
River Wye Preservation Trust, The 30, 157
Rivers, Ian 16–18, *17*, *233*
roach 52
Robins (boatmen) 160
Robins, Anthony 74
Robins, Sid 74
Rosina, Sister 228
Ross on Wye 4, 13, 16, 34, 37, 52, 58, 59, 82, 89, 103, 106, 113, 116, 123, 159, 204
   Benhall Pontoon 139, 140, *141*
   Gwynnes 37, 38
   Metcalfes 37, 38
   Beach 13, *13*
   Grammar School 57
   Regatta 138
   Rowing Club 13, 106, 112, 139–144, *140*, *144*, 210
   Wilton Bridge 99, 100
   Wilton Castle 19
Rotherwas 18, 54
   Island 210
   Munitions Factory 19, 20
Royal Yachting Association (RYA) 106
rowing 129–156
salmon 21–40, *27*, *29*, *32*, *33*, *35*, *45*, *47*, *59*, *75*, *78*, *80*, *81*, *83*, *93*
   'American Travelling Trunk' 31
   'ladies handbags' 31
   largest landed 31
   'portmanteau' 31, 32

salmon pools 2, 25
   Bert's Hole 25
   Bridge Run 2, 25
   Coldwell Rocks 2, 25
   Cowpond 31, 80
   Cowpool 25
   Dipples Pool 25
   Dog Hole 25
   Island Pool 2
   Martin's Pool 2
   Oak Run 2
   Oak Tree 25
   Pashley Crib 25
   Pope's Rock 2, 25
   Priors Pool 2
   Rock Pool 29
   Water Works, The 2

Sandy Bay 2, 169, 203
Saracen's Head ('Sags') 174, 176, 178, 181, 219–221
SAS 20, 157, 158, 187
Saunders, Jack 210
Scott, Keith 145
Scotts of Hereford family 16
Searle, Roger 120
Sellack 30, 186
    Bridge 186, 187, *187*
Severn Bridge 67
'Shanghai Heights' 145, 170
Sharpe, Captain 102
Shatner, William 73
Shaw, Richard 158, 173
Shoesmith, Ron 126, 127
Sid Wrights 35
Slatford, John 213, 215
Smith, Doug 218
Smith, George 40, 74, 86, 90, *232*
Smurthwaite, Pete, 79
Snead, Jim 213
snorkelling 19, 20
Socket, Bill 138
St Helier Evans, Revd H. 5
Startin, Malcolm 131, 133, 138
Staunton 126, 127
Strangford Bridge 201, *201*
Strangford End Fishery 26
Strawson, Rob 121
Stowfield Viaduct 183
Sugwas Boat 225
Symonds Yat 1, *4*, 19, 22, 34, 74, 106, 124, 127, 149, 160, *160*, 177–181, *177*, *182*
    Rock 4

Tabor, Bob 108, 110, 111
Teague, Cecil 74, 75
Tedstone, John 118
Terry, Mr J. 192

Thimblethorpe, June 191, 197
Thompson, Father Frank 228
Thompson, John Francis *33*, 34
Thompson, Ray 95–97, *96*, 100
Thornes (boatmen) 160
Timmins, H. Thornhill 185
Trier, Charlie 146
trow 108–112, *108*, *109*, *111*
Tunnel (beat) 74
Turner, Father ('Holy Joe'/ 'Bo Peep') 227, 228

Usk 90

Vaga, The 11, 55, 120, 145–147, *147*, 170, 200, 206, 219
Vaughan, Joe ' The Major' 217, 218

Walker, Bill 118
Wallace, Bruce 9–11, 54, 104, *105*, 129, 136, 138, *138*, 148, 151, 214
Walls Farm (see Hunderton Farm)
Wareham, Antony 225
Warham 128, 136
Warnes, David 194, *194*, *231*
Water Witch 103
Watts, Trevor 74
Weir End 74, 100, 124
Whalebone Inn 51
Whitefoot, Trevor 145
Whitney Court 66
Whitney-on-Wye 30, 151, 173, 193, 204, 207
    Boat Inn 99
    Bridge 193, *193*, *205*
    Toll Bridge 90, 193–195, *194*, 208
Whittingham, Jack 38, 81–85, *81*, *83*, *85*
Whittingham, Mike 38, 82, 84, 85, 99, 100
Wilce, Dennis 225

Wilce, Margaret 225
Wilcocks, Rear Admiral Philip 108, 110
Willersley 214
    Williams Brothers (boatmen) 160, 179, 180, *180*
Williams, Cecil 197
Williams, Chris 118
Williams, Frank 128
Williams, Harry 177
Williams, Ivor *32*, 74, 80, *80*, *178*
Williams, Roy 145
Williams, Trevor 177
Winforton 25, 31, 32, 66, 80
Woodman, Matt 11
Woodward, George viii, ix, 22, *22*, *23*, 25, *25*, 74–79, *75*, 93, *232*
Woodward, Lynn *25*, 74, 77–80, *78*, *232*
Wooley, Sam 196, 197
Woolhope Naturalists' Field Club 50
Wright, Tom 140
Wyastone Leys 16
Wye & Usk Foundation 30, 53
Wyebridge House 9
Wye Bridge 99, 210
Wye Ghillies Association 35, 78, 79, *79*
Wye Guild 136, 143, 148
Wye Rapids Hotel 34
Wye River Authority 40, 88
River Carnival 114, 117–121, *117*, *118*, *119*
Wye Tour 103, 159
Wye Valley Otter Hounds 95–102
Wye Valley Pools 132
Wyesham 74

Yggdrasil 106, *107*, 108
Yew Tree Inn (Wood Pub), Fawley 65, *65*, 221, 222

INDEX   245